EXPLORING OTHER WORLDS

Exploring Other Worlds

Margaret Fox, Elisha Kent Kane, and the Antebellum Culture of Curiosity

David Chapin

University of Massachusetts Press
AMHERST AND BOSTON

Printed in the United States of America

LC 2003027751
ISBN 1-55849-448-0 (library cloth ed.); 457-X (paper)

Designed by Dennis Anderson
Set in Sabon by Binghamton Valley Composition, Inc.
Printed and bound by The Maple-Vail Book Manufacturing Group, Inc.

Library of Congress Cataloging-in-Publication Data

Chapin, David, 1966–
Exploring other worlds : Margaret Fox, Elisha Kent Kane, and the antebellum culture of curiosity / David Chapin.
p. cm.
Includes bibliographical references and index.
ISBN 1-55849-448-0 (library cloth : alk. paper) — ISBN 1-55849-457-X (pbk. : alk. paper)
1. Kane, Elisha Kent, 1820–1857. 2. Fox, Margaret, 1833–1893. 3. Popular culture—United States—History—19th century. 4. United States—Intellectual life—19th century. 5. Explorers—United States—Biography. 6. Spiritualists—United States—Biography.
I. Title.
G635.K2C43 2004
910'.92'273—dc22

2003027751

British Library Cataloguing in Publication data are available.

Contents

Acknowledgments

A NUMBER of people have contributed their time, expertise, and advice in the creation of this work. I owe a great debt to the staffs of several libraries. The Dimond Library at the University of New Hampshire served as a home base during most of the time I was doing research and writing. I thank those in the reference, interlibrary loan, and microform departments for their help in locating and procuring countless materials. I also thank the staffs at the Dartmouth College Library, the New-York Historical Society, the University of Rochester Department of Rare Books and Special Collections, and the American Philosophical Society Library, especially Rob Cox, Beth Carroll-Horrocks, and Roy Goodman, for their interest in the project and for lending their expertise to my research. I am grateful to those institutions for permission to use materials in their collections.

I have benefited from the advice of a number of fine teachers over the course of many years. Art Worrall, Eugene Berwanger, and Ruth Alexander at Colorado State University all contributed to my desire to pursue the study of history. At the University of New Hampshire, Bill Harris, Jeff Bolster, Jan Golinski, Bob Mennel, and Briggs Bailey, all read and commented on early versions of this book. Thanks also to Jim Cullen, whose influence was felt at the very beginning and again at the very end of the process, and to Gretchen Adams, whose encouragement was greatly appreciated.

A full year of research on this project was funded by a fellowship from the University of New Hampshire graduate school, and a month of research in residence at the American Philosophical Society Library in Philadelphia was funded by a Mellon Fellowship. Portions of this book have appeared before in very different forms. A condensed version of chapters 2 and 4 was previously published as "The Fox Sisters and the Performance of Mystery," in *New York History,* and scattered parts of chapters 1, 3, and 9 originally appeared together as " 'Science Weeps, Humanity Weeps, the World Weeps': The Funeral of Elisha Kent Kane," in *Pennsylvania Magazine of History and Biography*. I am grateful to both journals for permission to republish that material here.

EXPLORING OTHER WORLDS

Introduction

A Culture of Curiosity

Remember then as a sort of dream, that Doctor Kane of the Arctic Seas loved Maggie Fox of the Spirit Rappings.

Elisha Kane to Margaret Fox, in *The Love-Life of Dr. Kane*

By the winter of 1853, Dr. Elisha Kent Kane was a young man with wonderful prospects. At the age of thirty-three, this short, almost frail navy surgeon was already making a name for himself as an explorer. The eldest son of a prominent federal judge, who mingled in the nation's highest social circles, Kane had traveled much of the world. In his twenties he had visited parts of South America, Africa, Asia, and Europe. He'd hunted elephants in India and climbed live volcanoes in the Philippines. Most recently, in 1850, he had been a member of the U.S. Grinnell Expedition, which had sailed north to the frozen regions of the Arctic in search of the lost British navigator Sir John Franklin. Kane's scientific researches while a member of the Grinnell Expedition had brought him membership in the prestigious American Philosophical Society. His world travels had also gained him a certain celebrity status with a wider American audience. Kane's popular lectures on the Arctic in eastern cities from Baltimore to Boston were attracting crowds who were thrilled by the young surgeon's dramatic descriptions of the frozen North.

Unknown at the time to his many admirers, Elisha Kane was secretly involved with another celebrated American, Margaret Fox, a "spirit rapper" whose mysterious life was shrouded in controversy. In 1848, according to believers, she and her sister Kate had begun to communicate with the dead by means of mysterious knocking sounds. Two years later these pale, dark-haired, dark-eyed teenage girls were holding séances in New York City. Hundreds of people came to see the Fox sisters and participate in their séances in the hope that they might contact dead loved ones and thus explore the unknown regions of the afterlife. Some excited witnesses thought that the activities of the Fox sisters heralded the beginning of a new age of spiritual enlightenment, while observers of a more philosophical bent believed that their séances revealed new mysteries about the workings of the human mind and human spirit. Still others, with more skeptical leanings, thought that the Fox sisters were con artists out to make a profit from deception. Despite these conflicting views, the Fox sisters were a sensation, and their séances attracted both hopeful believers and skeptical critics.

That Elisha Kane and Margaret Fox should have been romantically involved seems strange, as their outward differences were great. He came from one of the best Philadelphia families, while she had grown up in rural obscurity in western New York State. He was publicly heralded as a man of great virtue, while she was seen by many as a practicer of deception. He was embraced by mainstream American science, while she was rejected by most scientists as a symbol of irrational delusion. Despite these outward differences, in February 1853 Kane wrote to Margaret Fox, telling of the similarities he saw between his own highly respected career as an explorer and her disreputable one as a spirit-rapping medium: "When I think of you, dear darling, wasting your time and youth and conscience for a few paltry dollars, and think of the crowds who come nightly to hear of the wild stories of the frozen north, I sometimes feel that we are not so far removed after all."[1]

Elisha Kane was speaking with the condescension of a man sure of his own superiority but struck by a moment of self-doubt; he knew perfectly well that he and Margaret Fox differed greatly in status and reputation, but despite the success of his recent series of lectures, Kane was feeling dissatisfied with himself. He was having great success as a popularizer of Arctic science and exploration, but he sometimes feared that his appeal to public recognition demeaned him, just as spirit rapping demeaned Fox. When Kane continued his letter, telling his spirit-rapping love, "My brain and your body are each the sources of attraction, and I confess that there is not so much difference," he was reluctantly pointing to a conjunction of their two careers that transcended their personal relationship.[2] The respected explorer and the notorious spirit rapper were attractions that catered to the inquisitive tastes of the antebellum American public. The afterlife and the North Pole were equally unknown territory in nineteenth-century America, and Kane and Fox offered the chance to explore these mysteries. Their audiences, above all else, wanted to learn about the unknown; they wanted to be both educated and entertained by new knowledge, be it geographical, spiritual, or even, ultimately, personal. Public curiosity in antebellum America made celebrities out of women and men, like Margaret Fox and Elisha Kane, who helped Americans explore a myriad of "undiscovered countries."[3]

In their own ways Kane and Fox epitomized what can best be called a culture of curiosity. They both operated in a new world of commercial mass culture that appealed to curiosity about the unknown and justified new forms of amusement with older ideals of intellectual and moral betterment. This appeal to curiosity characterized the transition from Enlightenment ideals of republican virtue through public knowledge to a newer mass culture of commercial profit through public amusement. The culture of curiosity was reflected in the newspapers, the dime museums, the lecture halls, the books, and the pamphlets of this era. The interconnected lives of Elisha Kane and Margaret Fox offer a unique opportunity to study the meaning of this fascination with the unknown and how that fascination operated both publicly and privately for those who catered to it.

THE CULTURE of curiosity was made possible by the emergence of new kinds of audiences in antebellum America, particularly in growing cities such as New York, which reached a population of over half a million residents by 1850. Several other cities had populations of more than 100,000 and thus could provide audiences for a variety of novel cultural activities.[4] This was a time when the United States was moving toward an ever greater emphasis on a market economy, capitalism, and a wage labor system and away from the small-town farming culture that had dominated an earlier era. The skilled artisan was being transformed from the older paternalistic role of "master," who trained apprentices who would one day replace him, to the new role of employer, who hired workers and paid them wages. Industry was gaining ground, and countless men and women from rural backgrounds were moving into the cities. Some were entering a new middle class of professionals. Others were laboring in manufacturing jobs for wages.[5]

As both the middle class and the working class left behind the community-based rural culture to take part in the new mass consumer culture, they sought out activities to occupy their leisure time, and enterprising individuals supplied this need with new modes of entertainment. The theater, of course, had been around for years, but the antebellum era saw an expansion of interest in theater, particularly Shakespeare, among all classes in the city.[6] More specific to the era were the minstrel shows, in which mostly white performers would don blackface and give "authentic" African American–inspired performances for largely white working-class audiences. The minstrel shows drew upon African American culture yet degraded it in racist parodies.[7] Perhaps the best known of the antebellum showmen in New York City was Phineas T. Barnum, whose American Museum catered to as large an audience as it could attract, from genteel middle-class ladies to workers from the Bowery. Other forums such as newspapers like the *New York Sun* and *New York Herald* also sought mass circulation among this new urban population, becoming pathbreakers in the development of a true mass consumer culture.[8]

Showmen, newspaper editors, book publishers, lecture hall promoters, and others all wanted to attract this new mass audience to their products, and the appeal to curiosity became one of their most successful hooks. Mass entertainment was a new concept, and one that was not readily accepted. Entertainment for its own sake was still deemed somewhat disreputable. Like novel reading, mere entertainment seemed a waste of productive time, an indulgence for those who were weak in moral fiber. Satisfying curiosity, though, could be framed as a form of education. Barnum's American Museum could claim to perform a public service by making the wonders of the world available to the American people. The *New York Herald* could view itself as an educational institution as it brought before the public eye the latest sensational news of local crime, scientific discovery, or foreign travel. Even the minstrel shows could claim a certain educational value in their racist attempts to be ethnographically accurate.

Historians who examine the mass culture that was developing in the antebellum era have paid a great deal of attention to the showman Phineas T. Barnum. Some have called it the "age of Barnum," and in a sense Barnum does typify the era. Some of the entertainments he brought to the people of New York became legendary. His "Feejee Mermaid" for instance, had the head of a monkey and the body of a fish. Audiences suspected it was a hoax but could never manage to identify the exact spot where the two halves were connected, though they kept coming back to look harder. It was, after all, no less unbelievable as a specimen of natural history than the platypus that was exhibited in the same context. Barnum's exhibits were colorful, and in the jargon of the era they were often suspected to be "humbug." Barnum even encouraged the view that some of his exhibits might be fakes, because, as the historian Neil Harris has argued, the "operational aesthetic" of Barnum's humbugs was pleasing to his democratic audiences, who could participate in the intellectual challenge of trying to distinguish between truth and fiction. These famed humbugs get all the attention, but Barnum's museum included plenty of legitimate exhibits as well. Where else could one see a real live elephant or orangutan in New York City? Barnum's was a place for humbug, but it was also a good place to learn something about natural history and geography. The lines between science and sensation were fluid.[9]

This fluidity can also be seen in genres that we less readily associate with amusement such as the refined lecture. Notable gentlemen of science and letters such as Bayard Taylor and Henry Ward Beecher traveled from city to city entertaining and enlightening middle-class audiences with learned presentations—and they made a good living at it. While not crass like Barnum, these lecturers had to market themselves in order to attract audiences. Their financial need to pull in a mass audience led to some criticism that the lecture system had abandoned its intellectual roots and was watering down its content to the point where it had become superficial.[10]

Local literary societies and scientific associations sponsored lectures that drew curious audiences hoping for an evening of genteel diversion. This diversion, being of an educational sort, was thus deemed morally legitimate, yet it too was not without an element of sensation. Audiences might learn about ancient Egypt, medieval history, or the latest discoveries in chemistry. Some societies reached out to a broad middle- and working-class population in the hope that they could provide educational and thus morally uplifting information to an ever-growing democratic population. Education alone, however, was not going to draw large crowds. Public curiosity had to be aroused in order to bring in even the more genteel audiences.[11]

Elisha Kane and Margaret Fox were not in show business, but as Kane pointed out in his letter to Fox, they were attractions. Like Barnum, they both used mass marketing techniques to get themselves noticed; like Barnum, they held out to their audiences the chance to participate in the process of discovery and of separating truth from fiction. They even entertained, though unlike Barnum, they were not primarily entertainers. Yet it was this proximity to the baser elements of mass culture that made Elisha Kane uneasy. Kane wanted to be a scientist and an educator, not a showman. But how many people came to his lectures and read his books out of genuine scientific interest, and how many simply marveled at the wonders of the northern landscape he described?

There was a lot of new knowledge, both good and bad, available on the commercial curiosity market. On any give night in New York City one might be able to see a mummy from Egypt unrolled or learn about the new science of phrenology, which told character from the shape of a person's head. One could hear a lecture on natural history by the Harvard professor Louis Agassiz or one on mesmerism by a "professor" of animal magnetism. One could read in the paper the latest reports from far away, carried by the newly invented electric telegraph, or hear from the world beyond the grave via spiritual telegraph.

The culture of curiosity, built on knowledge of the world presented as both amusement and useful education, infused a growing commercial mass culture with a strong educational component that served as moral justification. Of course, education and commercial entertainment are not always an easy fit, and as the nineteenth century progressed, this became increasingly obvious. Curiosity could make the quest for useful knowledge stimulating, but it could also lead to voyeuristic sensationalism and entertainment for its own sake. It is the inherent conflict between these opposed aspects of the culture of curiosity that makes the story of Margaret Fox and Elisha Kane so compelling.[12]

WHAT FOLLOWS is a story.[13] It is about two individuals whose lives became intricately bound up with the antebellum culture of curiosity in a variety of ways. Fittingly, it is a personal narrative as well as an analysis of a rapidly changing world. By considering the public and the private in tandem, we can see a number of themes emerge in rich complexity. This was a time when new distinctions were being made between the public and private worlds. As celebrities, Kane and Fox were putting themselves on display before a nation of strangers, and they had to figure out how to do this without compromising themselves. Publicly, Kane and Fox used Americans' curiosity about the unknown to their advantage, but privately it overwhelmed them. Kane hungered for public recognition as a man of science, but he also recoiled from the intrusion of the often impertinent gaze of strangers into his private affairs. Fox, too, longed for the money, the independence, and the social advancement a lucrative life in the public eye could bring her. But the same public curiosity that helped her professionally could bring derision privately, especially for a young woman, since genteel women at this time were not supposed to have public lives. Intellectual curiosity spurred her career on, but the middle-class mores of her time did not support her way of life. Publicity and controversy threatened her respectability. Eventually she would attempt to escape from her public life to take refuge in middle-class gentility. Yet in doing so she cut herself off from the excitement and financial independence that her career had given her. Margaret Fox's private affairs demonstrate both the possibilities and the risks faced by a woman who became a celebrity in antebellum America. She struggled, sometimes successfully, but more often unsuccessfully, within constricted social boundaries.[14]

Many elements of antebellum cultural and social history emerge in Margaret Fox and Elisha Kane's personal story and can thus be explored through the window of their two lives. Issues of gentility, respectability, and authority came to define their relationship with each other and with the larger society, just as differing notions of male and female virtue influenced the public response to their careers. Larger historical questions of power, class, and gender were very personal issues for these two individuals. Their social context did not dictate the behavior of these two unique individuals, but their individual lives and the cultural setting in which they operated illuminate each other. Kane and Fox both often operated at the boundaries of their society. As they came into conflict with these boundaries, they revealed both the possibilities and the limits of individual agency in a changing world. A "thick description" of the relationships between Kane, Fox, and their audiences moves us toward a greater understanding of the diverse meanings antebellum curiosity had for different people within these specific social contexts.[15]

Their story marks both a union of opposites and a clash between disparate ideals. Popular culture brought together many varied elements of American society, and it allowed for Elisha Kane to see something of himself reflected in the career of the medium Margaret Fox; but popular culture did not obscure the serious social divisions that remained. While in some ways popular curiosity was a unifying force in American society, when it came to these individual lives, public scrutiny magnified social divisions.[16] Curiosity about the unknown made Elisha Kane into a great scientific hero who was honored by his entire nation. It raised Margaret Fox for a time toward middle-class gentility, but eventually it let her down, and left her largely forgotten by those who had once found her so intriguing.

1

Geographic Curiosity

Elisha Kent Kane's Early World Travels

It appears to me that nothing can be more improving to a young naturalist, than to journey in distant countries. It both sharpens, and partly allays that want and craving, which, as Sir J. Herschel remarks, a man experiences although every corporeal sense be fully satisfied. The excitement from the novelty of objects, and the chance of success, stimulate him to increased activity.

Charles Darwin, *The Voyage of the Beagle*

In the spring of 1844, a young gentleman from Philadelphia stood atop the Taal volcano in the Philippines looking down into the smoldering crater below. As his Filipino guides and his Prussian traveling companion secured the rope, he prepared to descend to the crater floor. Slowly he climbed down into the steaming depths, accompanied by a local man who told him stories of the crater's gods. Once within the crater he explored the bubbling mud and steaming pools. He took in the grand sublimity of the scene and pondered its creation. A short time later he was hauled back up, almost unconscious from the sulfurous fumes, having gained little for risking his life in this way except a water sample from a pool on the crater floor and a wonderful tale to tell when he returned home.

The young man who risked his life for science and a story was twenty-four-year-old Dr. Elisha Kent Kane, currently on leave from his post as physician to the U.S. diplomatic embassy to China. In his short lifetime Kane would set foot on four continents, collecting many stories as he went. He walked the streets of Rio de Janeiro, Bombay, Macao, Manila, Cairo, Athens, and London before he reached the age of thirty. Before he turned thirty-five, he had extended his travels to the coast of Africa, the battlefields of Mexico, and the frozen seas within the Arctic Circle.

Kane's descent into the crater of the Taal volcano was one of the more daring adventures of this restless and ambitious young man, full of boundless energy, arrogant daring, and a driving curiosity about the world. His friend Fletcher Webster, a fellow member of the embassy to China, recounted that when he met Kane on board the USS *Brandywine*, he "was at once struck by the activity and energy of the doctor, who was never for a moment idle, or seemed enervated by the climate." Webster went on to observe that Kane was constantly in motion both intellectually and physically: "He was very fond of the exact sciences, and was an indefatigable student,—evidently annoyed when not engaged in something, and always restless unless busy,—for hours in the state-room buried in mathematics, and then next seen at the mast-head or over the vessel's side."[1]

The restless curiosity that drove Kane to climb up masts and down into craters and led him around the globe also turned him into a celebrity in his homeland. Within a dozen years of his descent into the Taal crater, after his travels had taken him even farther afield, the name of Elisha Kent Kane would be known to any American who read a newspaper. His travels to distant parts of the world were seen as signs of American progress and expanding American power in an age that embraced the notion of manifest destiny, and his books and lectures were avidly consumed by his adoring fans, who were increasingly interested in the world beyond America's borders. He was heralded in the penny press as a great hero to the cause of humanity and science, and he was held up as a moral examplar for American youth. When he died tragically in the prime of his life, Americans from New Orleans to Boston mourned his passing. The story of the journey that brought Kane to the brink of a volcano on the opposite side of the globe from his Philadelphia home is not simply the story of a single traveler; it is also the story of a growing nation inspired by the sense of its own destiny and eager to leave its imprint on the world beyond its expanding borders.

ELISHA KENT KANE grew up in the midst of an upper-middle-class society that found gentility in the patronage of science and Enlightenment. He was the eldest son of John Kintzing Kane and Jane Duval Leiper Kane of Philadelphia. When Elisha was born in early 1820, his father was working hard to establish a successful law practice and forge a place for himself in a youthful nation. In 1814, at nineteen, he had graduated from Yale College, and after three years studying the law he was admitted to the bar. When their first son, Elisha, was born, John and Jane Kane were rapidly approaching the top ranks of the new professional middle class of the young republic. In 1828, when Elisha was eight years old, his father had the political sense to abandon his Federalist roots and become a strong supporter of Andrew Jackson for president. He soon became a leader in Pennsylvania Democratic politics. In time, John received lucrative political appointments, first as attorney general of Pennsylvania in 1845 and then as a federal judge of the U.S. District Court for the eastern district of Pennsylvania in 1846.

An ambitious man who thrived in the individualistic atmosphere of Jacksonian America, Judge Kane passed that ambition on to his sons. He and his family were reaching for ever greater social advancement, but their ambition could at times put their gentility in question. At least one Whiggish Philadelphia neighbor viewed the judge and his family with some distaste. The diarist Sidney George Fisher observed that Judge Kane "had ability, acuteness, some learning, plausibility, but he was without moral principle. He was unscrupulous as a politician and was a demagogue even on the bench. His manners were agreeable, kind & cordial, his conversation intelligent, flowing & genial, yet it was easy to perceive that he wanted truth & sincerity. His sons are like him."[2]

Despite this jaundiced view, John Kane was interested in more than just his career. He also had an amateur's interest in science. Like many men of standing, he found that cultivating a genteel scientific curiosity was a good way to become involved in the community and to establish a reputation for himself as a man of learning. In this he was successful. In 1825 he was elected to membership in the American Philosophical Society, the nation's premier scientific society, and he served as its secretary for twenty years before becoming its vice president in 1849 and, finally, its president in 1857, the year before his death.[3] John Kane was thus in a position to know some of the most influential men of his time in both intellectual and political circles. He was involved in an advisory capacity in many of the major scientific undertakings of his day, including the U.S. Exploring Expedition and the creation of the Smithsonian Institution. Though not a scientist himself, he was a man for whom the patronage of science, the cultivation of learning, was a sign of respectability and professional success. In time he would pass this genteel form of curiosity on to his eldest son, who would adapt it for a new era.

Elisha Kane was born in February 1820 in Philadelphia and baptized a Presbyterian. As a youth he attended private schools, was taught by private tutors, and was given the opportunity to study and prepare for any profession he desired. His life would be greatly influenced by the city in which he was raised. In 1804 Thomas Jefferson had described the citizens of Philadelphia as a "population, crowded, wealthy, and more than usually addicted to the pursuit of knowledge."[4] Although over twenty years had passed since the nation's capital had removed southward to the banks of the Potomac, in 1820 Philadelphia was still America's premier city for science and culture. In the eighteenth century it had been the heart of the Enlightenment in America, and when Kane was born, Enlightenment culture was still alive and well there. In prior generations such notables as Benjamin Franklin, John and William Bartram, and Charles Willson Peale had made Philadelphia their home, and they had left legacies in the form of institutions. The American Philosophical Society, the Academy of Natural Sciences, and Peale's American Museum all made Philadelphia the center of American intellectual life, especially in the realm of natural science.

As a child Kane would have been exposed to this culture. Perhaps he listened to his father's conversations with fellow members of the Philosophical Society about the latest discoveries in science, or browsed the rare plants to be seen at Bartram's gardens. Surely he would have visited Peale's great museum, where he could have seen such wonders as the bones of a great mastodon excavated from the soil of New York State. Peale's museum contained America's greatest collection of natural history artifacts, and was a repository of wonders of all kinds from the far corners of the earth, displayed in a manner designed to draw interest among a popular audience. As his father and his uncle Robert M. Patterson both spent time on the board of the museum, young Elisha must have visited there quite often.[5] Of course, he would not have been expected to become a scientist himself; the word "scientist" had not yet even been invented. Rather, he would have been expected to cultivate a gentleman's interest in science while pursuing a more lucrative professional career.

According to William Elder, a friend of the Kane family and Elisha Kane's earliest biographer, as a child Elisha was hard to control. He avoided schoolwork but had an intelligent, if undisciplined, mind that preferred independent investigation.[6] He was not averse to learning, but he seemed to have trouble focusing his attention on any one topic for long. When he became old enough, Elisha attended the University of Virginia, where he began to prepare himself for a career as a civil engineer. There he found that he was most interested in his studies in chemistry and geology. Though small in stature, Kane was attracted to activities that combined physical and intellectual effort, such as geological field trips into the Blue Ridge Mountains with the noted professor William Rogers.[7] Plans for a career as a civil engineer quickly changed, however, when, at the age of eighteen, Kane was struck with rheumatic fever. His symptoms included severe swelling of the joints and, more alarming, an inflammation of the lining and valves of his heart. For weeks he was expected to die; then slowly, he began to recover. Nonetheless, the effects of this serious disease would stay with him for the rest of his life, manifesting themselves in frequent periods of severe illness, and would ultimately contribute to his early death.[8]

Kane's illness led to a change in career plans. Instead of geology and engineering, he would now study medicine. Elder asserts that this choice was made because the chronically ill Kane and his friends felt "that he would be happier, or less unhappy, if he understood and could manage his own case."[9] Kane began to study medicine with a doctor in Philadelphia and enrolled as a medical student at the University of Pennsylvania. By the end of 1840, before he even graduated, the twenty-year-old was serving as a resident physician at Blockley Hospital.

William Elder reports that when Kane was recovering from his first bout with rheumatic fever and had to face the probability that it was going to lead to chronic illness and an early death, his father firmly told him, "Elisha, if you must die, die in the harness."[10] Although this seems a bit dramatic, it is true that Kane refused to lead the life of an invalid. While Elisha was finishing his medical studies, his father, apparently without his knowledge, pulled some political strings to get him appointed assistant surgeon in the U.S. Navy.[11] As a surgeon on a navy ship, Kane could have a steady career, much easier and financially more stable than a private practice. His father hoped that shipboard life would restore his son's health as well as provide him with a steady income. In addition to being the best thing for his physical well-being, a position as a naval surgeon would enable Kane to pursue his interest in geology and natural history, which he had developed while at the University of Virginia. Natural history could be his pastime, engaged in during his hours of leisure, while the navy would be his career.

Although his family's political connections got him the job, Kane did not lack qualifications for this position. Even if a medical education in the 1840s was not what it is today, Kane had worked hard and done well in school. His thesis had been so warmly received by the faculty that it was published on their recommendation, which was not common. His time in residence at Blockley Hospital in Philadelphia had also been successful, and he was well thought of by his more experienced medical colleagues.[12] Furthermore, the position of surgeon on board a naval ship was not at all unusual for someone like Kane with medical knowledge and an interest in science. It was the launching point for many scientific careers, including those of two of Britain's most accomplished men in the biological sciences, Joseph Hooker and Thomas Huxley. Hooker served as assistant surgeon and botanist on HMS *Erebus* during Sir James Ross's voyage of discovery in the Antarctic from 1839 to 1843, and Huxley served as surgeon on board the British survey ship *Rattlesnake*.[13] Growing sciences such as geology, botany, zoology, hydrography, ethnology, and the study of terrestrial magnetism all required travel as a means of doing research, and for those without substantial resources to pay their own way, the navy offered a good alternative.

Kane was probably thinking along these lines when he followed his father's advice to enter the navy. He passed the examination to become an assistant surgeon, but as there were no openings at the time, he had to wait before receiving a commission. In the meantime an opportunity just as good, if not better, came along. He sought and received a place on Caleb Cushing's diplomatic mission to China aboard the navy frigate *Brandywine*, commanded by Commodore Foxhall A. Parker. In May 1843, Dr. Kane was aboard the *Brandywine* as physician to the delegation when it departed Norfolk for China.[14]

The Cushing embassy was a sign of the United States' growing involvement in world markets and world diplomacy. China's distrust of foreigners had traditionally made commerce between the United States and China a delicate affair, yet trade persisted nonetheless until interrupted by the Opium War between China and Great Britain in 1840. In August 1842 the war was resolved with the Treaty of Nanking, in which China succumbed to most of the Britain's demands by opening five ports to British trade and ceding Hong Kong to Britain.[15] These new conditions affected U.S. trading interests. Through the efforts of Commodore Lawrence Kearny, China announced that the new trade regulations would apply to other Christian countries as well as Britain. This in effect opened China to trade with the United States, but a number of American diplomats thought that an independent Sino-American treaty should secure these trade rights. As a result, the veteran diplomat Caleb Cushing was dispatched to China in the spring of 1843.[16]

What mattered more than diplomacy to young Dr. Kane was the opportunity the mission offered to see the world and pursue his various interests. It was an opportunity he would exploit to the fullest. Despite persistent bouts of ill health that would recur throughout his life, he was a young man of tremendous energy and unbridled intellectual curiosity, even if he lacked discipline. He was only five and a half feet tall and for most of his life weighed no more than 130 pounds, but he made up for his small stature with a strong desire for knowledge and a willingness to push himself to both his intellectual and his physical limits. In preparation for the trip he read as much as he could on a variety of subjects from world history to natural history, hoping to supplement his book learning with firsthand experience during the voyage. He specialized in no single field; instead he was curious about everything from ancient religion to geology. Like his father, he cultivated an upper-middle-class interest in learning about the world, but he would take this interest in a very different direction than his father had.

In May 1843 the *Brandywine* crossed the Atlantic to the Portuguese island of Madeira, about four hundred miles west off the coast of North Africa, though Kane did not have the opportunity to disembark. It then recrossed the Atlantic to the Brazilian port of Rio de Janeiro. There the future world traveler found himself on what he called "my first and only foreign soil."[17]

Kane kept journals of all of his travels, but many of these accounts are now lost. Fortunately, a four-page account of his visit to Rio does survive. It was the first of many attempts by Kanc to document his travels in writing, a technique he gradually mastered over the course of his life. It may have been written as a journal entry or a letter to his family, or perhaps for possible publication in a newspaper or magazine at home, as accounts of this sort by American travelers were a staple of the antebellum literary trade. Kane's point of view in this account is that of an American searcher after foreign novelty and exoticism. He commented that the "general appearance of Rio was such as to greatly interest me; not so much by its intrinsic merit as by the constantly recurring conviction which it everywhere brought—of another people and another world."[18] As an American abroad, Kane was prepared to write about what he saw, as countless others like him did. Certainly he was aware that when he returned home to Philadelphia, his experiences would give him a certain status as a man of learning. A few intelligent observations printed in a magazine or delivered to a small group of genteel savants like himself would gain him the kind of reputation he desired.

The themes of an exotic landscape and exotic people characterize his account of Rio, which begins with a panorama of the local setting. "The general character of the scenery was wild and highly picturesque," wrote Kane, "the mountain ridges having an air of rugged grandeur which contrasted admirably with the placid character of its quiet waters." Then, with a mixture of curiosity and xenophobic horror, Kane moved from an overview of the wondrous landscape to a description of its strange inhabitants, "uncivilized looking mulattos" who, he later found with surprise, "to be the native and loyal citizens." In the true Jacksonian style, which was able to embrace ideals of political equality for white men alongside notions of racial inequality, he dwelt on the social and economic extremes of this Brazilian city. With more contempt than sympathy, he commented on the conditions of the poor in Rio, whom he called "a wretched herd of jabbering negroes," and contrasted them with what he saw as the aristocratic pretensions of the imperial court of the fifteen-year-old emperor Dom Pedro II, who, according to Kane "needed more than his gilded coat to make him *manlike*." Kane's description of Rio is an argument for American republican principles that scorned both poverty and excessive wealth: "Nothing can be more pitiably contrasted, than the gilded finery, and squalid rags, so curiously intermingled."[19] In this, his earliest writing on foreign places, Kane's depiction of Brazilian society reflected back on conditions at home, helping to define an American identity in contrast. America, to Kane, was a different kind of nation, one where such disparities of wealth did not exist—and where citizenship was for whites only.

Like many of his white contemporaries, Kane emphasized foreign inequality while ignoring the inequality that existed at home in the form of racial slavery and the removal of the Native Americans from valuable lands. Those who are not of European ancestry are part of the wonderous scenery to Kane. He rarely treats nonwhites as human individuals worthy of the same level of respect as whites; rather he depicts the native people of the regions he visits as curiosities, clearly unlike his readers at home. Despite his appeals to a democratic ideology of equality, being American to Kane meant being white and middle class, and his earliest writings reinforce this idea by painting all else in the mode of exoticism.

THE *Brandywine* progressed from Rio, rounded the Cape of Good Hope, and arrived in Bombay, India, on October 25. Here the ship had to wait three weeks for the arrival of the expedition's leader, Caleb Cushing, who was traveling by way of Suez. While the ship sat in Bombay, Kane took the opportunity to travel through the Indian countryside. He visited the Buddhist and Hindu temple caves carved into the rock of Elephanta Island near Bombay as well as those at Ellora and Daulatabad. He also traveled inland across the Ghat Mountains at Khandala to visit the Karla caves with a young midshipman from the *Brandywine*, William Weaver. Midshipman Weaver, like Kane, knew that it was appropriate to write down one's observations as an American witness to a foreign scene, and he did so as a writing exercise for his tutor on board the ship.[20]

Once Cushing joined the ship, the embassy proceeded on to the island of Ceylon (presently Sri Lanka), where, in early December, Kane traveled inland to its capital, Kandy, to hunt elephants in the countryside.[21] The Reverend George Jones, chaplain to the embassy, later described Kane at this point in his life. "He seemed to be all hope, all ardor, and his eye appeared already to take in the whole world as his own. . . . His conversation showed a great deal of such intelligence as is gained from books, and a great desire to learn all topics."[22] These travels in India certainly thrilled the young doctor. William Elder colorfully asserts that Kane "used to refer to this as a time of delightful excitement. The risk edged the relish of the joyance, and he feasted to the full upon the tropical wealth of novelty which everywhere surrounded him, multiplied in its effect by its infinite variety." Clearly this first opportunity for extensive inland travel in India stimulated Kane's desire to see more of the world.[23]

The *Brandywine* resumed its journey to China, reaching Macao Roads in the Bay of Canton by the end of February 1844. Here the slow process of diplomacy began, but Caleb Cushing, his assistant Fletcher Webster, and Dr. Peter Parker, a missionary who had spent many years in China, handled this task.[24] Kane had little to do, and day after day of idle ship life must have irked his restless spirit. To combat the boredom, he sought and obtained permission from Cushing to do some exploring on his own with a Prussian baron, Diedrick von Loë, whom he had met while traveling near Bombay. Finding their own transport, the pair traveled southeast across the China Sea to Luzon, the largest of the Philippine islands, then a colony of Spain. Kane seems to have planned for this journey even before leaving home, as he was prepared with useful letters of introduction to various political and ecclesiastical authorities in the Philippines.[25]

Kane and Baron Loë traveled extensively over the inland regions of Luzon and perhaps other islands of the Philippines. Scattered accounts of the earliest part of these travels survive in Kane's papers in what may be either a draft of a book or a much longer and more polished narrative for his family. We know that John Kane wanted his son to publish an account of his travels, and Elisha's younger brother Thomas often referred to the goal of publishing something, although there is no record of anything ever appearing in print until Kane's later Arctic travels.[26] This nevertheless reinforces suspicions that Kane's motive for traveling was not just personal curiosity; he clearly realized that a book or even a few articles on his travels could secure his reputation as a man of culture and learning. Whatever the purpose of these narratives, nine chapter-length sections survive, all of which bear the marks of later editing.[27]

Kane's language, describing his arrival in Manila, shows something of his romantic search for novelty in the exotic, typical of his style at this point, and typical also of the popular travel accounts found in the newspapers and magazines of this era:

> It was at the close of the monsoon, in the sultry month of May, a season notorious for its listlessness and sleepy calms that we anchored off the great capital of the Philippine Islands. I say *we* for I had one companion, who like myself was a wanderer and had his own reasons for making the East his field. We had met each other in the Hindu Ghauts near Bombay, he on his way seaward, bound for the Hills of Mahableshwer, I on a pilgrimage to the cave temples of Elloza and Carli. Again we met in Canton and Macao, and now by that strange sympathy which sometimes brings opposites together we had yoked forces and friendships to tramp over comparatively untrodden ground.[28]

Kane's Philippine narrative falls somewhere between an adventure story and ethnography, with surprisingly little comment, considering his later career, on the natural history and geology of the regions he passed through. As he and Baron Loë traveled over the countryside, Kane recorded picturesque descriptions of the landscape and the people who inhabited it, all with the goal of helping his reader to develop an accurate visual impression of this foreign scene. He also collected plants, minerals, and other objects of interest to him.[29]

Kane and Loë visited all of the sights of Manila. They went to the cockfights, looked in on the cigar manufacturers, and visited the city's architectural sites, but it is clear that they wanted to do more than just see what earlier travelers had described. In Rio and in India, Kane had traveled in places that were exotic but still well known to European and American travelers. If he really wanted to make a name for himself as a traveler, he would have to do something special enough to bring him notice. He wanted to branch out, to become an explorer as well as a traveler, so Kane and Loë received permission from the authorities to explore inland regions of Luzon, where few foreigners were allowed to go.[30]

The two gentleman adventurers traveled up the Pasig River to Laguna de Bay. They began "on one of those beautiful mornings which make you in love with life," wrote Kane, floating in a large dugout canoe called a *banka* propelled by three paddlers and a pilot. As they traveled upstream, Kane observed all the sights around him, both human and natural, and described what he saw in the voice of one sure of his own superiority. He was in good spirits, and his narrative has a lighthearted air. The two young men often seem more interested in the people than in the flora and fauna. "For a long time we amused ourselves by looking at the native women bathing in the stream," he noted. They flirted with the women, trying to get them to smile. Kane commented on the attractiveness of their raven-black hair, only to be both amused and disgusted to discover that the women's teeth were stained with the juice of the betel nut.[31]

From Laguna de Bay they continued their travels on foot into the mountains, sometimes sleeping out and at other times staying at the haciendas of Spanish landowners or with the Catholic priests in Tagal villages. Kane found his surroundings both wondrous and entertaining. While at times he ridiculed what he saw as the backward habits of the Filipinos, at other times he made fun of his own sense of being out of place in a strange and different land. The clash with exotic cultures that his trip often precipitated was for Kane an opportunity for humor, much like the displays of exotic "cannibals" and "savages" to be found in the dime museums at home.

On one occasion early in their trip Kane and Loë entered the village of Bay in the middle of the night. As strangers in the dark, they did not know where to sleep. They were led by their guide to a spot in a sleeping apartment to rest. Awakening suddenly, Kane was horrified to find a sleepy young Tagal woman's head resting on his chest. "There is a point beyond which even good nature cannot go," he wrote. "Remember too that I was very tired and to tell the truth a little (a very little) scared. I seized the unknown head by its dangling locks and started to my feet." Of course the woman cried out in surprise at having her hair pulled in the night by a strange man, and Kane was immediately surrounded by "fathers and grandfathers, mothers and grandmothers, aunts, sisters, and cousins of sizes ages and, alas! costumes entirely beyond my pen." Luckily for Kane, the village priest was able to sort the matter out, but Kane readily admitted that he was the foolish one for not knowing local customs, while the occupants of the apartment he had entered "listened most respectfully to the gibberish by which I tried to render simple the complicated presence of two strange and somewhat shabby gentlemen in their dormitory."[32] Either way, Kane's emphasis on strangeness and the distance between himself and those of other cultures made an entertaining story that he must have told often to friends and family back home. This was the era of amateur ethnography, and Kane differed little from other Americans traveling abroad, for whom cultural difference was enjoyed for its novelty but not appreciated as having any intrinsic value of its own.

Kane and Loë progressed inland, where they met and enjoyed the hospitality of an old Spaniard, Señor Don Inigo Gonzales y Azaola, who, according to Kane, had seen the volcanoes of Mexico with the famous German traveler Alexander von Humboldt. While staying at Don Inigo's hacienda, they explored the area. They climbed "El Monte de Mah-jai-jai," collected bird skins, and observed the people. Kane described sugar production on Don Inigo's estate, following this up with an account of an alligator hunt, which he found brutal, and then progressed to a discourse on the roles of the government and the Catholic Church in the Philippines.

In short, everything he observed in this far-off land was worthy of detailed description for the instruction and amusement of his readers.[33]

Kane's next goal, along with his companions and guides, was the Taal volcano, with its deep two-mile-wide crater, on an island in the middle of a large lake in southern Luzon. Of all his early travels, it is the trip to the Taal volcano to which biographers have paid the most attention. It is here that Kane's narrative first begins to emphasize the kinds of dangers that would come to dominate his later writings, and is also where, for the first time, he combined the elements of science, adventure, and exotic natural wonders—a recipe that would ensure him a popular following later in life.

Here he related another anecdote of intercultural miscommunication that he found humorous, but that was also tinged with a serious threat of danger. While his companions were having a midday siesta at the village of Taal, Kane borrowed a horse from the local priest and went by himself to see the volcanic lake. He was riding along, pondering the scenery, when "a large Indian rose suddenly before my horse and almost before I had recovered from the sudden start of the animal, he had seized him by the bridle. The man was armed by a long knife and although his language was a perfect jargon I knew enough by intonation and gestures that he was ordering me to dismount." Kane immediately drew his pistol and spurred his horse, knocking the man down, and galloped away down the path.[34]

He visited the lake as planned, but eventually he had to return to the village along the same route. At the place of his earlier encounter, he found a large group of islanders waiting for him. A chase ensued. Kane galloped away and tried to hide for a time in a thicket, where he gathered some small stones, then he remounted and galloped back through the surprised group, throwing the stones at his attackers. Soon it seemed as if he would be brought down by this mob, who he believed wanted to murder him as a Protestant heretic. "Some time had thus gone by and the infernal devils still preserved their ground," he wrote, "when I saw a second party well mounted and rapidly nearing me from the other direction. The party behind gave a loud shout of exultation—and pressed on—for myself I was in that stupid state of confusion which attends the complete absence of an [illegible] when I recognized the white cassocks and broad brimmed hats of the Padrés. A moment more and I was hugged, kissed, and congratulated by a regular posse of Augustines headed by Padre Poblacion, Loë, and Don Inigo."[35]

After recounting this dramatic rescue by a friendly ecclesiastical cavalry, Kane explained that the adventure was actually more ludicrous than dangerous. While he had imagined that the "Indians" were out to slaughter him, in actuality the man who had stopped Kane had been acting quite reasonably. The man, Esedro, had recognized the priest's favorite horse being ridden by Kane, who was unknown to him. In Kane's words, Esedro had seen him as "a very shabby suspicious looking, not foreigner, but Spaniard, a sort of vice sub-delagado hanger on of the tobacco inspection or some such respectable personage. In a word, I was not a persecuted heretic, but a run-away horse thief."[36]

One of the more appealing aspects of Kane's writings is the way that, in the midst of a largely ethnocentric narrative in which he casts himself as the civilized white man surrounded by primitive foreigners, he can suddenly turn the tables to show himself as the foreigner. Yet these moments of insight never last long, and he soon returns to the role of superior white man. The technique ultimately serves to distance himself and his readers further from the inhabitants of these foreign lands. One can imagine Kane, back home, entertaining the ladies and gentlemen who frequented the parlors of upper-middle-class Philadelphia with his wonderful stories of exotic adventures such as these. For the audience at home, the Tagal men and women became curiosities fit for the consumption of genteel American parlor entertainment. Their primary importance was to amuse.

Imagined danger soon turned to real danger, however, as Kane and his companions set off to visit the volcano. They hired an extra-large *banka* that took them, with a host of servants, including Esedro, now Kane's friend, to Taal Lake. Kane described it as unlike any lake he had ever seen: "The saline character of its waters gave it a darker tinge, but it was not on this account called by the natives 'the dark sea,' for the quantities of crumbled cinder and charred detritus which cover its bottom and line its shores are such as to make it literally *black*."[37] They sailed out into this "zone of desolation in the midst of fruitfulness," making their way to the island of Bonbong, which he described as "a mass of scoriacious ejections rising into a central cone, covered in some places by long runs of congealed lava and at others rent into angular gullies just as you would expect in any good orthodox volcano." No living thing could be seen in this landscape; the ground was littered with cinders, and from the crater "a lazy column of steam and smoke was slowly ascending."[38]

The party slept on the island that night, and in the morning they began to climb the volcano, finally arriving at the top, where they could look into the crater. "Crawling upon our hands and knees," wrote Kane, "the lava within six inches of our noses, suddenly our heads jutted up above the crest of the volcano, and the magnificence of the crater literally a coup d'oeil burst upon us." Below them lay a crater around two miles in diameter filled with spires of lava and lakes of congealed black mud. At its center another cone rose 150 feet, "and in its centre a boiling cauldron of fire, smoke, steam, and sulpher." Kane admitted that the sublimity of the scene was beyond his powers of description. As he and Loë lay there looking down into the volcano, the two travelers formed a plan to descend into it.[39]

The pair did not proceed right away. This section of the narrative ends with their first glimpse into the crater and resumes at some later date, with Kane and Loë returning to the island with a large group of islanders prepared for a journey into the crater. They again climbed the volcano and chose a place for their descent. Kane's account makes no mention of this, but at some point, most likely at the insistence of the baron or Don Inigo, he wrote a short note in pencil that still survives among his papers, absolving his friends of all responsibility for his dangerous actions.[40] Then, having nothing to secure their climbing rope to, they dug eight holes in the slope of the mountain, "and into each we deposited a pair of Indians who seated with their legs braced against the sides took charge of the rope upon which we hung our safety."[41]

After the baron threatened to shoot in the head any of the Tagala rope holders who did not attend to their duty, Kane, who at no more than 130 pounds weighed much less than his six-foot-four-inch Prussian companion, started down the 103-foot descent. After climbing and being lowered partway, Kane looked up to see Loë on a projecting crag fourteen feet from the top. They both agreed that it would not be a good idea for the larger man to trust himself to the rope, so the baron turned back. Elder asserts that, at this point, Loë urged Kane to give up the descent, but Kane makes no mention of this in his narrative. Instead, we learn from Kane's papers, Esedro took the baron's place. Elder's account, quite typically of nineteenth-century accounts of white men traveling among "Indians," makes no mention of Esedro. All later accounts incorrectly describe this as a solo adventure.[42]

Kane relates a local myth Esedro told him about the crater, then the account abruptly ends. Elder, however, the only other source for these travels, continues, asserting that once Kane reached the crater floor, he untied himself from the rope, collected some specimens from the crater's lake for later scientific analysis, and barely made it back to the rope in time to tie it around himself before almost losing consciousness from the fumes. He was then hauled out of the crater and carried home. Elder adds the rather dubious story that a "pygmy mob" then assailed Kane and his friends for desecrating the gods of the volcano, so that they had to hide in the bushes, firing off their guns until they were rescued by the local padres.[43]

We know no more of Kane's travels in the Philippines except for a brief account in an 1859 book on "eminent Philadelphians," which suggests that the travels extended further on Luzon and the Philippine islands of Camarinas and Mindoro.[44] By the end of June, Kane was back in Macao to participate in the more social aspects of the final month of the diplomatic expedition, but when the *Brandywine* left Macao in August, its mission over, Dr. Kane was not on board. He had resigned his post with the intention of setting up a medical practice in the Chinese port of Whampoa farther up the Canton River. Here he and his partner, an Englishman named Michael O'Sullivan, planned to tend to the medical needs of the crews of European and American merchant ships visiting that part of China. This endeavor lasted only a few months. Late in the year Kane became seriously ill with rice fever, and in January 1845 he left Whampoa.[45]

FROM JANUARY to April 1845, Kane's route is unclear. He may have spent some time exploring more of the interior of India. Some accounts describe him traveling through the Himalayas, but by April he was in Cairo planning an ascent of the Nile. A diary of his trip up the Nile can be found among his papers, yet it is a much less polished piece of writing than his accounts of his adventures in Rio and the Philippines. Far from the enthusiastic young explorer of the earlier accounts, this diary shows a tired and depressed man whose travels had perhaps gone on too long.[46]

Kane's interests focused on ancient Egyptology rather than the Egypt of his own time or even the natural sciences. He commented in his journal on various ancient sites and the discoveries by European scholars such as Sir John Gardner Wilkinson.[47] This was the golden age of European Egyptology, spurred on by the expansion of European colonialism in the nineteenth century. Since Napoleon's armies had descended upon Egypt with a corps of scholars at the turn of the century, Europeans had been visiting Egypt to view, and often take home with them, its great wonders. In the 1820s Jean-François Champollion had finally deciphered Egyptian hieroglyphs, paving the way for a greater understanding of ancient Egypt. The historian Brian Fagan has observed that, by the 1830s, Egypt had become a European fad, leading to what he calls "the rape of the Nile," as "diplomats and tourists, merchants and dukes, all vied with one another to assemble spectacular collections of mummies and other antiquities."[48] In the United States it was not unusual at this time to hear of "mummy unwrappings," in which a mummy that some traveler had collected while in Egypt would be publicly unwrapped for the benefit of public curiosity. Although Egyptian culture was quickly being consumed by a new Western consumer culture, this sort of consumption was legitimated by the pretext of scholarship.

Kane threw himself wholeheartedly into this scholarly and popular milieu. He read widely in preparation for his voyage and then searched out ruins mentioned by the authors. He seemed to see himself as something of an amateur Egyptologist. Traveling up the Nile by boat, he hunted for ruins, sketched the landscape, and copied hieroglyphs into his notebook. While "ruin hunting" near El Sheikh Sa'îd, he stumbled upon "the trunk of a king in fine marble, or alabaster. The cartouches on his girdle made him a Pharaoh." Feeling that his discovery was of some scholarly significance, he arranged to have the piece of statuary packed up and shipped to the American Philosophical Society in Philadelphia.[49]

Kane did not just acquire objects of art. A list of items he lost in a boat accident one day along the Nile indicates something of his collecting habits throughout his travels. The lost items included minerals, pressed plants, journals and papers of his time in Whampoa and Luzon, and, most disturbingly, a collection of human skulls of the different ethnic groups he had encountered, as well as the entire skeleton of a Chinese woman. These he had planned to present to the craniologist Samuel Morton on his return to Philadelphia. Morton was well respected at the time for promoting a uniquely nineteenth-century brand of scientific racism. His studies of the relative intelligence of the various "races" of mankind were based on measurements of the cranial capacity of skulls from around the world sent to him by travelers like Kane. This research was then used to justify different forms of racial oppression such as American slavery and the forced deportation of Native Americans from desirable lands.[50]

To Kane the skulls and skeleton were simply bits of inanimate booty to be collected and taken home for intellectual consumption by his fellow Americans. Non-Western peoples, their strange habits, and even their bodies were fit objects of interest for the culture of curiosity, like pressed plants and minerals. The essentially dehumanizing nature of antebellum popular ethnography such as Kane practiced placed other cultures in a passive role; they existed to be examined and studied as objects. This was the case with scientists such as Samuel Morton, and it was the case with the popular audiences who constituted the culture of curiosity. Americans were to be informed and entertained by the knowledge of other cultures, but always in a way that reinforced American superiority and diminished the object of study. Like the minstrel show, which used well-researched ethnographic details of African American life to create amusements for racist audiences, the travel accounts and collecting habits of Americans such as Kane used the knowledge of other societies as a way to demonstrate growing American dominance. Americans and Europeans were the ones who traveled, observed, and collected, while non-Western peoples were the inferior objects of the travelers' observation and collection.

As the summer of 1845 commenced, Kane began to weary of traveling, so he headed for Europe, and by mid-July he was in Paris. Apparently he toured much of Europe, but once again we have only the biographer William Elder to rely on for this part of his journey.[51] By the end of the summer the world traveler was home in Philadelphia, ready to embark on the next phase of his life.[52]

KANE'S INTEREST in faraway places and exotic people and landscapes was shared by countless Americans and was reflected throughout American culture. As one scholar has pointed out, "Almost every prominent American literary figure of the nineteenth century has written one type or another of travel book or based some of his literary output on his experiences of travel in foreign lands."[53] Scientists too produced travel accounts that reached a wide popular audience. Charles Darwin was known for his

Voyage of the Beagle (1839) long before anyone had heard of his theory of natural selection, and Americans avidly read the German traveler Alexander von Humboldt's *Personal Narrative* (1834). American explorers such as Charles Wilkes, John L. Stephens, and John C. Frémont made names for themselves with their descriptions of foreign places and people.[54]

Nineteenth-century Americans did not just read about travel. People could learn about the wonders of geography by going to hear lectures at their local lyceums or lecture halls.[55] Urban dwellers could visit dime museums such as Barnum's to see artifacts from faraway lands. They could even see strange "savage" people on display. In Barnum's cosmorama section, even the poorest class of citizen could afford to pay the quarter necessary to peer through peepholes at scenes from around the world.[56] Similarly, wealthy gentlemen could join the new scientific and geographic societies that emerged in this era, where science and exploration were discussed as a scholarly pursuit.[57]

Much interest in the wonders of the globe fell somewhere between the scientific and the sensational, as even intellectual entertainment was aimed at a mass audience. The announcement of "Professor Sattler's Panoramas" which appeared in the *Knickerbocker* in 1851 is fairly typical:

> Again have we of the Great Metropolis occasion to thank our stars that we can travel abroad, and see the rarest marvels of the earth, alike without fatigue, without sea-sickness, and (what is quite as much of an object) without money! The *Second Series of Professor Sattler's Panoramas* is now open to the public. There is even more variety in the second than in the first series; and nothing can exceed the exquisite truthfulness and beauty of the pictures which make up the present collection. Would you visit the sublime ruins of Karnak, in Upper Egypt, there they are, *as* they are in reality, before you. Would you visit the loveliest spot in all the Gulf of Naples? Lo! the Bay of Sorrento, by Moonlight; a scene of unsurpassed loveliness. Pause and look at "Damascus" in Syria, before you pass on to "Bethlehem in the Holy Land," crowned with hallowed associations.[58]

As the nineteenth century progressed, Americans' interest in distant lands and their belief in their superiority over the exotic people who lived in them became one rationale for the rise of American imperialism in some of the countries Kane visited. At home, showmen presented "savages" and "cannibals" for the entertainment of a mass commercial audience, while abroad native people were colonized and consumed by a growing American imperialism.[59]

When Elisha Kane embarked on his travels he became part of this milieu, and his travel writings conformed to the established conventions for describing foreign lands and non-Western people. The natural and human wonders he hoped to see were the same ones that thousands of Americans were curious about when they picked up a travel narrative to read or went to the local lyceum to hear a lecture. At home, to friends and acquaintances, he would have become an authority on the foreign lands he visited and an interesting companion for a genteel conversation even before he became a published author.

In time Kane would learn to tap into many popular forums to promote his own career as a famous explorer. He began his life in a center of the American Enlightenment, in the midst of genteel middle-class culture, but as he matured and was influenced by the commercial world of nineteenth-century America, he eventually learned to adapt that background for a mass audience. The stories he told of his early travels were only a starting point for his future career as a great popularizer of geographic exploration and ethnographic description.

THE GEOGRAPHY of the globe was not the only thing Americans were curious about during the antebellum era. They were also curious about the geography of the mind and soul. Only two years after Kane's return to the United States from his travels abroad, Americans would be exposed to one of the greatest wonders of the era. A phenomenon more marvelous than the pyramids of Egypt and more sublime than the deepest volcanic crater would be presented by three sisters from western New York State who knew little of science or Enlightenment. These sisters, however, were adept performers of mystery, and for a time they became master popularizers of one of the era's most controversial new theories: communication between the living and the dead.

2

"Come and Investigate"

Mysterious Rappings in Western New York

Lovers of the marvelous usually take great delight in tales of mysterious knockings. We have one now to tell.

Rochester Daily American, April 4, 1848

IN LATE MARCH 1848, a few months after moving into a new home in the small community of Hydesville, New York, John and Margaret Fox became the victims of a prank perpetrated by their two youngest children. Maggie, age fifteen, and Kate, age twelve or thirteen, enjoyed mischief and often teased both their mother and their niece, Lizzie Fish, who was also in her early teens.[1] Perhaps the girls were restless and bored after a long northern winter in a new home, or perhaps they were just naturally mischievous, but on a few nights in March, when they were supposed to be sleeping, they engaged in a little foolishness that would have consequences far beyond what they ever intended. Taking apples from the cellar, they tied string to the stems and bounced them on the floor next to their bed, producing sharp rapping sounds.[2] Naturally the girls' mother and father, who slept in the same room as their children that night, rose to investigate the sounds, but the girls, most likely enjoying their ability to make fools of their elders, denied any knowledge of the source of the knockings. The baffled mother recalled, "The night we heard the rapping, we all got up and lit a candle; and searched all over the house."[3] She found nothing, but the noises continued.

On Friday night, March 31, the girls decided to take the trick a little further. On this night, Mrs. Fox decided to go to bed just after sunset to catch up on lost sleep. Soon after, the noises began again. The children then imitated the sounds by snapping their fingers, and to Mrs. Fox's horror, the knocks soon seemed to respond to the children's actions. As Mrs. Fox later recalled, Maggie next said aloud, "Now do this just as I do. Count one, two, three, four . . . ," as she clapped her hands together. The knocks followed her lead. Then an alarmed Mrs. Fox spoke out asking the noises to count to ten, and they did so. "Then I asked the ages of my different children successively, and it gave a number of raps, corresponding to the ages of the children," she later attested.[4]

The raps had become more than random bumps in the night. Now they were communicating in an intelligent manner—but unbeknownst to Mrs. Fox, the intelligence was that of her two daughters. Maggie Fox would later admit that she and her sister soon "got the idea of producing with the toe joints similar sounds to those we had made by dropping apples with a string." She continued: "From trying it with our fingers we then tried it with our feet, and it did not take long for us to find out that we could easily produce very loud raps by the action of the toe-joint when in contact with any substance which is a good conductor of sound. My sister Katie was the first to discover that we could make such peculiar noises with our fingers. We used to practice first with one foot and then the other, and finally we got so we could do it with hardly an effort."[5]

Convinced, however, that she was communicating with a spirit from another world, the gullible Mrs. Fox tried to determine who this nocturnal visitor was. In doing so she allowed her own beliefs to provide the direction that the story would take, and unwittingly encouraged her daughters to continue the trick.[6] She asked if the visitor was an injured spirit and heard knocks in the affirmative. She went on to determine, by means of answering knocks for yes and silence for no, that the visitor was the spirit of a thirty-one-year-old man who had been dead for two years and was buried in the cellar. After receiving these disturbing revelations, Mr. and Mrs. Fox decided that it was time to call in the neighbors.[7]

At about seven-thirty or eight o'clock, John Fox went next door and brought back their neighbor, Mary Redfield. Mrs. Redfield had heard about the mysterious noises earlier from Maggie and Kate, but she thought it was all a joke. She went over to the Fox home "with a good deal of levity, saying that I would go over and have a spree with it, if it was a ghost."[8] Despite her initial jocularity, when she arrived at the Fox home, she found Mrs. Fox upset and quite in earnest, and it appeared to her that "the girls were much frightened." Mrs. Fox demonstrated the strange phenomenon for Mrs. Redfield by asking more test questions of the spirit, which were promptly answered with knocks.[9]

Soon more neighbors were summoned to hear the curious knockings and ask questions of the ghost, which at this point was not yet specifically identified with the presence of the girls. Mrs. Redfield went and got her husband, Charles, who in turn called in William Duesler and his wife. Mr. and Mrs. Artemas Hyde and David and Elizabeth Jewell also soon arrived on the scene. Mr. Duesler took charge of the dialogue, asking questions that focused on the identity of the spirit and the circumstances of its murder. These questions were answered, as before, by raps for yes and silence for no. "In the same way Mr. Duesler ascertained that it was murdered in the bedroom, about five years ago, and that the murder was committed by a Mr.———, on a Tuesday night, at 12 o'clock; that it was murdered by having its throat cut, with a butcher knife; that the body did not remain in the room next day, but that it was taken down cellar, and that it was not buried until the next night, that it was not taken down through the outside door, but through the buttery, down the stairway; that it was buried ten feet below the surface of the ground."[10] More questioning revealed that the victim was a peddler who had been murdered for the five hundred dollars he carried. The supposed murderer was identified as a former tenant in the house, John C. Bell, who was then living in nearby Lyons, New York.[11] These findings originated in part from the answers Maggie and Kate surreptitiously provided to questions, but mostly from the questions themselves, since Maggie and Kate had only the limited ability to answer yes or no. It is not surprising, then, that the story developed into a fairly typical tale of greed, murder, and an unquiet ghost.

That night, when the investigations were done, Mrs. Fox went to sleep at the Redfields' home, and Maggie and Kate slept at another neighbor's. Mr. Fox and Mr. Redfield stayed behind to keep watch at the house. On Saturday morning many people came to investigate, as many as three to five hundred by some accounts, but as long as the sun was up, they heard no knocks.[12] When darkness fell, however, the knockings resumed, and they continued throughout the next day. The excited community was eager to solve the puzzle of the raps and to uncover the murder, if there had been one. They asked the spirit what part of the cellar his body was buried in, and they started to dig in the cellar after receiving a reply. They wanted tangible proof to back up the strange sounds, but the diggers hit groundwater and had to stop at less than four feet.[13]

In the days that followed, as word spread of the mysterious sounds, hundreds of people came from miles around to satisfy their curiosity.[14] In the 1920s Adelbert Cronise, a citizen of the region, recalled that in his youth old witnesses to the scene still "told of the Saturday and Sunday crowds that came from far and near, filling the roads and lining the fences with horses and vehicles." Moreover, "they said that a small admission fee was charged by Mrs Fox."[15] Soon previous tenants of the house were telling of strange sounds they too had heard while living there. On a more sinister level, Lucretia Pulver claimed that, while working for Mr. and Mrs. Bell at the time of the supposed murder, she had witnessed what appeared to be signs of digging in the cellar, which Mrs. Bell had explained as rat holes. This, she said, was just days after a peddler had made a visit and then mysteriously disappeared.[16] All signs pointed to a grisly murder by John Bell.

To THE MODERN reader these events seem no more than the acting out of an eerie and rather typical ghost story. We have heard it all before: the restless spirit of a murder victim, buried under the house, emerges at night to disturb the sleep of the new family living there. The Fox family's house was thought to be haunted, just as scores of homes across the country were thought by superstitious minds to be haunted. Surprisingly, however, the events in Hydesville grew to become far more than a simple ghost story in the months and years that followed; they became the starting point for a new mass movement, called spiritualism, that would influence tens of thousands of people in America and Britain for the remainder of the nineteenth century. Spiritualism, in a variety of forms, became one of the largest popular movements of the time. It promised communication between the worlds of the living and the dead, first through simple knocks, then through more sensational phenomena created by mediums at séances. Spiritualism promised an end to the fear of death and loss of loved ones, and it offered the opportunity to investigate life's greatest mystery. Its influence would be felt from the working class all the way to the White House, and it would cross the Atlantic to become a mass movement in Victorian England as well.

When Kate and Maggie first began the rappings, the Fox family were living in a four-room rented house in Hydesville, New York, a rural farming community within the township of Acadia in Wayne County. The signs of a rapidly growing commercial society could be seen just a few miles south in Newark, where barges traveled the recently constructed Erie Canal on their way west toward the Great Lakes or east to the Hudson River, bringing the new products of western agriculture to the commercial markets in the East. Western New York epitomized the rapidly changing face of America in the first half of the nineteenth century. The "transportation revolution" of the 1820s, which had brought the Erie Canal to the region, meant that one could travel easily to the port of New York, and moreover, agricultural goods could be efficiently transported to urban markets. The communities that sprang up as a result of improved transportation were filled by families moving west from the more established regions of New England. Unlike the genteel society of Elisha Kane's Philadelphia, western New York was the home of people who had departed the towns where their parents and grandparents had lived in favor of setting out on their own and acquiring the cheaper land to be found in the West. This made it a site of rapid change and growth, and the fluidity of the region made it a place where new ideas, new movements, and new forms of inquiry were readily embraced.[17]

In the early 1800s, when evangelical religious revivals had spread throughout the country in what historians call the Second Great Awakening, western New York State was particularly affected. The fires of religious revival burned so hot there that it came to be called "the burned-over district." The historian Whitney R. Cross has described the "broad belt of land" flanking the Erie Canal as home to "a people extraordinarily given to unusual religious beliefs, particularly devoted to crusades aimed at the perfection of mankind and the attainment of millennial happiness."[18] Revivalist such as Charles Grandison Finney had found a welcome reception there, and more radical religious movements such as the Shakers and reform movements such as the abolitionist and women's rights movements also found a natural home in the region. A generation before the Fox sisters began their rappings, not far from Hydesville in the community of Palmyra, Joseph Smith received the revelations that would lead to the founding of the Mormon Church. The region was thus not unaccustomed to new religious beliefs or supernatural revelations that promised a brighter future. The spirit rapping came along at the tail end of this period, when much of the religious enthusiasm of a generation prior had simmered down. But just as Elisha Kane would adapt his Enlightenment background for a new era, the Fox sisters would adapt the waning enthusiasm of the burned-over district to a new age of commercial culture.

MAGGIE AND Kate Fox's backgrounds do not appear unusual for this time and place. Their father, John D. Fox, was a blacksmith and a farmer who was considered by his neighbors to be a respectable and trustworthy member of the community. His wife, Margaret, was a devout Methodist who had raised six children since their marriage almost thirty-five years before.[19] The Foxes were originally from Canada, according to some reports, but they had moved to western New York and settled at first in Rochester then moved east to Hydesville.[20] Of the six children, four were now adults living away from home. Margaret and John Fox had not lived together continuously since their marriage; after their first four children were born, John, who had problems with alcohol, had abandoned his wife and children. He returned years later, and he and Margaret had two more children. Margaret, who was called Maggie or Margaretta to distinguish her from her mother, was born around 1833 and was now fifteen. Her sister Catherine, called Kate or Cathy, was two or three years younger.

Like every region of the United States at this time, western New York had its local newspapers, and the editors of these papers played a major role in promoting curiosity in the Fox sisters' rappings. These editors were businessmen who peddled news and knowledge, some of it important and some simply peculiar. In many ways the newspapers were a central part of the intellectual life of a community. The editor's job was to inform the readership as well as to interest them in curious tidbits of information that inspired thought. Soon after Maggie and Kate began the rappings in Hydesville, nearby editors recognized that the curiosity generated by the Fox sisters was a marketable commodity, and several went to see for themselves. The authors of some of the earliest published accounts played up the mysterious nature of the knocks and invited their readers to draw their own conclusions. Others dismissed them as an April Fools' joke. All, however, expressed a desire to get to the bottom of the mystery, to find out whether the rappings came from this world or the next. A good mystery, after all, made good copy.

An editor from nearby Canandaigua, New York, E. E. Lewis, was the first who widely publicized the rappings for a reading public. In late April, less than a month after the initial events, he printed a pamphlet containing the signed statements of many of the principal witnesses. It remains the earliest and best source of information about the rappings, and most later accounts stem from it.[21] Lewis knew that the way to make his pamphlet sell was to follow the example of the sisters in offering a strange phenomenon without definitive explanation. Presenting himself as an impartial observer, he laid out the bizarre and unbelievable evidence and invited his readers to "step forward and solve the mystery, if they can." He even offered a $50 reward to anyone who could do so.[22] His pamphlet could be read as proof by those who believed in ghosts or as a challenge to those who sought to uncover a fraud. According to Maggie Fox, Lewis was not the impartial observer he claimed to be: "Much of the effect of the 'rappings' is greatly exaggerated in this statement which my mother was made to write," she later said, and which had perhaps even been dictated by "men who desired to make public the details of the 'rappings' and to make money by the sale of a pamphlet describing them."[23] As a journalist, Lewis knew that if he engaged his readers' interest by giving them a mystery to solve, they would buy his pamphlet. Spirit rapping, from the start, unlike earlier movements in the burned-over district, was thus propelled forward by commercial purveyors of information who were out to make money by catering to public curiosity.

Local newspaper reporters were more skeptical, but they also promoted the growth of the phenomenon. They invited readers to do a better job of detection than the foolish people of Hydesville. The *Rochester Daily American*, for example, adopted a superior and disbelieving tone, reporting that the superstitious residents of Hydesville were creating meanings for the sounds to fit their own preconceptions. With an air of sarcasm the paper noted, "We would not for a moment insinuate that the girl did it, because everybody was determined to consider it supernatural, and it is safest to go with the majority." Questions had been put and interpretations made in accordance with preexisting beliefs, so "by this time the story of a murdered peddler became current. No one doubted that his unfortunate bones were crying for vengeance. Questions were framed to meet the exigency, and answers were received in distinct knocks, which the excited crowd were at no loss to interpret." The mystery was not a supernatural one, in the eyes of this reporter, but it was still a challenge to figure out how the trick was done. This was an opportunity for intelligent men to prove that they were not fools by exposing the fraud.[24]

Despite the sporadic press coverage in nearby Rochester, the knockings in Hydesville were still primarily a local affair. Assorted versions of the story appeared in various newspapers, but there was not a great deal of emphasis placed on these accounts or even in getting the facts straight.[25] By April 22, the *Rochester Daily American* reported, "the excitement which this unparalleled humbug has created, has in a measure subsided, and the people who were a little credulous at first, are now beginning to countenance the idea that they have been unequivocally gulled." The paper speculated that perhaps the whole thing had been an April Fools' joke.[26] But the story did not go away completely, since the mystery had not been solved. Occasional reports continued to appear in the papers, but perhaps the excitement would have slowly disappeared had it not been for Maggie and Kate's older sister, Ann Leah Fish.[27]

LEAH, AS SHE was called, was the eldest daughter of John and Margaret Fox. At the time, she was making a living teaching piano in Rochester. In May the mother of one of her piano students showed her a copy of Lewis's pamphlet on the knockings. Apparently that was the first she had heard of her younger sisters' activities, and that night Fish boarded the Erie Canal packet boat to Newark to discover for herself what was going on. She found the family at her brother David's house in Hydesville, where they were all staying after fleeing the "haunted" house.[28] Unfortunately, the strange sounds had followed them to David's house. By this time the family had realized that the knockings seemed to be associated with Maggie and Kate, in whose presence they always occurred. Leah Fish was not fooled, as most people had been. As soon as she arrived from Rochester, she took her two younger sisters aside to interrogate them, asking how the raps were produced. She did not, however, choose to expose them. Instead she learned how to produce the sounds herself.[29]

Although not much is known about Leah Fish's life to this point, what we do know indicates a difficult existence. Born in 1814, she was still a young girl when her father deserted the family. There is no evidence that tells what the family did to support itself while John Fox was gone, but life could not have been easy for any of them. Leah, by her own report, was only fourteen years old when she married a much older man, Bowman Fish.[30] This marriage brought her a daughter, born when Leah herself was still a child. Her husband subsequently deserted her, leaving her to fend for herself. The life of a single teenage mother in nineteenth-century America was not an enviable one. Fish did what she could to make a living for herself by teaching piano, and her parents often helped out by taking the child, Lizzie, into their home.[31]

It is not surprising, then, that Leah Fish was looking for a way out, and she seems to have realized immediately that the raps had commercial potential. She soon became an active force behind the rappings, and as such she transformed the episode from a cliché-ridden ghost story into a much larger and more original phenomenon that would appeal to public curiosity about the unknown. Using the excuse that separating the girls might put an end to the sounds, she soon persuaded her mother to allow Kate to travel back to Rochester to live with her for a while. About two weeks after Fish had first arrived in Hydesville, she, Kate, and Lizzie took the packet boat to Rochester. Maggie, who seems to have had some reservations about her older sister, chose to stay with her mother. Fish later explained this separation of the sisters as an unsuccessful attempt to stop the rappings, but these only increased and became more elaborate now that she was in charge.[32]

According to her account, which she repeated to acquaintances in Rochester and published in a book almost forty years later, she and her family continued to be tormented by the spirits in Rochester, and however much they tried to discourage and ignore them, they persisted as a sort of curse. They produced terrorizing sounds, moved beds as the women tried to sleep, and hurled things through the air. Calvin Brown, a friend of the family, soon came to live with them, but he seems only to have become a target of the spirits. Soon Maggie and Mrs. Fox arrived in Rochester as well, and the activity of the spirits increased.[33]

Maggie Fox later claimed that her older sister forced her and Kate to continue the rapping, but this seems to be an exaggeration. While Leah Fish, as the eldest, was the most dominant of the three sisters, the younger girls seem to have enjoyed continuing the charade.[34] At least a month passed in Rochester during which Maggie, Kate, and Leah played their tricks on Mrs. Fox and Calvin Brown, perhaps with some reluctant help from Lizzie. The girls, who apparently saw the whole thing as a game, honed their skills of deception, using Brown and Mrs. Fox as practice.

They even added new tricks to their repertoire. According to Reuben Davenport, whose 1888 account was authorized by Maggie and Kate Fox:

> [Maggie Fox] remembers with tolerable distinctness the antics that distinguished this sojourn of her mother, herself and her sisters in the Rochester house. She and Katie did indulge in wild larks in the sleeping rooms of the family at all hours of the night. The "whispering" and "giggling," the "scuffling" and "groaning," and the tragic mimicry were natural to childish dare-devils like themselves, and one can well understand how, with the attendant "rappings," the showers of slippers hurled from the "green room," the shaking of Calvin's bed and the "banging" of him on the head, these things may have made the desired impression upon both him and the mother.[35]

The more the rapping went on, however, the harder it was to stop. So many people, including family and friends, had been fooled that to confess the trick became impossible. "So," according to Maggie Fox, "we went right on."[36]

During the summer of 1848 the sisters introduced their spirit rappings to a select group of Rochester citizens including Amy and Isaac Post. Isaac owned a local drug store, and he and his wife were active in many reform movements of the day, especially abolition. The fires of religious revival that had burned through Rochester during the 1830s and 1840s had advocated greater moral free agency of Christians and the ability of individuals to contribute to their own salvation and ultimately the coming of the Millennium. This drive toward Christian perfection fed into moral reform movements such as temperance and abolition.[37] The Posts, who were Hicksite Quakers, were at the heart of these movements in Rochester. Others who attended the first séances with the Fox sisters included evangelical Methodists, Quakers, and prominent reformers, such as Mr. and Mrs. Lyman Granger, Mr. and Mrs. Henry Bush, Elihu Grovers, and the Reverend Asahel H. Jervis.[38]

These pioneer spiritualists were a different sort from the Fox sisters or the people of Hydesville.[39] As respectable urban middle-class professionals and reformers, they believed strongly in moral and social progress and thought that the world could be changed for the better through their active agency. Leah Fish realized that if the rappings were going to have a future, this was a good group with which to start. She did what she could to present the rappings as part of a progressive age of reform, and many of the reformers soon came to believe that the raps were simply additional evidence that a new era of history was about to begin through the agency of reform-minded Christians like themselves. By associating the rapping with people like the Posts and Grangers, the sisters would go a long way toward turning it from mere fodder for ghost stories into the dawning of a new and better age.[40] As in Hydesville, the audience was invited to explore and then determine the meaning of the raps. But this audience would understand the raps differently. What had been a common ghost story to rural farmers became a sign of moral progress to these urban middle-class professionals.

The Posts were especially important to the spread of spiritualism, since they had contacts throughout the national abolitionist network. Amy Post in particular was in regular contact with movement leaders such as William Lloyd Garrison and Frederick Douglass. Abolitionist speakers and activists often passed through Rochester and stayed with the Posts; when Douglass first arrived in Rochester, he stayed at the Posts' house.[41] As a result, after Amy and Isaac began to attend regular séances with the Fox sisters, the word quickly began to spread throughout the national abolitionist community of this strange new phenomenon. Douglass, in fact, was an early witness to the rapping, but it did not appeal to him. Not all, or even most, abolitionists joined the Posts in their spiritualist beliefs, but they did become interested, since the idea of spirits coming back to earth to guide humanity to a new age seemed consistent with their firm belief in human progress and perfectibility. The Boston abolitionist William Cooper Nell visited Rochester sometime in early 1849 and attended a séance with the Posts, Maggie and Kate Fox, and Leah Fish. He was not yet convinced, but, as he later wrote Amy Post: "I would give worlds *to know*. Yes to *know*. That's the word. *What* it was that pulled my coat on that memorable night." He also reported that William Lloyd Garrison had heard of the rapping and was becoming interested.[42]

The connection between reform movements such as abolitionism and spirit rapping should not be overemphasized or misunderstood, however. Spirit rapping cannot be equated to the many reform movements of the era. The Fox sisters used the reform movements to their advantage, but there is nothing to indicate that they had moral reform as a motive for their activities. Moreover, other reformist friends of the Posts expressed doubt and concern about the Posts' involvement in such a dubious-sounding fad. Fellow Quaker John Willis wrote Amy Post that, while at meeting, he had told friends who inquired after her that "thee and Isaac . . . was as much like a balloon as anything that I could compare you to, ready to be taken any way the wind should blow." Willis made no secret of his distaste, calling spirit rapping "the most absurd and ridiculous thing that ever was believed in on the face of this earth."[43] Spirit rapping is thus not best understood as a reform movement itself; rather, the sisters were creating a marketing relationship with the reformers by attaching their performances to the social circles created by the reformers. Their performances encouraged preexisting philosophies of human progress and perfectibility but did nothing to promote the positive changes desired by the reformers. Some of the Posts' reform-minded friends seem to have realized this.

With some serious caveats, the historian Ronald G. Walters has nevertheless, included spiritualism in his study of antebellum reform movements, yet he also acknowledges that the Fox sisters themselves did not concern themselves much with reform philosophies of human progress.[44] Ann Braude takes a similar approach in her study of spiritualism and the women's rights movement, seeing strong links between spiritualist believers and women's rights advocates but at the same time dismissing the Fox sisters as unimportant.[45] This is a contradiction that can best be understood if we separate spirit rapping from the spiritualist philosophies it fostered in the people who can be described as its customers. We need to draw a distinction between performers (spirit rappers) and audience (spiritualist believers and curious nonbelievers). The activity of spirit rapping, as performed by the Fox sisters, can then be understood as a consumer commodity that successfully marketed itself to reformers along with other audiences as they came along. This becomes increasingly clear as the sisters moved from one market to another in the first few years after the rappings began at Hydesville, gradually expanding their exposure and their appeal to ever larger audiences. While the first rappings in Hydesville did not seem to have had a financial motive, as the sisters expanded into urban markets, a financial basis for continuing would soon establish itself as well-off urban professionals took an interest.[46]

One can only speculate as to what the three sisters hoped to get out of the rappings at first, because it took several months before they gained any financial benefit that can be documented. It is clear that Leah Fish craved respectability and the admiration of those above her on the social ladder. The rappings may have seemed to her to be a pathway to middle-class status. She was very careful to expose the spiritualist rappings only to respectable citizens, a point that she repeatedly emphasizes in her later writing.[47] While spiritualism has often been portrayed as a middle-class movement because of the dominance of people such as the Grangers and the Posts, the case is actually a bit more complicated. The Fox sisters' relationship with these middle-class reformers set a precedent, often repeated, of working-class spirit rappers appealing to a middle-class audience of believers. Rapping thus became a ticket to the middle class for women like Maggie and Kate Fox and Leah Fish.[48]

The idea of using and deceiving people to gain status did not seen to bother Fish, and for the younger girls the rappings were a way to gain love and attention. Perhaps they justified their marketing of the raps in the same way that Isaac Post justified marketing bogus cures for consumption and hair loss in his drugstore. It was a matter of meeting a demand. Both Maggie and Kate Fox formed close relationships with Amy Post while deceiving her into believing in the spiritual origins of the rappings. At this point in their youth the rappings were fun, something that made them the center of a community of caring people. Perhaps they even convinced themselves that they were helping those they fooled by giving them consoling "messages" from loved ones and confirmation of their reformist beliefs in a better age to come. There is also a possibility, considering their father's history of alcoholism, that their home life in Hydesville had not been a happy one. Their removal from what was perhaps an unpleasant environment to a more nurturing one in Rochester may have encouraged them to continue the deception. There is no evidence that John Fox was not a loving and supportive father, other than reasonable speculation based on his history of alcoholism, but it is clear from their surviving correspondence that Amy and Isaac Post were warm people who formed very close relationships with those who were part of their movement. By rapping, Maggie and Kate Fox and Leah Fish became part of this intimate community.

A letter Maggie Fox wrote to Amy Post while on a visit back to Hydesville during the summer of 1849 shows that her relationship with the Posts was characterized by sincere affection rather than purely cynical manipulation. In little more than a year Maggie had come to see Rochester as a better home, even though much of her family, including her father, remained in Hydesville.

> Dear Amy you can't think how lonesome it is out here. I think if you were here the time would pass more swiftly. It seems as if I have been here three months instead of three weeks. I am anxious to get back to Rochester again. Rochester is my much loved home, but after all Amy I have some [illegible] times here. If mother could only be with me then I should be happy, but I know she can't be there all the time. Oh Amy, it is a very gloomy day. It has been raining all forenoon. Oh how still and silent it is here today. I love the noise and confusion of the city, but I am something like the woman that became so accustomed to her husband's snoring that she could not get to sleep without it.[49]

Very soon after arriving in Rochester, the sisters, led by Fish, developed the format of what would become the spiritualist séance. An explanation was devised for visitors that the sisters had special qualities that made them "mediums" through whom the worlds of the living and the dead could be brought into contact. This was why the raps occurred only in their presence. Forgoing the random and uncontrolled format of the rappings they had performed at Hydesville, the sisters began to organize controlled séances with rules for proper conduct. Séances would begin with a prayer, while the party sat around a wooden table in a darkened room. If a spirit made its presence felt, participants could ask it yes-or-no questions, or the spirit might "call for the alphabet" by knocking five times in rapid succession. If this happened, someone would recite the alphabet until a knock was heard at a particular letter. The process would be repeated until words and sentences were spelled out. The spirits had to be treated with great respect or else they might refuse to participate.[50]

The earliest séances were private affairs, and as a result few records remain to tell what went on. But in June 1848, three months after the first raps were heard, a Congregational minister, Lemuel Clark, from Worcester, New York, visiting the Grangers' home in Rochester, became a skeptical participant in and observer of some of these early performances. Lyman Granger and his wife, wealthy Methodists, had by this time become convinced of the spiritual origin of the raps and believed themselves to be in communication, through the Fox sisters, with their daughter Harriet, who had died less than two years before. The Reverend Clark described the séance to his brother in a letter that November.[51] The group, which met at the Grangers' home, was made up of Mrs. Elihu Grover, Calvin Brown, Leah and Lizzie Fish, Kate and Mrs. Fox, as well as Mr. and Mrs. Granger and their fourteen-year-old daughter, Elizabeth, who was soon to become a medium herself. They sat down around a large cherry table for refreshments, and Clark was asked to say a blessing. As he did so, he heard sounds. He recounted to his brother, "To all the more devotional parts of the service it responded by rapping." As the participants drank tea and ate cakes, they began to converse with the spirits, who responded to questions with raps for yes and silence for no.[52]

The first spirit to appear was the murdered peddler from the house in Hydesville, whose name had by now been determined through "calling for the alphabet" to be Charles Rosna. He retold the same old story, but then, led by the Reverend Clark, moved on to issues of greater theological importance. When asked by Clark, "Did God send you?" the spirit responded in the affirmative. This prompted the minister to ask, "But what can have been his object, has He any important purposes to accomplish, the fulfillment of which depends on such manifestations from the spirit world as you are now making?" The spirits answered this with louder than usual raps.[53] Clark next saw the table move while no one seemed to be in contact with it, and then the spirit of Harriet Granger joined them to converse with her parents about her mysterious death. The parents seemed to believe, and the spirit seemed to confirm, that she had been murdered by her husband, who now intended to harm her parents as well. When Clark questioned Harriet's spirit, she told him of heaven, the resurrection, and her growing awareness and moral understanding.[54]

During the next two days at Fish's house, Clark heard strange sawing and planing noises, as if, he said, a coffin were being built out of pine boards, and he communicated with the spirits again. Skeptical yet baffled, he was soon hearing raps even when the sisters were not present. "This affair astonished me more than anything or everything I had witnessed," he reported. "I knew not but some of the company, at other times had practiced legerdemain, but it would be impossible to convince me that Liman Grainger [sic] practiced it, nor can I perceive how it is possible that any person could have practiced deception upon us under those circumstances and in that way."[55] While it is impossible at this late date to tell exactly how the sisters produced all of these phenomena, it is apparent that they were adept at telling people what they hoped to hear, for it is easiest to deceive people into believing that which they most want to believe. Perhaps this is why reformers were an easy early target: they were the ones with the greatest desire to believe that something new and transformative was coming to the society in which they lived.

The rappings continued in this way for over a year. In addition to performing private séances in Rochester, the girls traveled and demonstrated their ability as mediums in homes around western New York State. Kate lived for a time in Auburn, New York, with Mr. and Mrs. Eliab Wilkenson Capron. Eliab Capron was a friend of the Posts who had first heard the raps in November 1848. Capron was also a dedicated reformer who served as secretary to the Auburn National Reform Association.[56] He gradually became convinced of the spiritual nature of the raps and eventually played an important part in the development of spiritualism. In Auburn the rappings caught on strongly. The phenomenon did not confine itself to the Fox sisters, either. "Mediums" seemed to be popping up all over. In Rochester, Elizabeth Granger, the daughter of Lyman Granger, was soon showing signs of being a medium, as were a number of women in Auburn.[57] In early 1850 Capron described the spread of the spiritual phenomenon "The first of its being heard in this city [Auburn] was when the youngest daughter of Mr. Fox [Kate] visited our boarding house. After she returned it was heard for some time in the presence of several who had heard the sounds in her presence, and in a few months spread to several families where it has gradually grown more free. . . . We are informed of at least six families in Auburn who hear more or less of the same sounds."[58]

These new rappers may not all have produced sounds the same way the sisters did, and we do not have the evidence to discount them all as tricksters, but there was undoubtedly more religious fervor among the Fox sisters' protégés than among the sisters themselves. Theological speculation and religious enthusiasm by this point were moving beyond the sisters' control. Some of these new mediums may well have been believers themselves, caught up in the excitement of the moment, while others were undoubtedly frauds, but all looked to the Fox sisters for a model of performance.

SO FAR THE sisters's spirit rapping had taken place primarily within a private setting, but an important transition occurred in the fall of 1849, when "the spirits" demanded that their manifestations be demonstrated publicly. To make planning such a demonstration easier, the spirits insisted on directing the whole affair. First, supporters of the Fox sisters were told, they should rent Corinthian Hall, the largest hall in Rochester. There Maggie Fox and Leah Fish would act as mediums (Kate Fox was visiting in Auburn), while Eliab Capron would deliver a lecture recounting the history of the rappings since they first began in Hydesville a year and a half earlier. Presumably the material for Capron's speech came from the sisters. Another supporter, George Willets, "was to act as friend and business man, doorkeeper, etc." Five respected citizens of Rochester, all supporters of spiritualism, were to sit on the platform with the sisters to lend gravity to the whole affair. They were the Reverend Asahel Jervis, Lyman Granger, Simeon Draper, Mrs. Sarah D. Fish, and Mrs. Pierpont. In addition, the audience was to choose five individuals to act as a committee of investigation. For their part, the spirits promised to make their raps loud enough to be heard in the large hall.[59]

The advertisements for the demonstrations, which appeared in the local paper, appealed to the curiosity of the public rather than to any religious or reform beliefs. This was early evidence that spirit rapping did not have to confine itself to reform circles. The sisters could reach beyond the limited audience of moral reformers to a larger public by using the techniques not of reform but of mass marketing. The advertisements, mixing appeals to sensation with appeals to investigation, were framed as a challenge to the intelligence of the public: "Let the citizens of Rochester embrace this opportunity of investigating the whole matter, and see if those engaged in laying it before the public are deceived, or are deceiving others, and if neither, account for these truly wonderful manifestations. . . . Come and investigate." The price was twenty-five cents, but after the performances on Wednesday and Thursday, the admission charge was reduced to half for the final two shows.[60] This is the first indisputable documentation of the sisters charging a fee; whether they received any money for their earlier private performances is unclear, but not unlikely.

To demonstrate a new phenomenon in an urban performance hall was not unusual. Such public demonstrations of novelties were central to the culture of curiosity and could be found in every community of any size. In this democratic age, new ideas were often presented for public debate. Sciences (or pseudo-sciences) like phrenology, which claimed to judge personality by reading the shape of a person's head, and mesmerism, an early version of hypnotism, were demonstrated publicly as a combination of education and entertainment. Traveling phrenologists and mesmerists went from city to city giving demonstrations of wonderful feats, as did practitioners of more established sciences such as chemistry. Mesmerists, phrenologists, and later spiritualists allowed a glimpse into the mystery of the human mind. They claimed to reveal recently discovered aspects of the mind and to resolve the relationship between mind and body and between matter and thought.

The people of western New York were therefore very familiar with these kinds of demonstrations. In December 1848, for example, citizens of Rochester and Auburn could go see "Professor Rogers" and be amazed by "his miraculous experiments and illustrations" in mesmerism and phrenology.[61] Or they could read about "'Miss Bertha' the clairvoyant who 'reads without eyes.'"[62] Just two months before the Fox sisters' demonstration at Corinthian Hall, residents of Auburn were able to observe experiments in magic and ventriloquism by "Mr. Gester," along with a "magnificent diorama of the conflagration of Moscow."[63] Or they could take classes in phrenology and mesmerism in the basement of the local Universalist church with Mr. H. E. R. Lewis.[64] These sorts of demonstrations were not without controversy. Mr. Lewis had to defend himself in the newspapers from the Reverend H. Hicks's charges of being "an Infidel."[65] More controversy and debate in the form of letters to the editor of the *Auburn Daily Advertiser* erupted a month later when a Dr. Dods arrived to lecture, to give demonstrations, and even to cure disease with "Electrical Psychology," his version of mesmerism.[66]

So it was not without precedent when, on the evening of Wednesday, November 14, 1849, the first commercial public demonstration of spirit rapping commenced. Apparently the spirits had a good bit of talent for show business, for their plan to publicize the rappings worked wonderfully, drawing "a few of 'all sorts of people'" to Corinthian Hall to see the show, according to the *Rochester Republican*.[67] First, Eliab Capron rose to speak. He recounted the history of the mysterious noises, then, according to the *Rochester Daily Democrat*, went on to discuss the scientific "discoveries of Gallileo, Newton and Fulton, and how their substantial invention and discoveries were laughed at long ago, when Science was in its infancy."[68] Clearly, Capron wanted to deflect ridicule by presenting the rapping as a new scientific discovery rather than as an occult phenomenon.

R. Laurence Moore, who has studied the way spiritualism reflected the cultural authority of empirical science in the nineteenth century, convincingly argues that spiritualists rejected supernatural or occult explanations of spiritual phenomena in favor of an approach that borrowed the methods and language of science. The séance was thus modeled after the scientific experiment in the hope of rationalizing religion by replacing faith with proof. Spiritualism, Moore concludes, may thus be considered a sort of democratic psuedo-science in which individuals were invited to draw their own conclusions on the basis of their observations.[69] We see this theme demonstrated in the lecture by Capron, which combined his reformist leanings with a strong faith in progress through science. Capron believed that science could explain more than just the material world; he thought that a scientific examination of the rapping phenomenon could provide answers to difficult spiritual questions.

Capron linked spiritualism with the mesmerist philosophies that were then current. Developed by an Austrian, Franz Anton Mesmer, in the eighteenth century, by the 1840s mesmerism was experiencing a resurgence of popularity in England and the United States. Mesmerism involved putting subjects into a trance state, which was often called "mesmerizing" or "magnetizing" them. This state was, and still is, only partially understood, but mesmerized subjects showed themselves to be very susceptible to suggestion and could be made to believe almost anything suggested by the mesmerist. On a practical level mesmerism was often used to relieve pain, but it also branched out to embrace beliefs in phenomena such as clairvoyance, or the ability of the mind to leave the confines of the body to communicate with the minds of others or to "see" things far away. It was only a short step from such ideas to the belief that mesmerism could help bring out people's latent mediumistic abilities by making them more sensitive, more in tune with the "magnetic fluids" or "ether" which was supposed to surround all things. If a mind could communicate with another mind while separated from the body, why should this communication not continue after the body had died? Edgar Allan Poe had toyed with this very subject in one of his stories.[70] Capron was at the forefront of those who saw spirit rapping as the logical extension of mesmerism and clairvoyance.[71] The central idea was that a whole other world, which could be explored by the mind, existed beyond the bounds of the physical plane. Just as Elisha Kane explored other geographic worlds, mesmerists, clairvoyants, and now spiritualists would explore other worlds of the mind and soul. Like terrestrial explorers, they would map this world and present their findings to the people in commercial democratic forums such as the newspaper and the lecture hall.

Meanwhile, at Corinthian Hall, Leah Fish and Maggie Fox appeared on the stage and produced knockings that continued throughout the performance, "to the great astonishment of those who had gone thither, with gaping ears, to catch the mysterious sounds."[72] Each night the audience elected a committee of five to investigate further and to report their findings the next night. These committees were allowed to meet privately with Leah and Maggie to investigate. In this way the sisters became the objects of scientific inquiry, as the *Rochester Daily Democrat* noted:

> Several questions were put here and answered, not altogether right, nor yet entirely wrong; but the rapping indicated to the committee that if they would go to Mr. Post's house, it would do more for them than it could where they were. So the committee went, as requested. When at Mr. P's, the rapping was heard on the outside of the front door, after they had entered, and on the door of a closet. By placing the hand on the door, there was a sensible jar felt where the rapping was heard. One of the committee placed one of his hands upon the feet of the women, and the other on the floor, and though the feet were not moved, as far as he could perceive, there was a distinct jar on the floor. Placing the women on an elevated settee, *no sound was heard,* and this failure also happened *when they were placed on a bed.* On the pavement, and on the ground the same sound—a sort of a double rap, as of a stroke and rebound—was distinguishable. When the women were separated, at a distance, *no noise was heard, when a third person was interposed between them, it continued.* The women seemed to be very ready to give every opportunity to the committee to investigate the cause fully, and would submit to a thorough scrutiny by ladies.[73]

This "thorough scrutiny" by ladies involved having the sisters undress so that their clothing and bodies could be examined.

Each night, after these examinations, the committee would come back without answers. Respectable and seemingly intelligent members of the community could not meet the challenge of the Fox sisters and had to admit their defeat publicly before raucous crowds. It would almost have been easier to admit a belief in spirits than to admit to being stumped by a pair of mere girls. One newspaper described the riotous scene when the committee reported on its lack of findings one night: "They concluded that they were no wiser then than they were when they started the search of the ghost.—At this announcement popular feeling began to effervesce, and several gentlemen rose to remonstrate, while the lay members of the committee attempted to explain—all were subdued by the general tumult that ensued."[74] Who knows if any in these audiences were converted to a belief in spiritual communication; probably not, but certainly they all had a good time investigating the matter in such a democratic forum.

Fox and Fish played their roles well. They made no extravagant claims, and they drew no attention to themselves as individuals. Instead they appeared as innocent and guileless young creatures, unable themselves to account for the mysterious noises that seemed to follow them around. They allowed themselves to be examined, and surrounded themselves with sincere, reform-minded men and women whom they had fooled, like Eliab Capron and Amy and Isaac Post. They let Capron and the others draw all the attention, do the overt marketing, and make claims about theological and scientific meaning, while they receded into the background, producing their knocks. As a result, accounts of these performances at Corinthian Hall feature Capron, the knocking, and the committees of investigation, but Leah Fish and Maggie Fox are barely mentioned. In many sources, such as the newspaper reports of the Corinthian Hall demonstration, the sisters remain vague figures seen only through the veil of spiritual phenomena.

The Corinthian Hall performances were the launching point of spirit rapping as a widespread commercial success. From here it moved outward beyond the confines of the reform community into the larger culture of curiosity. Shortly after the performances, Capron and his friend George Willets wrote a long letter to Horace Greeley at the *New York Tribune*, published on November 29, 1849.[75] The result was an avalanche of public debate in the *Tribune*, one of the nation's more influential papers, about the significance of what had happened. None of the previous manifestations had been noted in the large New York City newspapers, but now that changed. With four successful public demonstrations of the rappings in the fall of 1849, they grew from a local craze to an object of national curiosity. The next step was the big city itself and then a national tour.

The Fox sisters never formulated any philosophies to explain their rappings, but others did so wherever they appeared. Historians, generally more interested in spiritualist believers than in spirit rappers such as the Fox sister, have tried to explain the rise of spiritualism in the wake of the sisters' rise to fame. Spiritualism embraced a diverse set of ideas that were prevalent in the antebellum era and the later nineteenth century, the common denominator being that living humans could communicate with the dead. There were spiritualists of all sorts, so it has been difficult for historians to pinpoint any one characteristic that made someone a spiritualist. R. Lawrence Moore has studied spiritualism's emulation of science, Ronald Walters has considered spiritualism as a reform movement, Ann Braude has examined the strong connections between spiritualism and women's rights, and Bret Carroll has looked at the theological beliefs of spiritualists.[76] These historians have observed that spiritualism had its start as a popular movement with the knockings at Hydesville, but in light of this, it is surprising how little significance they have found in the persons of Maggie and Kate Fox, who actually initiated the knockings. Most historians have essentially dismissed the Fox sisters themselves, emphasizing instead the religious, philosophical, and social views of those who went to their séances and became convinced of the spiritual nature of the raps. The sisters never took a leadership role within any spiritualist organization. They never advocated a particular theological or scientific point of view or attempted to explain the mysterious knockings at all. Braude, who actually gives more attention to the sisters than others, puts it bluntly: "Although the Fox sisters converted many influential people and provided the model for other mediums, they never participated actively in the movement they began. Their own lives . . . add little to an understanding of the role of Spiritualism in American history."[77]

This view has some justification if we are looking at spiritualism as a set of ideas; but the problem with this perspective is that it stresses the content of spiritualist philosophy to the exclusion of the performance and form of the rappings themselves. Spiritualism, after all, was rooted in the activity of the séance, not in a set of beliefs. Most studies take as their focus those who identified themselves as believers in spiritualism, but spirit rapping was larger than that, appealing not only to believers but to the curious as well, as when the sisters performed at Corinthian Hall. In fact, when we concentrate on the Fox sisters rather than on spiritualism's believers, the picture we get changes from ideas to performance. Maggie and Kate Fox were crucial to the development of the séance in the United States. They created a form and structure for spiritual manifestation and investigation. They were also skillful marketers who knew how to attract a diverse audience. The audiences of the culture of curiosity might be believers or they might not, but they all eagerly paid to see the sisters nonetheless. The Fox sisters offered participants an intriguing puzzle which allowed people to create their own meanings for the strange phenomena they witnessed. In doing so, and in charging a fee for the service, the sisters positioned spirit rapping squarely in the midst of an emerging commercial mass culture. This was their greatest contribution, and it was one of form not content.

Spirit rapping was a process of active exploration into the unknown. Just as Elisha Kane presented his discoveries and experiences to the world through his writing, the Fox sisters became guides who led their audiences on explorations of the "undiscovered country" beyond death. The sisters never dictated what would be found in the world they explored, but as skilled performers, they inspired the investigation. By looking at the Fox sisters' performance rather than the intellectual content derived from it, we see that, in the way they appealed to American popular culture, Margaret Fox's spirit rapping and Elisha Kane's explorations would prove to be not so far removed after all.

Of course, at this early stage in their careers, the Fox sisters and their rappings were still far from the realm of genteel scientific investigation. But Maggie Fox and Elisha Kane were headed in the same direction. Theirs was a road that led toward the rising urban centers of a new mass culture in America—places like New York City. Each was learning to tap into the antebellum American love of the unknown. Each was learning how to perform, how to tell stories in a way that the American mass audience found interesting. Elisha Kane, coming from a world of Enlightenment and gentility, had not yet found a broad audience for his stories of exploration. Maggie Fox was coming from a far more disordered and dynamic world of reformers, performers, and followers of popular pseudosciences. As each began to engage a larger audience, their careers would increasingly converge. Although they came from very different backgrounds, they would soon find that they shared a common audience.

3

Humboldtean Science and the Search for Franklin

The First Grinnell Expedition

Elisha has gone to the North Pole.
Diary of Bessie Kane, May 26, 1850

FROM THE beginning of their spirit rapping career, the Fox sisters were masters at performing for a curious public interested in exploring the workings of the mind and the nature of death. At the same time, Elisha Kane was slowly learning a similar approach toward interesting a wider democratic audience in his geographic explorations. His presentations, linking science and humanitarianism within a framework of thrilling adventure, would ultimately bring him the admiration of thousands. He, like the Fox sisters, would become an attraction, but he also won the personal respect of the American public to a degree that far surpassed what the Fox sisters were able to achieve.

Kane's early travels had been those of a restless young adventurer with a gentlemanly interest in various branches of science. In the years following his return from those youthful journeys, Kane learned to focus his interests, to the point where he could become accepted by the scientific community as a colleague and, at the same time, by the public as a celebrity, a humanitarian, and a popular scientific hero. Two interrelated developments helped make this transformation possible. First, Kane became increasingly exposed to the moral, methodological, and popular paradigm of "Humboldtean science" which dominated the field in mid-nineteenth-century America. Second, the American press was growing increasingly interested in the fate of the British Arctic explorer Sir John

Franklin, who, with his entire crew, had disappeared into the strange icy regions near the North Pole on a quest for the greatest of all geographical mysteries: the Northwest Passage. Many Americans began to support a humanitarian mission to help find the lost explorer.

Both developments combined science, morality, and popular sensation in a uniquely nineteenth-century way which Kane would learn to exploit when he became a member and chief chronicler of the U.S. Grinnell Expedition, sent out in search of Franklin. The book he wrote about this expedition made him a well-known public figure and served as the launching point for his subsequent career as an Arctic explorer. Like the Fox sisters, he played on themes of mystery and investigation of the unknown in order to appeal to public curiosity. In doing so, he became as much a performer as Maggie Fox, but unlike Fox, he carried the weight and cultural authority of mainstream American science.

FOR FOUR years after Kane returned from his world tour, his activities were varied and adventuresome. He served on a navy ship stationed off the coast of Africa for a time, and this enabled him to explore the coastline of yet another distant continent. He then played a small role in the Mexican War, and was wounded in a skirmish with a group of Mexican officers. Next he was assigned to a navy store ship, delivering supplies to American ships in the Mediterranean. In this job Kane grew to hate navy life, and especially naval discipline, which he saw as arbitrary and despotic, while the tedium of the daily routine at sea grated on his restless nature.[1]

In December 1849 Kane was assigned to duty that was more suited to his interests and that would have a great influence on him: the U.S. Coast Survey. None of Kane's biographers make much of Kane's four or five months with the Coast Survey. Yet, considering his later career as a popularizer of science, this experience was of vital importance to his development as both a man of science and a celebrity. The U.S. Coast Survey was founded in the early nineteenth century to map harbors and coastlines as an aid to navigation and maritime trade. But as the historian Hugh Richard Slotten has shown, from 1843 to 1867, under the direction of Alexander Dallas Bache, "the Coast Survey became the largest and most important institution supporting science in antebellum America."[2] In particular, Bache and the Coast Survey became the primary organized force in America behind what has been called "Humboldtean science."[3]

The historian Susan Cannon has perceptively shown that, around the middle of the nineteenth century, much scientific inquiry was characterize by a search for global interconnections among all natural phenomena. This view, she argues, was best represented by the German scientist and explorer Alexander von Humboldt. Humboldt was one of the first European scientists to explore much of the interior of South America during a five-year trip from 1799 to 1804. The Humboldtean approach, which grew out of his explorations, was to travel the world to measure a variety of physical phenomena on a global scale, often using instruments such as barometers to gauge atmospheric pressure, thermometers and theodolites to gauge temperature, and dip needles to gauge terrestrial magnetism. The data collected by these means could then be tabulated with the data of hundreds of other researchers around the world, with the ultimate goal of discovering global patterns and interconnections.[4]

This approach advanced beyond mere collecting, which had been prevalent among travelers for decades, to become a form of global data correlation. Humboldtean science was geographic in focus, but it also included areas not now understood as aspects of geography, such as geology, geomagnetism, hydrography, astronomy, meteorology, oceanography, and even, to a lesser degree, zoology and botany. Bache used the Coast Survey to advance this approach. As one contemporary observer pointed out, the survey "was made to cover almost the whole range of . . . science, from the structure of the microscopic dwellers in the bed of the ocean, up to the improvement of lunar tables and the determination of positions of fundamental stars."[5] When Kane was assigned to the Coast Survey, he became a part of the Humboldtean process of gathering scientific data, and he would remain a part of this process even after leaving the survey. The diversity of his own scientific interests, combined with his restless nature and love of travel, made him the ideal Humboldtean.

On December 24, 1849, Kane wrote to Bache that he had reported to the secretary of the navy for work on the Coast Survey and requested instructions.[6] He was sent south to the Gulf of Mexico, where a team was surveying the delta of the Tombigbee and Alabama rivers.[7] No detailed accounts of Kane's experiences in the Coast Survey exist, yet from Hugh Slotten's descriptions of its unique scientific culture, we can get a good picture of what the project was like and how it would have influenced him.

Building on Cannon's description of Humboldtean science as a method, Slotten has shown that this approach, especially as practiced at the Coast Survey, had cultural and ethical as well as methodological components. Bache adopted a paternalistic attitude toward his assistants and a moralistic attitude toward science. He expected his assistants, some of whom were naval officers like Kane, others of whom were civilians, to be hard workers and morally upstanding men. Much of the work was done outdoors, and the survey crews often slept in tents for long periods, which Bache considered a wholesome environment. The detailed work of surveying and triangulation seemed to Bache to promote virtuous attributes as well. In Slotten's words, Bache "viewed scientific progress in republican terms that subordinated individual interests to the common good. As a large-scale cooperative activity, the geographical research pursued by the Coast Survey supported this ideal by involving a large number of practitioners in the search for truth—by building a community of like-minded, truth-seeking inquirers."[8]

In Kane's case the paternalistic approach of Bache may have been intensified by personal connections. Bache and Judge John Kane were friends, and the judge had even helped Bache get his job. This no doubt contributed to Elisha's decision to join the Coast Survey. But regardless of how he got there, the survey's approach to science as a virtuous activity dedicated to the advancement of the common good was of great value to Kane when combined with the Humboldtean emphasis on travel. His early travels had been mere wanderings with no greater purpose than the satisfaction of his own petty curiosity. Now Kane had a model for travel and exploration that merged scientific significance with a high moral purpose, even if that purpose was vaguely defined as the advancement of knowledge and the "common good." He could now pursue both science and travel as a calling rather than just a gentleman's pastime.

Kane was not the only one influenced in this way by Humboldt's approach. Charles Darwin took a copy of Humboldt's *Personal Narrative* with him on his voyage on the *Beagle;* John C. Frémont named a river in California for him; John Muir as a young man admired Humboldt and aspired to become a traveling naturalist.[9] To these naturalists and explorers, Humboldt's influence was inspirational as well as methodological. Humboldt was held up as a searcher after truth who sacrificed his own safety and comfort in traveling to remote regions of the earth, all to increase the store of human knowledge.

The influence of Humboldtean science extended beyond scientific travelers and institutions like the Coast Survey to reach a wide-ranging public in America and around the world. Humboldt himself was elevated to the status of a popular hero. To his contemporaries he seemed to have special abilities that allowed him to contribute to the progress of human knowledge and to the ultimate unveiling of life's mysteries. He brought science to a general audience through books that described his extensive travels and offered scientific descriptions of human life and physical phenomena in exotic parts of the world.[10] Non-scientists admired Humboldt to a degree bordering on hero worship. Edgar Allan Poe dedicated his prose-poem "Eureka" to him, and stories about him often appeared in the popular press.[11] The *New York Daily Times* called him one of "the most world-renowned men of the last half century."[12] The *New York Herald* called him a hero of science.[13] Statues were erected in his honor, including a bust in New York City that still stands at Seventy-seventh Street and Central Park-West. But perhaps the travel writer Bayard Taylor was the most emphatic, bluntly asserting, "Alexander von Humboldt is the world's greatest living man."[14]

Writers in the popular press praised Humboldt for advancing the causes of both science and humanity. Such an achievement had wide romantic and sensational appeal. An article in *Eclectic Magazine,* invoking sensuality and religious ecstasy to describe Humboldt's scientific gaze, was typical:

> He has looked upon nature in her aspect of the apparent, and he has investigated her in her essence. All her forms of beauty are to him familiar forms; all her combinations are to him distinguishable, although, to less analytical and less comprehensive minds, they are lost in a great and bewildering unity. . . . Nature, in all her moods and aspects, has been familiar to him; science, in all its painful and delightful phenomena, as illustrated in himself and declared by himself, and he has taught all nations, by his depositions concerning the phenomena and essence of this wondrous world, to admire and better know its Almighty and glorious Author.[15]

An important aspect of Humboldt's approach was his appeal to the public's sense of both wonder and virtue. Humboldt described sensational things that were sublime and awe-inspiring, such as the volcano of Chimborazo, yet he contained these descriptions within a scientific framework. Just as a mythic hero is made greater by the caliber of the trials he overcomes, the scientific hero is elevated by the sublime wonder of the natural world he describes and explains.

The public admiration extended beyond Humboldt as a single personality to include many who practiced his brand of science. One cannot understand Kane or nineteenth-century American popular attitudes toward science without understanding that the search for knowledge about the physical world was imbued with moral overtones. Popular forums reveled in the ideals of human intellectual and moral progress through Humboldtean science. The American people made romantic heroes out of those who seemed to contribute to that progress by explaining nature's wonders. Humboldt was the model, but others, like Kane, followed in his footsteps.

KANE'S UNDERSTANDING of science and exploration matured during his exposure to the Humboldtean approach of the Coast Survey, but he still needed an opportunity to practice what he had learned and to get his own name before the public as a heroic explorer. This opportunity came when the U.S. Navy, with the financial backing of New York merchant Henry Grinnell, decided to send out an expedition in search of the lost explorer Sir John Franklin. Kane volunteered to serve as surgeon on the expedition, and by May 1850 he was on board the brig *Advance* as it set sail for the Arctic regions.

The history of polar exploration dated back to the sixteenth century, when European explorers first set out to discover a Northwest Passage around North America to Asia. By the nineteenth century, sailors and geographers knew that such a route, if it existed, was impractical because of the ice that blocked the channels even in summer. But in 1818 the British Admiralty decided to explore more of the Arctic and renew the quest for this elusive passage. The British quest was motivated by a blend of scientific curiosity along the Humboldtean model, national pride, and a desire to employ a navy left idle after the end of the Napoleonic Wars. By 1845, under the direction of John Barrow, second secretary of the Admiralty, most of the route had been mapped, and quantities of scientific data had been collected by British naval officers such as John and James Ross, George Back, Edward Parry, and John Franklin. By 1845 little remained to complete the search for the Northwest Passage, and the next expedition was expected to succeed.[16]

The Royal Navy fitted out a large expedition consisting of two frigates, the *Erebus* and the *Terror*, and 129 men equipped with three years' provisions. The veteran Arctic explorer Sir John Franklin was placed in command with two accomplished captains, F. R. M. Crozier and James Fitzjames, serving under him. The expedition departed England on May 19, 1845. Two months later they communicated with a whaler in Baffin Bay. They were never heard from again. The fate of Franklin became one of the nineteenth century's great mysteries. Reference to it even found its way into Henry David Thoreau's *Walden,* where Thorean uses geographic exploration as a metaphor for, and contrast to, introspection.[17] Where had the expedition gone? While practical minds no doubt realized that the ships had most probably been crushed by the ice and sunk, the aura of mystery around the disappearance intensified public curiosity.

In the spring of 1848, while there was still some slight hope that the members of the expedition could be found alive, stranded somewhere on the ice, the Admiralty sent out three search parties, one from the east through Baffin Bay and Lancaster Sound, one from the west via the Bering Strait, and one across Canada and down the Mackenzie River to the Arctic Sea (see maps following illustrations). By autumn 1849, however, they had found no sign of the lost ships. Concern mounted, especially the concern of the captain's wife, Lady Jane Franklin, who equipped additional ships at her own expense to search for her husband and urged America, with its large commercial whaling fleet and experienced Arctic sailors, to join the search.[18]

Lady Franklin's appeal took the form of a personal letter to President Zachary Taylor in April 1849. The letter, which was subsequently published in the newspapers, spoke of American humanity and pride—not to mention the £20,000 reward being offered by the Admiralty to any expedition that could find and assist the lost explorers.[19] Secretary of State John M. Clayton responded to Lady Franklin in a public letter, expressing his belief that "the name of Sir John Franklin has been endeared by his heroic virtues and the sufferings and sacrifices which he has encountered for the benefit of mankind." He assured her that the American people were deeply concerned for her husband's fate and that the president would do all he could to help.[20] A few days later, responding to rumors of an American expedition, the *New York Herald* declared that the American public would enthusiastically approve of such a mission. The Department of the Navy, however, reluctant to spend its limited resources looking for lost British sailors, claimed that no ship was available on such short notice. As May and then June 1849 passed, no expedition was sent, and the opportunity for a mission that summer was gone.[21]

Despite the failure to send an expedition, popular American interest in the missing explorers only increased. The American press gave sympathetic attention to the plight of Franklin and his crew, who were imagined to be yet alive, huddling together for warmth amidst the perpetual Arctic snows. Franklin seemed to embody popular ideals along the Humboldtean model of moral and scientific progress made possible by discovery and sacrifice. Arctic exploration, especially discovering the location of the magnetic pole, was seen as an important part of the international process of collecting data for the advancement of science, and as a missing martyr to this endeavor, Franklin soon developed into a popular hero. His fame was intensified by the romantic appeal of his being lost in the strange and sublime landscape of the Arctic, while his faithful wife waited for him at home.[22]

Perhaps American sympathy for the lost British expedition had more than a little to do with pride in the nation's role as a fledgling world power. The United States was a continental nation by 1849, its dreams of a "manifest destiny" to stretch from sea to sea recently fulfilled. When not embroiled in ever-increasing and troublesome sectional strife, America could look outward beyond its own boundaries. England was still the world's greatest maritime power, but the American commercial maritime presence was already strong. For the small U.S. Navy to rescue a pair of British frigates would be a coup for the nation and a clear sign of a growing international presence.

The value of such a mission was clearer to newspaper editors than to the navy, however. The *New York Herald* castigated the Navy Department for its lack of enthusiasm for the project, claiming that officials had "thrown themselves in the way of a high and noble enterprise in the cause of science and civilization."[23] Once again the images of scientific progress and moral advancement combined in the popular press in the figure of the explorer Franklin, this time heightened by the drama surrounding the fate of his expedition, lost somewhere in the distant Arctic.

HAVING FAILED to send an expedition in 1849, the Americans were not about to let another opportunity pass. During the winter, plans were made for an expedition in the spring of 1850. As the navy remained reluctant to contribute to the search, a wealthy New York shipping merchant, Henry Grinnell, who was also a founding member and later president of the American Geographical and Statistical Society, offered the use of two of his ships.[24] With this prompting, the navy provided the men and officers.

Learning of the expedition while working for the Coast Survey in the Gulf of Mexico, Kane volunteered to join it, but for months he heard nothing from his superiors. He knew that his involvement in such a dangerous undertaking would upset his family, yet he confided to his brother Thomas his plans to go if chosen: "Seldom, dear fellow, in the routine of our naval profession does self sacrifice and privation connect itself with reward and self approval, and God knows both are involved in a volunteer expedition such as this."[25]

As spring approached, interest in the expedition mounted. The *New York Herald* took the opportunity to stress patriotic and expansionist themes. European nations, it asserted, had explored the globe for self-interested reasons associated with empire. American explorations were different: "They have not only furnished to older nations truer systems of exploration, but have incited in the breasts of our people a heroic ardor to penetrate into the most distant regions." These explorations, and the free commerce that followed, would, according to the *Herald,* civilize the barbarous regions of the world.[26] Volunteers for the expedition were not lacking among either officers or crew.[27]

Kane did not receive orders to join the expedition until May 12, so he had little time to prepare. In his narrative he described receiving the dispatch assigning him to the expedition while "bathing in the tepid waters of the Gulf of Mexico. . . . Seven and a half days later, I had accomplished my overland journey of thirteen hundred miles, and in forty hours more our squadron was beyond the limits of the United States."[28]

The expedition, commanded by Lieutenant Edwin J. DeHaven, was composed of two rather small "hermaphrodite" brigs, two masted vessels whose foremasts were square-rigged while their mainmasts were schooner-rigged. The *Advance* had four officers, including Kane as surgeon, and thirteen men, while the *Rescue*, commanded by passed-Midshipman S. P. Griffin, had four officers and twelve men. When Kane arrived in New York, he later wrote, he "could not help being struck with the universal sympathy displayed toward our expedition. From the ladies who busied themselves in sealing up air-tight packages of fruit-cakes, to the managers of the Astor House, who insisted that their hotel should be the free head-quarters of our party, it was one continual round of proffered services."[29] Midshipman Robert Randolph Carter, of the prosperous Virginia family, served as first officer on the *Rescue*. He observed in his own journal that everyone expected great success for the expedition, although he was not as optimistic himself, having been pressured into volunteering for the journey by his friend Griffin.[30]

The expedition departed on May 24 from the Brooklyn Navy Yard with orders to proceed northward through Davis Strait to Baffin Bay and then west through Lancaster Sound and Barrow Strait. As the brigs passed by the city, its wharves and ships were crowded with well-wishers come to see them off. Kane observed, "Cheers and hurrahs followed us till we had passed the Battery, and the ferry-boats and steamers came out of their track to salute us in the bay."[31]

Soon, however, the realities of shipboard life overcame the rhetoric of heroic endeavor. Robert Carter, whose enthusiasm for the expedition was minimal, complained in his journal of the unseaworthiness of the *Rescue*: "Did anyone ever see such a beast. She is certainly Amphibious. She takes water in whenever she can, seems to delight in rolling to windward so as to get a whole sea aboard, then by rising forward throws it aft with a rush. Confound this business. . . . Again I reflect what a fool I am to expose myself to such discomforts and vexations."[32] On board the larger brig *Advance*, Kane was horribly seasick, so much so that Captain DeHaven proposed to Kane that he return home a month into the journey, when they made port at Whale Fish Island in Danish Greenland. Yet Kane's unbridled enthusiasm for exploration outweighed his bouts with ill health, and he insisted on remaining.[33]

The American expedition proceeded north as ordered, entering a strange realm of icebergs, polar bears, and continual summer sunlight. They stopped at some settlements on the west coast of Greenland to acquire last-minute provisions and furs, then attempted to cross to the western side of Baffin Bay to Lancaster Sound. Here they ran into what is known as the "Middle Ice." Even at the height of summer in Baffin Bay, miles of ice float down from the north and clog the middle of the bay. Before the days of icebreakers, ships attempting to sail from the eastern to the western shore of the bay could cross at the south, middle, or northern passage, although the most common and safest route for whalers and explorers alike was to the north. This preferred route entailed following the west coast of Greenland north almost to Smith Sound and then crossing to the west in the relatively ice-free "North Water." As an alternative route the middle passage was more direct, yet more often blocked by huge fields of ice, which could become packed together, often trapping ships for weeks or even months.[34]

The *Advance* and the *Rescue* sailed north, with the Greenland coast to the east and the pack ice to the west. Soon after passing the Danish settlement Uppernavik, at around 73 degrees northern latitude, the men saw to the west a vast expanse of ice-free water. They were still in the region of the middle passage, yet the temptation of open water as far as they could see was strong. On July 7, over Kane's respectful objections, Lieutenant DeHaven decided to try the middle passage. By the next day they were stuck fast in the Middle Ice of Baffin Bay and would remain trapped, vainly trying to cut their way out, until finally being released by a shift in winds on July 28, still on the eastern side of Baffin Bay.[35]

Three weeks wasted in the middle of the already short Arctic summer was a great loss. They had not even traveled as far into the Arctic as the typical commercial whaler. One can tell from letters he sent home soon after this that Kane, with his desire for personal glory, did not tolerate the delay happily. In these letters he blames DeHaven for not following his advice.[36]

The *Advance* and the *Rescue* sailed northward to the "North Water" and finally made the crossing to the west. On August 19 the two American brigs approached the entrance to Lancaster Sound, which would take them west into the Canadian archipelago and the site of the search. Here they sighted two ships of Captain William Penny's squadron, the *Lady Franklin* and the *Sophia,* which had come from Britain in search of Franklin. Soon within Lancaster Sound, the Americans were in contact with more British ships, all on the same mission. The British ships had been delayed by ice as long as the Americans. Sir John Ross commanded the *Felix*. Three Royal Navy ships, the *Resolute*, the *Assistance,* and the *Pioneer,* formed the squadron of Captain Horatio Austin. The schooner *Prince Albert* was there also, sent out by Lady Franklin under the command of Captain Charles Forsythe.[37]

All of these searchers, now in almost continuous contact, proceeded west together until they finally came to a halt in Barrow Strait. Routes to the north, south, and west were all blocked by ice, so there was nowhere to go, but the combined expeditions did find evidence of the lost mariners.

On Cape Riley they discovered two stone cairns and signs of British sledge travel and encampments. The American expedition was at Beechey Island on August 27 when men from one of the British ships made the most important discovery to date, Franklin's winter quarters and the graves of three members of Franklin's crew: W. Brain of the *Erebus* died April 3, 1846, John Torrington of the *Terror* died January 1, 1846, and John Hartnell of the *Erebus*, whose grave was undated. There was no other written record left by Franklin at this winter encampment, as was usually done. He had presumably departed this place in a hurry in the spring, as soon as the ice broke up, neglecting to leave the customary record.[38]

This discovery nevertheless indicated that Franklin and most of his crew had survived their first winter in the Arctic, but the question yet remained where they had gone once spring arrived. They could have sailed north up Wellington Channel, west to Melville Sound, or south toward King William Land. Each of these routes was thought possibly to lead to the Northwest Passage. Kane was convinced that they had gone north, but there was no way to prove any of the theories, since all routes were equally clogged by ice.[39]

The Americans and British spent their time looking for clues, hunting the occasional polar bear, and getting to know one another. Since all the ships were quite close together most of the time, they had plenty of opportunity to visit from ship to ship. Kane was particularly impressed by Sir John Ross. Ross was seventy-three years old in 1850 and had been engaged in Arctic exploration for over thirty years. He had commanded the British expedition of 1818 and had been the first to explore much of Baffin Bay. At that time, mistakenly thinking that Lancaster Sound was only a bay, he had failed to explore it deeply. His lieutenants had disagreed, and on later expeditions proved their former captain wrong, seriously injuring Ross's career. Many years later Ross had set a record by surviving four winters in the Arctic when his ships remained frozen in through the summers. When his friend Sir John Franklin failed to return to England by 1847, Ross had been the first to urge the Admiralty to send out rescue missions, but his initial offers to lead such an expedition had been spurned. Finally he had arranged an expedition of his own.[40]

Kane made many other acquaintances among the British officers, and even became reacquainted with a Lieutenant Brown, whom he had last met "among the tropical jungles of Luzon."[41] Kane's account presents a picture of gallant camaraderie among the searchers from both nations, yet there was also an undercurrent of competition between them. The Americans, in their cold, often wet little brigs, were somewhat envious of the larger and warmer British ships with their superior equipment. Both Kane and Carter also jealously asserted the American share in the discoveries made on Beechey Island and occasionally complained of self-interested glory seeking, especially by Captain Ommanney of the *Assistance*, Austin's second in command.[42] It is clear that while international scientific cooperation in the Humboldtean model was the ideal, national rivalries did not disappear.

When not looking for clues to Franklin's fate or socializing with the British officers, Kane spent most of his time in scientific observation. From the start of the expedition, he had taken every opportunity to observe, collect, and catalogue the local flora and fauna. On entering Baffin Bay he observed the marine life, and when the ship first made port in Greenland, he took the opportunity to "botanize."[43] His observations of the local plant and animal life continued throughout the trip. He was often joined by Benjamin Vreeland, the *Rescue*'s surgeon. Vreeland, who, like Kane, conformed to the model of the naval surgeon–naturalist, was also keenly interested in science. His particular field was ornithology, and he spent much of his time shooting and stuffing birds. Most of the other officers seem to have been happy to assist in the shooting (and the eating), and the expedition did its part to decimate the local bird population, even killing one of the last surviving great auks, if Carter's identification is correct.[44]

Kane behaved like a model Humboldtean on the voyage. He observed and recorded the Arctic geology, which was his favorite field, mapped ocean currents in Baffin Bay, kept meteorological records, and pondered the processes of iceberg and glacier formation.[45] When discussing these topics in his narrative, he regularly demonstrated his familiarity with scholarly authorities in all these fields and reflected on a variety of established theories. Every aspect of Arctic science came under his gaze, including ethnology, when the expedition had brief encounters with the Inuit. Kane was interested in kayaks and native hunting techniques, but he was generally disgusted by the people themselves. As in his earlier contacts with people from other cultures, he was both curious and contemptuous. In mid-August, when he met some "genuine, unmitigated Esquimaux" near Smith Sound, in contrast to the "adulterated breeds of the Danish settlement," he observed that "these poor animals were as fat as the bears which we killed a few days ago."[46] Ironically, a few years later these "poor animals" would keep him from starving to death on his second trip to the Arctic.

As winter approached and it became clear that no more discoveries were going to be made that season, DeHaven decided that the wisest course would be to return home for the winter and resume the search in the spring. The expedition attempted to do so, yet after little more than a day's sailing back toward the east, the two brigs became trapped in the ice in Barrow Strait. Helpless in the face of miles of thick, slowly drifting pack ice, and alone now that they had left their British friends, the Americans drifted with the ice, first north into Wellington Channel, where they were able to map some new territory not known to have been visited before by explorers, and then east as the ice moved slowly on its annual migration toward Baffin Bay and the Atlantic. They remained in this helpless position, with nothing to do but wait and hope that the brigs would not be crushed, from September until early the following June.

For the members of the expedition, these were nine months of terror and boredom. Surrounded by huge expanses of constantly shifting ice, the ships were in perpetual danger of being destroyed. At times the men slept in their clothes with packs full of provisions ready in case they had to abandon the brigs on short notice. Yet they eventually became numbed to the continual fear and found ways to occupy themselves through the long darkness of winter, including lecturing to one another on their particular areas of knowledge, publishing a newspaper, and putting on a play.

Kane continued to spend much of his time in scientific observation. Both Kane and Dr. Vreeland were interested in making regular and precise astronomical observations, an effort that could at times annoy other officers less interested in science. In the middle of October, Robert Carter complained of the work involved in collecting astronomical data for these two Humboldtean scientists:

> Star shooting or observing is a very cold and troubles[ome] sport, embittering the extremities of Arctic cruisers, especially on cold windy nights, sometimes resorted to by those unfortunate men . . . to swell the pages of a narrative or as in our case for the amusement of old asses who sit at home in comfort wondering why we didn't make ten thousand other observations with which they might gull the people in their meteorological tables and other scientific works on Arctic and other spots rarely visited by men and never without falsifying all their far fetched theories about winds, currents, tides, temperature &c. About equal to our doctors who having by some

> means obtained twice as much clothing as any of us, that they may be enabled to go or stay below whenever they please, criticize the logs, and dont hesitate to say that they are useless, not correct because the hourly observations on temperature, Barometer &c are not taken always at the minute appointed.[47]

Spring eventually came and released the ships without serious damage, but by this time the crew were in poor health. Many, especially the captain, had been affected by scurvy. They obtained fresh food at the Greenland settlements. Then DeHaven tried to return the ships to Lancaster Sound to resume the search, but the ice in Baffin Bay prevented them, so they turned toward New York. The *Advance* arrived home on September 30, 1851, and the slower *Rescue* soon after.

WHEN DESCRIBED in such straightforward terms, the first Grinnell Expedition hardly seems worthy of much attention. Little had been accomplished that would not have occurred without the American's participation. No great discoveries had been made, nor any great sacrifices. But this view does not take into account the aura of sublime wonder that surrounded popular nineteenth-century conceptions of the polar regions. The Arctic was one of the strangest places on earth, with its severe temperatures, mysterious optical phenomena, and perpetual night in winter and perpetual day in summer. Here the fantastic was real, and science entered the realm of fantasy. It inspired as much grand speculation as the moon or the planet mars would in later years or that other galaxies do today. Elisha Kane would make the most of these themes when recounting his experiences with the Grinnell Expedition, yet he also contained them within a framework of Humboldtean inquiry.

As with popular interest in the sciences and pseudo-sciences of the mind such as phrenology, mesmerism, clairvoyance, and spiritualism, elements of the wondrous and fantastic mingled with reasoned scientific theory from the beginning of the Grinnell Expedition. When Lieutenant DeHaven received his sailing orders, they specified that "having passed Barrow Strait, you will turn your attention northward to Wellington Channel, and westward to Cape Walker."[48] This seems peculiar, since Franklin's instructions from the Admiralty had been to proceed southwest, not north, after passing Barrow Strait. The navy, however, ordered the expedition to turn north because of the popular geographic theory of a mild Open Polar Sea, or "Polynia," surrounding the North Pole. Many scientists believed that the coldest region of the globe lay between 70 and 80 degrees north latitude, so that if a ship forced its way north through a barrier of ice in this region, it would emerge into a warmer open sea that supported plant and animal life. Some hypothesized that Franklin had made his way into this sea, had been trapped, and was living there still.[49]

Many of the organizers and members of the Grinnell Expedition, including Kane, believed in the Open Polar Sea theory, but it did not originate with them. The idea that there was a large body of open water at the North Pole had been discussed in geographic circles since the sixteenth century, though not surprisingly, every explorer who sought to find it had been thwarted by ice.[50] In England, Second Secretary of the Admiralty John Barrow championed the theory, while in nineteenth-century America its most influential proponent was the oceanographer Lieutenant Matthew Fontaine Maury, head of the Naval Observatory and Hydrography Office. Because of Maury's influence, a search for this mythical sea became part of Lieutenant DeHaven's orders.[51]

There was a variety of evidence that contributed to the Open Polar Sea theory. Explorers had noticed that areas covered by ice one year would be open the next, and regions far to the north were sometimes observed to be free of ice. The Russian word *polynia* (or *polynya*) is still used for these patches of open water. Witnesses had also observed animals migrating to the north in far northern regions. Some theorized that the warm currents of the Gulf Stream eventually found their way to the North Pole, or that ice could not form far from land, or that the continual sunshine of an Arctic summer would melt all ice. Maury supported the theory that the earth was flatter at the poles, so they were closer to the heat of the earth's core, as well as the theory that heat was produced at the North Pole from the friction of colliding ocean currents.[52]

While it is easy to heap scorn on such disproved theories with the benefit of hindsight and satellite imagery, some beliefs about open water at the poles were well reasoned and plausible, though mistaken. Maury was an accomplished scientist, not a crank, and he is today considered one of the founders of modern oceanography. But theories of an Open Polar Sea, like theories about the workings of the mind, had great imaginative potential that quickly spread beyond science into the realm of popular culture, where they could be used to explore any convenient theme. The Open Polar Sea was used symbolically by a number of nineteenth-century writers of fiction. Mary Shelley begins *Frankenstein* with an Arctic explorer who is obsessed with sailing to the North Pole, just as Victor Frankenstein is obsessed with creating his monster. Edgar Allan Poe, pushing the boundaries of scientific possibility, describes variations of the Open Polar Sea theory in his short novel *The Narrative of Arthur Gordon Pym*, and two of his short stories, "Manuscript Found in a Bottle" and "Hans Pfaal." Later in the century writers as diverse as Jules Verne and Sarah Orne Jewett would make use of the theory in their fiction.[53] Whatever the scientific merit of theories about the poles, their imaginative potential made them subject to American popular curiosity. In many ways the Open Polar Sea theory resembled contemporary theories about phenomena such as mesmerism, clairvoyance, or even spiritualism; it had more speculative potential than scientific data to support it, and it crossed the line in its appeal from enlightened savants to a popular culture of sensationalism. A vaguely defined unknown world could become a setting for the exploration of any number of themes, from a justification of European and American expansion to a critique of the Faustian quest for knowledge. It represented the progress of human knowledge as the unknown was made known, but as yet the nature of that knowledge remained obscure.

Other nineteenth-century speculation about the poles also clearly departed the realm of rational science and, like spiritualism, entered that of fantasy and even mysticism. Such theories did not directly influence the organizers of the Grinnell Expedition, but they did influence popular interest in the endeavor. One such theory was that of "Symmes Hole." In 1818 John Cleves Symmes Jr. declared to the world his belief that "the Earth is hollow and habitable within; containing a number of solid concentric spheres, one within the other, and that it is open at the poles twelve or sixteen degrees."[54] This idea was widely disseminated, if not believed, and versions of it were picked up by the earliest writers of science fiction, including Edgar Allan Poe in the United States and Jules Verne in France.[55] Poe used the Open Polar Sea theory, the Symmes Hole theory, and ambiguous, sometimes mystical combinations of the two in his stories. Like mesmerism, these were among the many outlandish scientific theories he used for literary ends. Even in our own day, popularizers of the "unexplained" sometimes place the lost continent of Atlantis at the South Pole. Interestingly, the historian William Stanton has shown a connection between the Symmes Hole theory and the motivating force behind the U.S.

Exploring Expedition of 1838–42, the first major government-sponsored American scientific exploring expedition. This connection can be extended to the Grinnell Expedition through Edwin DeHaven, who had commanded one of the ships of the U.S. Exploring Expedition.[56]

A number of contemporary newspaper reports also linked the Open Polar Sea theory, the theory of Symmes Hole, and the search for Franklin, showing that, on a popular level, the lines between science and fantasy were thin. A story on the front page of the *New York Evening Post* discussed the recently departed Grinnell Expedition, Matthew Maury's theories, and Symmes Hole, making little distinction between reasoned theory and fantastic speculation: "Polina, that northern world, unvisited hitherto, except by 'beast and fowl,' be it open sea or terra-firma, or, as Capt Symmes believed, the open passage to another concentric world within the earth, will become an object of public solicitude scarcely inferior to Sir John himself."[57] On the expedition's return, Symmes's son even wrote to Kane asking for information relating to his father's theory.[58]

Speculation about the North Pole and the fate of Franklin also attracted mystics and the proponents of many of the new pseudo-sciences of the mind. On May 22, 1850, in an article that appeared next to a piece on the recently departed Grinnell Expedition, the *New York Herald* reported that a friend of the mystic Andrew Jackson Davis, who would become a leading figure in the spiritualist movement, was claiming to have "passed from the Earth, through the opening at one of the poles," and in this way traveled to other planets.[59] The fate of the Franklin Expedition also became a favorite topic of clairvoyants who would "travel" with their minds to the Arctic regions and hold conversations with the lost explorers and report back on their whereabouts.[60] Even the fledgling spirit rapping movement, inspired by the continuing success of the Fox sisters, had something to say about the search for Franklin. A rapper in Cortland County, New York, knocked out the message that the Franklin Expedition had completed the Northwest Passage after much hardship, but had then stopped in Japan for supplies, where it was attacked and its members taken prisoner.[61]

Believers in the Open Polar Sea theory were not bad scientists, but at this time there was no clear line between scientific and fanciful beliefs about the North Pole, especially when science was being presented to popular audiences. The North Pole was a mysterious realm subject to speculation and investigation but not as yet to direct observation. The

Americans who picked up the newspaper and read a story about polar exploration or the Grinnell Expedition, or who later read Kane's narrative, might also be exposed to all sorts of more bizarre accounts. The popularity of the Grinnell Expedition stemmed not only from its humanitarian and scientific appeal but also from its appeal to sensational romantic fantasies. It invited unlimited speculation but no definitive conclusions, just as the spirit rappings of the two girls from Hydesville did.

WHEN THE Grinnell Expedition returned home, Commander DeHaven declined the privilege, as leader of the expedition, to write anything more than his official report to the navy on the meager results of the trip. Kane, however, had other ideas. He became the expedition's historian, writing a personal narrative of the journey that appealed to public interests in travel, adventure, and the heroic pursuit of science, as well as to public curiosity about the Arctic. Kane's book is a textual panorama of the Arctic landscape. Since most of the trip was spent trapped in the ice with little action worth describing, Kane dwelt in minute detail on every aspect of the strange region the expedition passed through.

The United States Grinnell Expedition in Search of Sir John Franklin: A Personal Narrative is a multifaceted book. On its surface it is a personal account of the expedition, but more important, it is a work of popular Humboldtean science. Most of the text is taken up with detailed descriptions of a variety of physical phenomena. Geology, oceanography, botany, zoology, astronomy, glaciology, geomagnetism, meteorology, and hydrography all come under Kane's consideration, with brief interludes for hunting polar bears and looking for relics of Franklin's voyage. Lengthy appendixes contain meteorological tables giving daily entries from the log book on latitude, longitude, direction of ocean currents, and wind, air, and water temperature, barometric pressure, and weather.[62]

Mixed in with the science is a heavy dose of the strange and sensational. The overarching theme of the book is the tension and interplay between mystery and science. Kane capitalized on public perceptions of the Arctic as a world of wonders. He describes polar bears, perpetual light and perpetual dark, icebergs, and the northern lights—phenomena that seem to defy the laws of nature or to belong to another world. At times he seems to be describing something from a fairy tale. Yet in the end he always explains these things rationally, or, if he cannot fully explain them, he subjects them to rational inquiry, thus containing the fanciful within the bounds of human understanding.

The best example is his discussion of refraction. In the Arctic, visual perceptions are often severely distorted because of reflections caused by large fields of ice and ice crystals in the atmosphere. Objects that are far away often appear to be close, and it is even possible for objects below the horizon to be reflected above the horizon, sometimes upside down. Some of Kane's most picturesque language is reserved for his descriptions of this phenomenon. Early in the trip he observes: "No effort of the imagination was necessary for me to travel from the true watery horizon to the false one of refraction above it, and there to see huge structures lining an aerial ocean-margin. Some rusty, Egyptian, rubbish-clogged propyla, and hypaethral courts—some tapering and columnar, like Palmyra and Baalbec—some with architrave and portico, like Telmessus or Athens, or else vague and grotto-like, such as dreamy memories recalled of Ellora and Carli."[63] His description of fantastic apparitions in the sky is juxtaposed with his objective consideration of refraction, which takes into account the theories of scientists such as Louis Agassiz: "Professor Agassiz has described a similar class of repeated images upon Lake Superior, limited, however, to two—one inverted, and above that the same erect. He suggests that it may be simply the reflection of the landscape inverted upon the surface of the lake, and reproduced with the actual landscape."[64]

Kane was aware of this tension between science and wonder, and, unafraid to appeal to his readers' imaginations as much as to their reason, he was able to balance the two. A phenomenon such as refraction, which seemed to deny the scientist the use of his ordinary senses, was a particularly appropriate vehicle. While Kane often used scientific instruments and scientific language, he also commented on their inadequacy. "Voyagers speak of the effect of Arctic refraction in language as exact and mathematical as their own correction tables," he wrote. "It almost seems as if their minute observations of dip-sectors and repeating-circles had left them no scope for picturesque sublimity."[65] Kane, by contrast, had room for both dip-sectors and sublimity, and he presented both to his readers.

Kane's descriptions of the Arctic in *The U.S. Grinnell Expedition* show that imagination and an emotional sense of wonder do not stand in opposition to science. Rather wonder and imagination provide a context for science, especially the Humboldtean variety of science. Wonder provokes intellectual curiosity. The unexplained marvel is fascinating to Kane. He continually seeks out "picturesque sublimity" so that he can first marvel at it and then explain it rationally. For Kane this becomes the ultimate justification for a scientific approach to knowledge, and the science itself is elevated by the grandeur of that which it explains. This approach was made popular by Humboldt, but Kane easily adapted it to his observations of the Arctic landscape and the search for Franklin.

KANE HAD found his audience. When American readers picked up Kane's first book, distant regions of the earth were revealed to their understanding, as they gazed at engravings of sublime landscapes and read Kane's explanations of the natural mechanisms that created these wonders. It is impossible to know exactly what emotions they experienced as they read. Perhaps they felt pride that American perseverance and sacrifice could lead to such discoveries, and hope that in the future ever greater discoveries would be made, leading ultimately to the inevitable advancement of mankind. Perhaps, too, they were inspired to think of the United States in global terms and to embrace an expansionist view of the American future as the nation headed into the second half of the nineteenth century. Kane's descriptions of this sublime Arctic world were thus a sign of both human and national advancement. One by one the mysteries of nature were yielding to understanding, and Kane's readers experienced the thrill of discovery as the unknown became known.

Kane's book ended with a call for further exploration. He laid out the scientific arguments developed by Maury in favor of an Open Polar Sea, and skillfully blended them with the humanitarian effort to locate Franklin. He announced his plan to return to the Arctic at the head of another expedition to find both. In the *Advance*, he and his party would sail north as far as possible, then set out across the ice with sledges and portable gutta-percha boats to the mythic sea: "Once there, if such a reward awaits us, we launch our little boats, and, bidding God speed us, embark upon its waters."[66]

4

The Spirit of Inquiry in New York City

The medium is the message.
Marshall McLuhan

SOON AFTER the Grinnell Expedition sailed off for the Arctic regions in the late spring of 1850, some of New York City's most accomplished literary men gathered at the Broadway home of the Baptist minister, journalist, and editor Rufus Griswold for an evening of exploration of their own. They had come to meet "the Rochester ladies," whom the New York City newspapers had been discussing on a regular basis ever since hearing of their demonstration of spirit rapping in Rochester's Corinthian Hall. Maggie and Kate Fox and Leah Fish, with Mrs. Fox, Eliab W. Capron, and Calvin Brown, had recently arrived in New York City and were staying at Barnum's Hotel, where they invited visitors to come and investigate spiritual communication for a dollar per person.[1] They also arranged to give a special private demonstration for an influential audience at Griswold's house.

Griswold's guest list for this "Post-Mortuum Soiree," as it was called by one of the guests, the writer Nathaniel P. Willis, was a veritable who's who of New York City's literary elite. It included, among others, the acclaimed writers James Fenimore Cooper, William Cullen Bryant, and Henry Tuckerman; historians George Bancroft and the Reverend Francis Hawks; physician Dr. John W. Francis; and newspaper editors John Bigelow and George Ripley.[2] This gathering of literary fame and distinction represented a cross-section of social and political views. The group included Democrats as well as Whigs, conservatives as well as radicals. According to George Ripley, the literary editor of the *New York Tribune*, "several gentlemen were invited who had been known to express the most entire skepticism with regard to the extraordinary nature of the sounds, believing them to be the result of contrivance and imposture." Others, like the radical Ripley himself, a founder of the transcendental community Brook Farm, were probably predisposed to give the rappings an open-minded hearing. Clearly this was going to be an important performance for the sisters. To convince even one of these men, "whose general character for intelligence and probity, was a guarantee against their being deluded by hasty impressions," would be a significant accomplishment.[3]

As the demonstration commenced that night at Griswold's home, no raps were heard for over half an hour, but eventually, as the company drew closer around the table into a "compact circle," they heard faint sounds from under the table which soon increased in volume. When Fish asked the spirits to communicate, the knockings indicated that they were now prepared to answer questions put by a guest named Marcy. His investigation, and those of the other guests at Griswold's home that evening, followed a format that the sisters had developed over the past several months. The questioner thought of a dead person with whom he wished to communicate. He then asked the spirits questions, either silently or aloud. Usually the spirits knocked for "yes" or remained silent for "no" as alternatives were spoken by the questioner or pointed to on a piece of paper with a pencil. At other times the spirits would "call for the alphabet" and spell out the answers. Marcy "inquired whether the spirit with which he wished to converse was a relation—was a child—and what was his age at the time of its death." The spirits responded correctly to these questions with knocks, according to Marcy, but "nothing worthy of special notice was elicited."[4]

Next, according to one observer, questions were put by Henry Tuckerman, a well-known literary critic, essayist, and poet. Tuckerman thought of a dead person with whom he wished to communicate but did not say the name aloud. He then began to ask test questions of the spirits. Had the person lived in New York? he asked, but no answer came. "In Baltimore? In Cambridge? In Boston?" At the name of this last city three raps responded indicating that he had lived in Boston. "Mr. T. continued, 'Was he a lawyer? A merchant? A physician? A clergyman?' Knocks. 'Was he an Episcopalian? A Presbyterian? A Unitarian?'—going over the names of the principal sects. No answer. At the suggestion of a gentleman, Mr. T. asked, 'Was he a Christian?' Knocks." Tuckerman then asked about the person's age at death by naming increments of ten and was answered at sixty. "'Has he left a family?' Knocks. 'Children?' Knocks. 'Five? Three? Two?' Knocks. 'Did he die in Boston? In Philadelphia? In Albany? In Northampton? In Bennington?' Knocks. 'Did he die of consumption? Of fever? Of cholera? Of old age?' Knocks." At the end of this questioning Tuckerman revealed that he had been thinking of William Ellery Channing, the Unitarian minister from Boston who had died in Bennington, Vermont, in 1842 at age sixty-two. While Channing was well known as a Unitarian, according to Ripley, who recounted the story in the *Tribune*, he preferred simply to be called a Christian.[5]

The sisters were unsuccessful with the Reverend Hawks, but then correctly identified the poet Robert Burns as the person Dr. Francis had in mind. But their greatest success came when they were questioned by the novelist, Cooper. According to Willis, "For no one, were the spirits half so willing to repeat their revelations twice over, or half so explicit."[6] Cooper was thinking silently of his sister, who had been tragically killed by a fall from a horse fifty years earlier. He asked questions about his unidentified subject, which were all answered correctly by the raps.[7] Leah Fish would later claim Cooper as a convert, saying that on his deathbed little more than a year later he wrote: "Tell the Fox family I bless them. I have been made happy through them. They have prepared me for this hour."[8] There is, however, no independent support for this dubious claim. The only verifiable mention Cooper made of the evening was in a letter to his wife in which he wrote, "I am deep in the Rochester Knockings, which are making a great deal of noise, just now," confirmation that his curiosity had been aroused, though not exactly the ringing endorsement of a convert.[9] Cooper's response was fairly typical of the effect the Fox sisters had on the citizens of New York: they aroused curiosity and interest in many more than they persuaded to believe in spirits. Of course, they were always ready to claim as converts any who showed interest in the mysterious sounds, especially if they were famous.

The guest list for this "Post-Mortuum Soiree" had clearly been drawn up with an eye toward generating the greatest possible publicity for the spirit rappers in New York City and national periodicals. George Ripley was the prominent literary editor of Horace Greeley's *Tribune*, William Cullen Bryant and John Bigelow were co-editors of the *Evening Post,* and N. P. Willis was the editor of the *Home Journal*, a New York weekly. Others were established writers whose essays often appeared in print. This group was well positioned to spread the word about the rappings and turn the sisters into big-city celebrities. They could tap directly into a growing American mass culture while lending the sisters an aura of respectability by their attention. This is exactly what happened.

On June 8 the *New York Tribune* printed a two-column article by Ripley recounting the evening at Griswold's, and a week later Willis printed an even longer story in the *Home Journal*. Neither of these pieces endorsed the rappings. They simply reported a mysterious story and left it up to their readers to decide. Ripley ended his article by "recommending our readers to see for themselves," while Willis concluded, "There is no end to the speculation on the subject, and we leave it with our readers."[10] Though not endorsing the spiritual origin of the mysterious sounds, they did endorse exploration. These accounts clearly encouraged further speculation and interest and ensured that a flood of curious New Yorkers would visit Barnum's Hotel, hand over their dollars, and hear the knocks for themselves.

To some, however, Ripley's and Willis's accounts did indeed read like endorsements because they did not condemn the raps outright as fraud. An unidentified guest at Griswold's that night, unhappy about seeing his name in the *Tribune* in association with such a questionable activity, wrote to the more reserved *Evening Post,* whose editors, William Cullen Bryant and John Bigelow, had declined to publicize the event. He made clear that none of the gentlemen present "to my knowledge, recognizes any supernatural agency in the affair."[11] His opinion was that the whole story was being blown out of proportion and that the distinguished names of Griswold's guests were being used to lend respectability to foolishness. He was right in part, but he did not understand what Fish, Capron, and the Fox sisters clearly did. As long as the rappings could get publicity, and as long as no overwhelming evidence showed them to be fraudulent, public interest would only increase. New Yorkers had a mystery on their hands, and their curiosity would not subside until it was solved.

THE FOX SISTERS' extraordinary journey from rural anonymity to the fashionable parlors of Manhattan was made possible by an ever-increasing discussion and debate about the "Mysterious Knockings" that had begun over six months before the "Post-Mortuum Soiree" at Griswold's. This debate was initiated when Eliab Capron and George Willets wrote to the *New York Tribune* about the Corinthian Hall demonstration in Rochester. On November 29, 1849, the *Tribune* devoted over a full column to a letter in which Capron and Willets claimed that the evening had been a total success. Capron and Willets presented spirit rapping as the latest evidence of American progress, suggesting that they might signal "the commencement of a new era of spiritual influx into the world," and called for further investigation.[12] A week later Horace Greeley wrote a front-page editorial in the *Tribune*. Responding to a letter he had received from a reader, he laid out his own opinions on the matter and endorsed open-minded investigation: "We cannot regard with any other feeling than respect that natural instinct of the heart, which in one way or another affirms a world of spiritual existences at no impassable remove from our natural life; and we have little sympathy with such unscientific presumption as passes the verdict of 'humbug' upon every fact it does not understand." Linking the rappings with mesmerism and clairvoyance as areas worthy of intelligent investigation, he offered to publish "all new facts that may be supposed to have a bearing on the subject." If this was something new and progressive, then the people should investigate. They should rely on their own good sense to judge the matter for themselves. But Greeley also expressed some serious reservations, pointing out that the substance of the rappings, even if genuine, did not amount to much: "It is difficult to understand why spirits, who act with as little reason as children or idiots, should be treated with any more consideration."[13]

Greeley had invited a public dialogue, and that is what he got. Throughout the winter and spring leading up to the sisters' visit to Manhattan, letters, articles, and editorials about spirit rapping became regular features in the *Tribune* and other New York papers such as the *Sun* and the *Express*. Two books on the history of the rappings also went on sale, one written by Eliab Capron and Henry Barron and the other by the Rochester publisher D. M. Dewey. With this influx of popular information, speculation of all sorts abounded. Some declared it all a fraud, while others speculated that the raps might signal the dawning of a new age. But one thing was clear: for New Yorkers truly to make up their minds about this strange phenomenon, they would have to witness it for themselves.

Back in Rochester, in the months after the demonstrations at Corinthian Hall, the small group surrounding the sisters became increasingly aware of the growing interest in the mysterious noises outside their own community. Amy and Isaac Post began to receive letters from people they had never met asking about the raps. Valentine Nicholson, a friend of a friend of the Posts', wrote from Ohio requesting that the Posts ask the spirits for advice: he wanted to know if he should buy his mother-in-law's farm, if he should continue to live near neighbors he did not like, and whether he should remain a farmer or take up the tinner's trade.[14] As further evidence of the growing interest, in April, Isaac Post's business partner, Edmund Willis, on a visit to New York City, found that he was constantly accosted with questions about the raps by those who had seen Post's name in the newspaper.[15]

At this point Eliab Capron once again emerged as the chief publicist for the sisters. As the dialogue in the New York papers increased, and as word of the rappings spread throughout the country, Capron began to push for a visit by Kate and Maggie to New York City. Apparently Mrs. Fox was somewhat hesitant to send her two young daughters off to the big city, and despite Capron's appeals, in early February she decided not to allow it.[16] Capron, however, did not take no for an answer. He wrote to Mrs. Fox telling her that "the persons who have sent for her [Kate] from there [New York City] stand among the first in the nation for science and influence. It would be of great advantage to your family to have such men satisfied in regard to the family, and it would *forever* clear all who are now being ridiculed and lied about from all charges of fraud."[17] Capron was corresponding with a number of men in New York, including Andrew Jackson Davis, the famed mystic, and the phrenologist Orson Fowler about a possible visit by the "Rochester Knockers." Another correspondent who, Capron told Mrs. Fox, "wishes his name kept a secret for the present" may have been Rufus Griswold or perhaps even Horace Greeley.[18]

Capron had set himself up in the position of the Fox family's agent, publicist, and defender, and he seemed particularly intent on taking Kate to the city. Although he claimed that the reputation of the Fox family and the importance of spreading the word about the manifestations were foremost in his thoughts, he had committed himself strongly to the phenomenon in a letter to a nationwide publication and in his recent book on the rappings, so his own reputation was at stake now as well. "Seriously," he told Mrs. Fox, "I do think it would end in great advantage to all of us for us to go. They offer no pay except to pay our expenses but there are always persons who will make presents to *girls*—besides money is not always the *greatest* advantage to be gained by a good-deal."[19] Of course, money eventually did emerge as a powerful motive when, four months later, the Foxes were charging curious New Yorkers a dollar a head to visit them at Barnum's Hotel.

From November 1849 to April 1850, while debate about the knocks grew in the New York City papers, Maggie and her sisters remained in the vicinity of Rochester and Auburn, giving séances for local citizens and for others who traveled to Rochester to see them. Leah Fish was most likely enjoying the status the rappings gave her. She had moved from a marginal existence as a single mother giving piano lessons to a new role as the focus of attention of prosperous middle-class men and women. Kate and Maggie Fox, by contrast, were still in their teens. To them the rappings were more a source of fun than of status or money, and they seem to have enjoyed playing mischievous tricks on those who came to their séances. As mediums they could behave in ways that were impossible in their ordinary roles. They could knock adults on the head and tell them absurd things and then blame it all on playful spirits from another world.[20]

Unfortunately for Kate and Maggie Fox, as the movement quickly grew, the fun and games must have diminished. The deeper they got into it, the less control the girls could exert. Scrutiny only increased, as did the cost of exposure. Soon the girls became trapped in their own game, forced to spend tedious hours as the object of public curiosity and gossip. This is probably when Maggie and Kate began to resent their older sister, who now controlled much of their lives. This resentment would finally bubble to the surface years later when they renounced spiritualism and blamed the fraud on Leah Fish.[21]

Sporadic reporting at this time mentioned rappings that were occurring in a variety of locations outside the sisters' influence. In the home of the Reverend Eliakim Phelps in Stratford, Connecticut, that March, witnesses heard raps and saw objects hurled through the air in the presence of an eleven-year-old boy. These "spirits" seem to have had more malevolent intentions than those at Rochester. Objects often struck witnesses and caused damage, leading the Reverend Phelps to conclude that "wicked spirits" were at work, and that "their communications are wholly worthless" and "devices of Satan."[22] Other rappings were heard in Newark, New Jersey, while strange, unexplained movement of objects was reported in both Richmond, Virginia, and the West Indies.[23] Clearly the sisters' hoax was taking on a life of its own.

During this time an independent spiritualist movement had emerged, inspired by the activities of the Fox sisters but dedicated to philosophies that had developed independently of the Rochester knockings. The foundations for this spiritualist movement predated the events in Hydesville, but it had enjoyed little national success before the Fox sisters generated publicity. The sisters, however, had little interest in or control over such a movement themselves.[24] Performance, not philosophy, continued to be their forte. In the midst of discussion and speculation, the Fox sisters began to travel, giving demonstrations of the mysterious knockings. Having originated the idea of the raps and the method of communication, they now became the first to turn them into a traveling road show.

CAPRON, WITH help from Leah Fish, finally won over Mrs. Fox, who granted permission for her daughters to travel. At the direction of the spirits, according to Fish, they first went to Albany and neighboring Troy at the end of April or beginning of May to give public demonstrations at Van Vechten Hall in Albany and Apollo Hall in Troy and private séances at the Delavan House Hotel and the Troy House Hotel. Professor R. P. Ambler accompanied them to Troy and gave lectures on spiritual communication and the spiritualist philosophy. The citizens of Troy, however, according to the *Troy Daily Whig*, were more interested in the raps than in the professor's lecture.[25]

For the public séances, which Fish called "promiscuous circles," the family charged a dollar per person per hour. Private séances for two or more people cost five dollars. The local citizens willingly paid these sums, for when the editor of the *Daily Whig* went to the Troy House to see the sisters, he found the hotel's parlors full of people waiting to get in ahead of him. He was disappointed at being to be put on a waiting list for the next day.[26]

From Albany and Troy, the party went on to New York City at the end of May.[27] In Manhattan they set themselves up in Barnum's Hotel (not to be confused with P. T. Barnum's Museum, with which it was not connected) and began to accept visitors at specified hours in the morning, afternoon, and evening. By this time they had established a consistent set of rules for receiving guests, which they posted on the door to the parlor where they received their visitors. They specified the admission fee, and advised that guests were to sit where instructed during the séance and were to comport themselves as in a "solemn religious assembly."[28] The sisters were careful to present themselves in a way that would appeal to an upscale clientele and exclude the lower classes. Indeed, Fish wrote that they considered raising their fee to five dollars to "keep the rabble away."[29]

The parlor in which they held their seánces contained a long table around which thirty people could sit. There they gave three public sessions a day, each lasting two hours or more. Most of their visitors were members of the professional middle class who could afford the not insubstantial admission fee, which was several times the cost of a theater ticket.[30] Each would wait his or her turn to ask questions, generally about dead loved ones or famous people.[31] The more skeptical class of visitor posed questions designed to test the sisters, while others, who wanted to believe, sought comfort and reassurance about the afterlife. Sometimes the spirits would oblige with answers, while at other times they remained silent. Often they gave correct answers to questions, but they were often wrong as well. The wrong answers were usually attributed to "bad spirits."

Most of the city papers sent representatives to report on the knockings. Horace Greeley went with a friend to observe for himself the phenomenon his paper had been reporting on for months. His own questions were answered correctly by the spirits, but those of his friend were answered incorrectly in all but one case. He did not believe that any overt deception was involved, but still, Greeley was not ready to declare himself convinced one way or the other. He stated his suspicion that some form of mesmerism was involved. Greeley's greatest difficulty, however, was in believing "that spirits have nothing better to do than make fruitless revelations by means of thumps and raps."[32] He longed for answers to serious philosophical and theological questions, not the continual repetition of mundane information about the recently dead. Not content with performance alone, Greeley wanted a practical philosophy, but the Fox sisters were not about to give it to him; so he suspended judgment and decided to continue investigating the matter.[33]

A writer for the *Evening Post* also visited Barnum's Hotel in the first week of the sisters' visit but recounted a very unsatisfying session with the spirits. None of the visitors at the time he was there received acceptable answers. This failure was explained by Fish as the result of "some mischievous little spirits present who . . . seemed desirous of amusing themselves by annoying and confusing the audience."[34] These "mischievous little spirits" were undoubtedly her two younger sisters, who most likely interrupted the growing tedium of day after day of constant séances by taunting not only their customers but their older sister as well, under whose control they increasingly found themselves.

Unlike these observers who did not commit themselves one way or another, a writer signing himself H. W., presumably a junior editor at the *New York Herald*, unhesitantly declared the "conviction on my mind is that it is a deception." Although some of those present when he visited the hotel had received correct answers, he had not. Furthermore, when he tried to look under the table during the séance, all rapping stopped. Fish explained this to him as the result of his "disposition not to believe" or his "desire to detect and expose a deception." H. W. was forced to conclude that "a dollar might certainly be spent worse, but, as I now think, not much worse."[35]

THESE REPORTS offer a composite picture of the Fox sisters near the beginning of their public career. While, for the most part, they were successful in directing attention away from themselves and toward "the spirits," some writers became interested in the young women at the center of this new sensation. These sources reveal that the deportment and appearance of the sisters were for many the most convincing part of the phenomenon. "Their manner," remarked Greeley, "is quiet and refined, and all their actions are marked by entire propriety. . . . They seemed at perfect ease, and their whole deportment exhibited an apparent frankness and sincerity which would dispose one to acquit them of any intent to deceive."[36] George Ripley agreed with this assessment, remarking, "The manners and bearing of the ladies are such as to create a prepossession in their favor." Ripley went on to note the apparent passivity of the sisters. "They have no theories to offer in explanation of the acts of their mysterious attendants, and apparently have no control of their incomings or outgoings."[37]

The sophisticated editor and author Nathaniel Willis was also impressed by the sisters, noting that they were "considerably prettier than the average." Willis admired not only their looks but also their passive and obliging behavior. Speaking on behalf of all the guests at Rufus Griswold's house, he noted that "throughout the evening, we were struck with their combined good-humor and simplicity, and the ease and unpretendingness with which they let their visitors (from both worlds) have their own way. They evidently won the respect and liking of all present, as the evening went on."[38] Even the writer for the *Herald,* who expressed his belief that the whole thing was a fraud, took time to remark on seventeen-year-old Maggie Fox's appearance and behavior: "She is a very pretty, arch-looking, black-eyed, and rather modestly behaved young girl."[39]

This favorable attention to appearance is of particular importance when we take into account contemporary beliefs in physiognomy which linked physical appearance to character. Honest, modest appearance was believed to reflect an honest, modest character. Reinforcing this evidence were beliefs about gender that assigned reason to men and passivity to women. The proper feminine deportment of the sisters was an indication that the girls fit the accepted rules for their gender. It therefore followed that they would not have the intellectual capacity to deceive the gentlemen who came to investigate. It was difficult to believe that pretty, well-behaved young ladies could attempt gross deception, let alone carry it off successfully in the presence of well-educated, rational men. The Fox sisters projected an image of sincerity, which in the antebellum era was a badge of middle-class gentility. When the men wrote that the sisters were "modestly behaved," "pretty," "at perfect ease," they were saying that they were sincere, a quality that carried more weight then than it does today. In their demonstration it was acceptable to answer a few questions incorrectly, but it was not acceptable to appear shifty, shrewd, or even intelligent. This was a test of character as much as it was a test of technique.[40]

The cultural historian Karen Halttunen has described the American preoccupation during this period with the issue of deception. Americans feared the confidence games of the trickster in the swiftly expanding cities. But they imagined the confidence man to be a savvy veteran of urban life, not an innocent-looking teenage girl from the countryside. Women were considered by their very nature to be more sincere than men and less able to mask their true feelings. Sentimentalists, according to Halttunen, believed that "true women were constitutionally transparent, incapable of disguising their feelings."[41] Thus two young women from Hydesville were aptly suited for the task of deception precisely because they were the type thought least capable of fraud.

By contrast, those writers who recognized intelligence in the spirit rappers also recognized the capacity for deception. Generally they acknowledged intelligence in Leah Fish first. While she was the least proficient at making the sounds, she was the one who generally directed the séances.[42]

Greeley noted that Fish "seemed to be on the most familiar terms with the knocking," meaning that she often directed questions to the spirits and interpreted the knocks for visitors.[43] Critics of the spirit rapping observed, too, that Leah Fish was a shrewd judge of human nature. J. Stanley Grimes, a leading mesmerist and phrenologist who believed the spirit rappings a fraud, saw in the two younger girls "very little of the ability to take a leading part in such a performance," but in Fish he observed "a masculine and energetic temperament," which led him to believe that she was at the center of the deception.[44] These comments indicate that the sisters were walking a fine line between gentility and notoriety. They were the latest public craze, yet they also had to maintain the deportment proper to young ladies. The location of their séances in the parlors of city hotels were neither fully public nor fully private. They were semiprivate settings that they chose as a way of mitigating the increasingly public nature of their activity.

By 1850 the Fox sisters, like Elisha Kane, were engaging Americans in the process of discovery. Like Kane, the sisters were presenting something that their audiences could see as a sign of human advancement. But more important, they were also promoting a moral context for their appeal to popular curiosity. Kane used the image of the Humboldtean explorer making sacrifices for the advancement of knowledge, while the sisters cultivated their image as transparent mediums through whom others communicated. In the long run their images were more important than the theories they represented. But unfortunately for the Fox sisters, they had a tougher job ahead of them. As long as they could maintain the perception that they were respectable, sincere young women rather than professional public performers, they would remain successful; but while male respectability could be cultivated in the public sphere, female respectability was largely understood to be private. The Fox sisters could not remain genteel for long if they also remained in hotels and performance halls. Their task, then was not just a matter of avoiding detection. They also had to avoid the dangers associated with being women in public life.

TO JUDGE from the accounts in the newspapers, most of those who visited the sisters at Barnum's Hotel during this first trip to New York City were men of the middle and upper classes. Those of reformist leanings, like Greeley and Ripley, were most prevalent, but interest was not confined to this class. The most striking departure from this trend came in early July, when Captain Isaiah Rynders visited the sisters. Rynders was notorious throughout New York City as the leader of the Empire Club, an organization associated with Tammany Hall, whose membership, according to one historian, "was made up of a choice variety of picked worthies who could argue a mooted point to a finish with knuckles."[45] Far from sympathizing with reform causes such as abolition, Rynders was a Democratic supporter of the urban working class and recent Irish immigrants, and a staunch enemy of evangelical reformers. Just two months before meeting with the Fox sisters, Rynders had caused a near riot at an abolition convention by mounting the podium and encouraging racist hecklers.[46] This was not an isolated incident; the Empire Club routinely broke up Whig, and especially abolition, meetings with violence and intimidation.[47]

Rynders was not about to believe in spirits. He went to see the sisters out of curiosity and with the intention of trying to expose their tricks. But after visiting with them several times, he wrote to the *Herald* to confess that, while he still did not believe in spirits, he could not discover how the thing was done. Rynders's letter is interesting in that he genuinely seems to have admired the sisters, while at the same time he believed them to be swindling the public. Acknowledging Maggie and Kate Fox to be beautiful and intelligent women, he expressed his admiration: "If they humbug you, they do it in the most amusing and agreeable manner, and it is well worth five dollars, instead of one, to witness their superior tact in confounding all attempts to disconcert or detect them, besides experiencing the pleasing impressions they leave upon every unprejudiced mind."[48]

Rynders's curiosity about the rappings represents a little-studied aspect of spirit rapping. Although most historians place it firmly within the context of the perfectionist reform and religious enthusiasm emerging in upstate New York at the time, spirit rapping moved beyond that context to find a natural home in the fast-paced urban world of New York City. Because the rapping started in western New York, the tendency has been to emphasize that region as its natural home; but spirit rapping found a more welcoming home in New York City than it ever had in Hydesville or Rochester. If we are to speak of spirit communication as a truly mass movement, its date of inception is June 1850, when the sisters reached the city, not March 1848, when it was still a little-noticed ghost story. The testimony of the antiabolitionist Rynders is a good indication of this fact. Rynders had nothing but scorn for the evangelical and perfectionist movements of the burned-over district, but he did not see spirit rapping as an outgrowth of those movements. To him it was a wonderful puzzle, an intellectual exercise. The rapping might be a scam, but it was an entertaining one. The New York City of Isaiah Rynders was a place where people got what they wanted by using their wits. It was at the forefront of a growing capitalist economy that stressed competition. If you could separate a fool from his money, why not do it? When Rynders looked at the Fox sisters, he saw three women making an excellent living at the expense of weaker minds. They were entertaining, they were clever, and they made the Whiggish reformers, whom Rynders despised, look like fools.

Rynders's article in the *Herald* gave a detailed description of his own session with the sisters and those of others he observed. He recounted how easily swayed some people were, such as the man who needed smelling salts after the sisters accurately rapped out his age, even though "any intelligent child twelve years of age could have guessed his age within a year or two."[49] Others, according to Rynders, would receive one wrong answer and declare the whole thing a sham unworthy of further investigation. Rynders delighted in the mystery, and he was convinced that the rapping was caused by human agency, yet that did not diminish its appeal. Like the thousands who went to Barnum's Museum to try to spot the stitches that connected the Feejee Mermaid's fish tail to its monkey body, Rynders enjoyed the rapping and admired the Fox sisters for their ability to make a fool even of him.

IN APPEALING to America's love of a good controversy, the Fox sisters drew support from the growth of the mass circulation newspapers that got their start in the 1830s and expanded during the 1840s and 1850s. In the past, each newspaper had been the organ of a specific political party and was designed to voice that party's official position, while providing political, economic, and foreign news. The antebellum era saw the rise of a new kind of newspaper commonly called the penny press, inexpensive papers sold daily on the street. They sought a broad readership by catering to the curiosity of the public with stories emphasizing conflict and sensation. Unlike the earlier partisan papers, the penny press appealed to the working classes that were swelling the population of eastern cities such as New York. These papers sought to educate as well as entertain their readers by providing a variety of information on a wide range of topics in a lively manner. New York papers such as the *Sun*, the *Herald*, and the

Tribune gained large circulations because they lowered prices and provided news of interest to a broad spectrum of readers.[50]

One technique used to increase circulation was to generate controversy over a mystery. James Gordon Bennett of the *Herald*, for example, had tripled his paper's circulation by taking a controversial stance in the sensational murder of the prostitute Helen Jewett in 1836, and defending his position against the contrary opinions voiced by the other city papers.[51] More recently, the grisly murder of Dr. George Parkman and the subsequent arrest, trial, and execution of his killer, John Webster, a Harvard professor, had filled the columns of the penny press. These articles appeared alongside stories of mysteries such as the fate of Sir John Franklin's Arctic expedition, and strange and exotic happenings from the unwrapping of a mummy to accounts of geographic explorations such as those of the Grinnell Expedition.[52] The papers carried serious political, economic, and foreign news as well, and their sensationalism certainly did not rival that of a later age, but they differed from their predecessors by embracing the goal of profit by means of mass circulation. They appealed to public curiosity, while at the same time that they created even greater attention to the stories they highlighted.

The case of the "Mysterious Knockings" was just the sort of story to catch readers' attention and sell papers. It offered both a puzzle and a controversy, not to mention three pretty young women, and it gave the different papers an opportunity to define themselves in relation to one another by the positions they took. Some papers dismissed the knockings out of hand as just another piece of fanatical idiocy coming out of a region notorious for its religious crazes. The *Herald*, under the direction of Bennett, led this attack. As a paper on the Democratic side of the political spectrum, it frowned on anything that smacked of "fanaticism," a term it used to describe all that was new or politically radical, including abolition and women's rights. It was not surprising, then, that the *Herald* portrayed the rappings as an instance of fraud and delusion. "There are many queer people and queer things in Rochester," the *Herald* observed, pointing out that anti-Masonry as well as Mormonism, two movements of which Bennett and the *Herald* disapproved, had originated in that region.[53] The *Herald* steadfastly maintained that the knockings were produced by knaves and listened to by fools. Bennett tied the rappings to other radical ideologies, such as Fourierism and socialism, with which he disagreed, and used them to attack rival papers, claiming that the knockings were "supported chiefly by the *Tribune* and the *Sun*, those organs of all kinds of isms and humbugs."[54] In one article Bennett dismissed the spirit rappings as ventriloquism and accused Rufus Griswold of trying to make money off them.[55] Bennett and his newspaper perhaps best represent the competitive and aggressive yet socially conservative spirit that typified the growing urban capitalist society of places like New York City.

As we have seen, Horace Greeley's *Tribune,* which tended to represent the reform branch of the Whig Party, took a different approach, calling for further investigation of the rappings. After Greeley's editorial inviting dialogue on the subject, readers from around the country responded, expressing a variety of views. A man signing himself "W" argued that the content of the communications did not matter so much as the fact of the communications, which he claimed contributed to the fight against "dogmatism." As a champion of human inquiry over religious authority of any sort, he asserted that the rapping "teaches what all men ought to know, namely, that they should never for a moment surrender their own rational powers in the acquisition of truth."[56]

"W" was not alone in his thirst for investigation. It appeared "most extraordinary" to "L.M.," writing in January, that in the face of the rappings, anyone could "relinquish inquiry and investigation till all is explained or the limits ascertained that restrict our knowledge. Meanwhile let us prepare ourselves for advancement of knowledge by leaving the citadel of Prejudice, though we retain the sword of Reason and the shield of Faith."[57] This correspondence was soon followed by a three-column editorial in which Greeley reviewed Eliab Capron's new book, then on sale in New York for 25 cents. Capron gave a positive version of the history of the mysterious noises and presented the rappings as a reconciliation between spirituality and materialism. Greeley weighed the evidence offered in the book, and in the end found himself unable to draw conclusions one way or the other. He continued to call for active yet skeptical investigation.[58]

These writers were all using the rappings as a way to debate philosophical issues in a popular forum. Most prominent were issues surrounding the relationship between science and religion and between mind and matter. Capron, for example, in a pamphlet published early in 1850, claimed that the greatest mistake of conventional forms of science and religion was the distinction they made between spirit and matter. Spiritualism, he claimed, showed that such a separation was not valid.[59]

Soon more writers to the *Tribune* began to offer their speculations as to the origin and meaning of the rappings. "W. F.," who had witnessed the rappings in western New York, wrote to the paper giving a brief history of the belief in spirits by a variety of mystics and philosophers including Confucius, Zoroaster, Plato, Jesus, and Swedenborg. He suggested that the spirits might be controlling electricity in order to produce rapping sounds. Even if the raps were produced by spirits, both "W. F." and Greeley felt it necessary to quote Scripture's warning, "Believe not every Spirit," in case these spirits came from below rather than above.[60]

As Karen Halttunen has argued, the fear of being defrauded by "confidence men" had New Yorkers on their guard in the antebellum era.[61] By the beginning of 1850, even before the Fox sisters arrived in New York, a new class of "antispiritualists" had emerged, dedicated to uncovering deception and proving the rappings a fraud. In late January and early February these antispiritualists began to make themselves heard. Letters from Rochester appeared in city newspapers claiming that the success of the Corinthian Hall performances had been greatly exaggerated and that only "a deluded set" in Rochester actually believed in the spirits.[62] One critic wrote that in the séances he attended in Rochester, he "never saw any manifestations of superior intellect, but very many that would be beneath the capacity and acquirements of a girl twelve years old." While admitting that mesmerism could be involved, he was very suspicious that the so-called manifestations and communications always occurred in the dark. And nine times out of ten, he said, the answers to questions put by investigators were incorrect.[63]

In Halttunen's terms, what these writers were claiming was that the Fox sisters lacked the sincerity that was essential for true middle-class respectability. The same critic, assailing the notion that the sisters were honest and genteel, characterized them instead as dishonest and thus perpetrators of fraud:

> I have had a conversation with something purporting to be the disembodied spirit of my brother, when in fact all my brothers are living. I have had information about family affairs, that was as far from truth as light from darkness. I have heard the "spirit" play upon an accordion when I *knew* who was doing it. I have heard rappings on men's heads when I knew whose hands were at work. I have seen the names of persons designated when I

> knew the signs by which they were communicated to the girls. I have seen the girls talk to each other with their fingers, when one knew what the other did not, and I have heard them deny all knowledge of matters about which I had myself informed them a short time before.[64]

He stated that even believers in spiritualism had a low opinion of the honesty of the sisters, and that Kate Fox "would rather lie than tell the truth." Apparently the sisters had drawn some suspicion on themselves when the spirits instructed séance participants to buy the girls new shoes and make them new dresses.[65]

Side by side with this damning letter, the *Tribune* printed two others that continued to maintain belief in the spirits and the dawn of a new age, leading Greeley to ask: "Is the world running mad, or getting sane?—stricken with judicial blindness, or just beginning to see? We must take time to consider and investigate one of these days."[66] If critics thought that these attacks would stifle public curiosity about the rappings, they were mistaken. Discussions of the mysterious knockings were only fueled by the added controversy, demonstrating the old adage that there is no such thing as bad publicity—unless, of course, one aspires to gentility.

Before the girls' visit to New York City, Eliab Capron had remained their most vocal supporter in the press, but once they arrived and began to give successful performances, many others, unable to detect any deception, came to the sisters' defense.[67] Interestingly, many of these defenders did not yet believe in the spirits. A surprising number who remained puzzled by the raps were simply convinced by the girls' deportment that they at least were sincere and thus were not causing the sounds intentionally. The most prominent of these defenders was Greeley. At the end of their visit to New York City in August, the sisters spent almost two weeks in a series of private homes, including Greeley's, to allow more detailed examination. At the end of this visit, Greeley wrote an editorial stating that he was "convinced beyond a doubt of [the sisters'] perfect integrity and good faith." While many have interpreted this to mean that he believed in the spirits, that is not the case. Greeley made it clear that he was only willing to rule out fraud.[68]

Others, however, were not prepared to take that step. As the fame of the Fox sisters grew through the latter months of 1850 and into 1851, a group of men emerged to capitalize on their activities by denouncing them. Ironically, these critics probably helped the growth of spirit rapping more than they hurt it. The most prominent members of this group were Stanley Grimes, Chauncey Burr, and a trio who would come to be known as "the Buffalo Doctors." In one sense the spiritualists and antispiritualists were in opposition, but in another they were all part of the same phenomenon. Both sides appealed to the popular love of investigation and mystery. All felt that it was the prerogative of citizens of a democratic nation to debate serious issues, and that is what they were doing.

The first eminent antispiritualist, Stanley Grimes, was one of the country's best-known lecturers on mesmerism and phrenology. He had spoken in many cities and towns in western New York while the rapping was getting under way. By his own description, his lectures centered on "Phrenology, Physiology and Mesmerism as parts of one great science of Human Nature."[69] Grimes believed in the power of both mesmerism and clairvoyance, but when it came to spiritualism, he balked.[70] At first he seems to have believed that the Fox sisters were clairvoyant; but after further investigation, he came to the conclusion that they were clever frauds. He claimed to have drawn a confession out of one woman in western New York who, said Grimes, had learned her tricks from the Fox sisters.[71] Grimes did not pretend to have discovered exactly how the sisters fooled people, but he gave a skeptical account of his own visit to one of their séances, pointing out that the rules were "such as are calculated to prevent rigid scrutiny."[72] He used phrenology to explain both the gullibility of one believer, the shape of whose head "indicated that it was well adapted for the habitation of superstitious ideas," and the cunning of Leah Fish, whose head indicated "courage, cunning, skepticism and a ready practical skill."[73]

Grimes became the focus of debate in the *Tribune* about the spirituality or non-spirituality of the knocks. One rebuttal implied that Grimes was afraid that spiritual revelations from mediums would undermine his own career as a lecturer on "animal magnetism," and that he had probably elicited a false confession from the medium in western New York by mesmerizing her. Other charged that Grimes was simply trying to advance his own career.[74] The argument, which lasted through the summer of 1850, included a series of letters that appeared under the headings "Grimes on Knocking" or "Knocking on Grimes." It was not a friendly scientific disagreement. Writers increasingly accused their opponents of fraud, delusion, and plain stupidity. Spirit rapping was becoming a controversial topic that drew bitter accusations from both sides. Capron's friend Henry

Barron wrote defending himself from what he called a "calumny of foul abuse heaped upon my friends and myself," while calling Grimes a false "aspirant for fame."[75] Another correspondent, writing to the *Evening Post* but responding to the debate in the *Tribune,* lamented the "moral weakness displayed by the principal part of the audience" at séances he had attended.[76] Clearly it would be difficult for the sisters to maintain their aura of innocent gentility within such a milieu.

C. Chauncey Burr, the editor of the *Nineteenth Century Review*, also put himself before the public as an antispiritualist. In addition to being an editor, Burr, with his brother Heman, gave lectures under the title "Imagination and Ghost-seeing," in which they demonstrated the susceptibility of the human mind to mesmeric powers of suggestion. From the start Burr had believed the spirit rappings a fraud, but he did not become concerned, he later said, until he saw "many imaginative persons driven to the wildest extravagances, and some to absolute insanity, by the phenomena."[77] Spurred on by his concern for the mental well-being of the nation, he began to visit mediums and investigate their performances. Soon he found that he could reproduce the "knockings" quite loudly by cracking the joint of his big toe, and he could explain the medium's ability to influence participants by his previous study of the imagination.[78]

Burr decided to add an antispiritualist element to his lectures on imagination and "ghost-seeing." In January 1851 he presented a new lecture "Spiritual Knockings Exposed," in an engagement that ran for three nights at Hope Chapel on Broadway.[79] Burr showed how he could produce raps with his big toe loud enough for everyone to hear, while his brother demonstrated his ability to control the imagination and will of audience members chosen at random. Horace Greeley attended the last of these performances, but remained unconvinced that fraud was proven.[80] Burr continued to spread his antispiritualist message on the lecture circuit, though he was unable to persuade those who believed in the raps to change their minds.[81]

A more convincing blow to spirit rapping was struck in late February 1851. The sisters had returned to Rochester in the fall of 1850 after their successful summer in Manhattan, but soon they began to receive calls to appear publicly again. By the end of the year Kate Fox, accompanied by her mother, had gone back to New York to stay for a time in various private households, while Leah Fish and Maggie Fox took a trip to Buffalo to hold public séances at the Phelps House Hotel. For a time, Maggie and her older sister gave successful and convincing performances. After some weeks, however, they were surprised to find in the columns of the *Buffalo Commercial Advertiser* a stunning exposé that accused them of fraud and claimed to reveal the secret of the "Mysterious Knockings."

The article, written by Dr. C. B. Coventry, Dr. Charles A. Lee, and Dr. T. M. Foote, who came to be known as "the Buffalo Doctors," was written in the most authoritative-sounding scientific language these experts could muster. They claimed that, driven by curiosity, they had visited the sisters at the Phelps House and had come up with a logical explanation for the raps. The doctors had arrived at the conclusion that the rapping was a fraud by "the application of a method of reasoning much resorted to in the diagnosis of disease—namely, the reasoning *by way of exclusion*."[82] Since the knockings could not be regarded as spiritual if they could be accounted for physically, "we are thus to *exclude* spiritual causation in this stage of the investigation."[83] They also "excluded" artificial machinery hidden in the sisters' dresses and the use of the vocal cords. Therefore, the sounds must come from the "action of the will, through voluntary muscles, upon the joints."[84] They thought that the knee joint was the most likely, and claimed to have found a "highly respectable lady" in Buffalo who could in fact produce such sounds with her knee.

The doctors' exposé was actually no more impressive than that of Chauncey Burr, but it was delivered with pompous self-assurance and soon appeared in a medical journal, causing many to take it more seriously. Instead of backing down in defeat, the sisters mounted a vigorous challenge. This was actually not so hard to do, for the strength of the doctors' argument was also its weakness. That is, they spoke with authority, but people attracted to spirit rapping were usually dissatisfied with explanations provided by sources of authority. Furthermore, the assumption of their argument "by exclusion" was that spiritual explanations were inferior to material explanations, hardly an argument likely to convince the many supporters of spirit rapping, who believed that the dichotomy between matter and spirit could be reconciled. To Fish, reflecting on the episode years later, the doctors represented "the materialistic bigotry of modern science . . . in arms against us and the Spirits."[85]

The women refused to retreat like exposed confidence men. Instead they boldly sent back a challenge to the doctors via an open letter printed in all the local papers, in which they rose up to defend not only the rapping but also, more important, their own female honor. "As we do not feel willing to rest under the imputation of being impostors," they wrote, "we are very willing to undergo a proper and decent examination." Professing absolute innocence and a desire to get to the bottom of the mystery, the sisters agreed that "it is due to the world that the investigation be made, and that the 'humbug' be exposed."[86] With this simple challenge they skillfully turned their "exposure" into an opportunity for further investigation. This publicity ensured that for weeks following they would have ample business as crowds came to see for themselves. When they finally left Buffalo, Leah Fish would conclude, "in a financial point of view, we had never met with an equal success."[87] Yet such boldness was risky, too, for it exposed the women to accusations of not being respectable.

Here again, the sisters were using female gentility in much the same way that Kane used Humboldtean science—to lend moral validity to their roles in the public sphere. Neither could rely solely on the search for knowledge to validate their explorations; rather, both Kane and the Fox sisters needed to clothe their actions in social virtue. Without their image of sincerity and gentility the Fox sisters were nothing, just as Kane would be nothing without his assertions that his explorations promoted humanitarianism and the common good.

A few weeks after their triumph in Buffalo, the sisters were assailed by another exposé. Chauncey and Heman Burr, continuing their antispiritualist investigations, somehow obtained a deposition from Mrs. Norman Culver, a relative of the Fox family who lived in Arcadia, New York. In her statement, dated April 17, 1851, Mrs. Culver claimed that at first she had believed in the rappings but had soon began to suspect fraud. To test her theory, she approached Kate Fox and offered to assist her in answering test questions and making the raps. Fox revealed to Mrs. Culver that the raps were produced by the toe joints, and showed her how to do it. According to Mrs. Culver, Fox then explained to her that it was usually easy to guess the correct answers to questions by careful observation of a person's body language. At times, she said, the girls were also assisted by a Dutch servant girl who would go down to the cellar and knock with her knuckles or a broomstick on the ceiling.[88] After this deposition appeared in the papers, the sisters simply denied the charges, saying that Mrs. Culver was only a distant relative by marriage and that she held a grudge against the Fox family.[89]

Leah Fish and Maggie and Kate Fox were clearly the driving force behind the emergence of spirit rapping as a popular phenomenon in antebellum America. They skillfully marketed their abilities to successive audiences, yet remarkably little emphasis has been placed on their role by either their own contemporaries or historians. Their story is generally represented as a preliminary to later and more important developments, with the Fox sisters depicted as more or less witless children who unintentionally made history. One historian who did extensive research on the Fox sisters and believed them to possess actual unknown psychic abilities has gone so far as to claim that they did not even understand "their own mediumistic experience,"[90] in other words, that they had no active agency in their own affairs. The larger story of spiritualism is often told with little more than a passing reference to the sisters, while emphasizing instead the experiences of their audiences. The reason for this neglect is that they played their roles so well. The sisters, led by Leah Fish, judged the temperament of each audience and manipulated it to their advantage. The rappings repeatedly changed form. First they were presented as a ghost story performed for rural farmers; next they became a sign of moral awakening for urban reformers; then a demonstration of the latest theories in the sciences of the mind; and finally a challenge to the curiosity and intelligence of Rochester, New York City, and the nation.

The sisters were successful as spirit rappers for much the same reason that their role is often passed over: their success depended on their own agency remaining in the shadows. They had to appear passive, guileless, and innocent, while in actuality they were keenly perceptive observers of human nature who devised a very original form of presentation. They *actively* created themselves as passive objects of investigation, thus conforming to their audiences' beliefs about gender and gentility. The sisters made no bold claims to higher knowledge or power. They presented themselves only as mediums who were not even acting on their own behalf. They even, for a time, masked the overtly commercial aspect of spirit rapping, offering themselves as scientific exhibits rather than the skilled performers they had become.

One particular element of the Fox sisters' performance for which they seldom get credit was its appeal to the new mass culture of curiosity. The sisters invited observers to explore, to question, to investigate, and ultimately to provide their own answers, thus giving their audience the active role. The rapping seemed to promise answers to life's great questions, but this was only a tease; instead they manipulated participants to create their own answers to suit their own particular beliefs. The movement could thus go on indefinitely. While some historians have noted this technique as an attribute of spiritualism in general, no one has given the Fox sisters any credit for developing it.

As the Historian Ann Braude had observed of spiritualism, "The interpretation of investigators, rather than the manifestations themselves, provided the content of the new religion."[91] Braude is correct in this if we limit ourselves to the religious side of spiritualism and ignore the rest. But spiritualism was not just a religion. It was firmly grounded in the practice of séances, which were skillfully marketed to a broad American audience and presented by skilled performers. The three Fox sisters created a thriving business for themselves, having successfully identified a vast market for the commodity they provided. That commodity was neither religion nor science but rather a mode of presentation.

Historians of nineteenth-century spiritualism have tended to recognize that there were two sides to it.[92] One consisted of seekers after truth, who were drawn to the scientific, philosophical, and theological implications of communication with spirits. Andrew Jackson Davis, for instance, popularly known as "the Poughkeepsie Seer," predated the Fox sisters. He wrote a number of books on spiritual issues and claimed to be in spiritual contact with the Swedish mystic Emanuel Swedenborg. The side of spiritualism represented by Davis and by dedicated Christian social reformers like Amy and Isaac Post and Eliab Capron was intellectually and religiously driven.[93]

The other side of spiritualism was commercial and sensational. This aspect of spiritualism offered the public unexplained wonders, and charged an admission fee to see them. It challenged its audiences to understand the phenomena produced by mediums. It also, at least part of the time, engaged in conscious deception and fraud, like the showman P. T. Barnum, seeking publicity any way it could get it. It is not surprising that some historians have mistakenly identified Barnum as the Fox sisters' publicist. In fact they were never associated with him, but they did use many similar publicity techniques. Like Barnum, they mixed scientific investigation with sensationalism to attract a paying audience. And like Barnum, they appealed to the culture of curiosity.

Many historians have seen the intellectual and religious side of spiritualism as more historically significant than the commercial, sensational side. But this dichotomy should not be taken too far, for the very essence of the culture of curiosity was the combination of the two. When the Fox sisters performed séances, the intellectual and sensational sides of spiritualism held hands around a darkened table. That was their intention.

By the middle of the nineteenth century, knowledge about the world had become a matter of broad public debate. In a democratic society, the authority of popular opinion, derived through individual investigation, now determined truth more than the authority of tradition or experts.[94] This was what made spiritualism possible both as a religious and intellectual movement associated with reform and as a popular sensation that appealed to public curiosity. Spirit rappers such as the Fox sisters invited ordinary people to "come and investigate," and thus to become actively engaged in determining the truth for themselves. Nineteenth-century Americans did come and investigate, but they did not all arrive at the same conclusions. Where some found humbug, others found God. But what they found is less significant than their ability to investigate and to satisfy their curiosity. In this sense spiritualism stands out more for the interactive structure of its performances than for any of its varied philosophical content.

By mid-1851 there were probably few Americans who had not heard of the "Rochester knockings." When the Fox sisters came to town, some would go to see them to communicate with the departed, but others would go to see the show, to test their wits against the skills of the "knockers," and to try to detect how the noises were produced. Depending on one's perspective, different issues were raised. Some saw spirit rapping as a return to the superstitions of an earlier era, while others saw it as a way to combat the closed-minded dogmatism of both established religion and materialist science. The opportunity the Fox sisters offered for the public to explore these issues continued to draw in crowds. No exposé, no matter how well founded, would be able to stop the rapping.

The sisters were able to survive for a time in this competitive world by clothing themselves in ideal images of female innocence, virtue, and gentility. But when they entered the public world, their sincerity came into doubt. To those who were not convinced of their honesty, they became the worst sort of women. Deception was an ugly thing to antebellum Americans; it was unappealing in men and positively repulsive in women. If the Fox sisters were found to be deceivers, all the gains they had made since beginning their rappings over two years before could be lost.

5

Curiosity and Values in the Antebellum Lecture Hall

There is no better intellectual discipline than the habit of hearing the different sides of important questions discussed, in a dignified yet earnest way, by persons who represent the most adverse positions. If truth is not always sifted from error by this process, the mind of the listener, at least, is discharged of its bigotry and prejudices, and put in a condition to weight evidence properly, and draw correct conclusions.

"The Lecture System," *Littell's Living Age*, January 14, 1854

WHEN ELISHA KANE returned from the first Grinnell Expedition in the autumn of 1851, he immediately went to work to keep alive the public enthusiasm that had driven that endeavor. Writing to Lady Jane Franklin, still waiting to learn of her husband's fate, he observed that the "tone of the press is favorable to continued search and it will not be difficult to keep the subject sufficiently prominent" to promote further expeditions.[1] Although many members of the expedition spoke to the press, giving accounts of the marvels of the Arctic seas, Kane's quickly became the dominant voice. By all accounts he was a charming man and could tell a good tale. He, more than the others, summoned up for listeners at home the thrill of Arctic adventure.

Within a few months of the expedition's return, the winter lecture season began, and Kane decided to try this forum as a way of generating both publicity and money for further exploration. He delivered his first series of lectures at the Smithsonian Institution in Washington, D.C., in late December. The Smithsonian had been founded less than six years before, dedicated to the "increase and diffusion of knowledge." Here he had the opportunity to address some of the most prominent minds in the country, including Joseph Henry, the superintendent of the Smithsonian.

Interest in his lecture, however, clearly went beyond the scientific elite. The *New York Daily Times,* one of the new penny papers, devoted a remarkable four columns to Kane's lecture, indicating that this was a subject with broad appeal.[2]

Kane began his series at the Smithsonian with a brief history of Arctic exploration dating back to the European discovery of the Americas. He moved on to a discussion of the important geographic discoveries made by past polar explorers and reviewed the theory of the Open Polar Sea. He then turned to the history of the Franklin Expedition and expressed his conviction that Franklin had sailed, or drifted in the ice, northward through Wellington Channel into this northern "Polynia." Using maps, he laid out a very convincing (though entirely mistaken) argument, based on his observations while on the Grinnell Expedition, that Franklin's course had been to the north. His arguments seemed to one newspaper reporter to be "almost conclusive."[3] He then moved on to the question of whether or not any of the men from the Franklin Expedition remained alive. "The consideration of this question was made exceedingly interesting by the lecturer," observed the *New York Daily Times*.[4] Kane reviewed the conditions he had observed in the polar regions and expressed his opinion that Franklin's ships, the *Erebus* and the *Terror*, could not both have been crushed and sunk. Furthermore, he observed, the Arctic afforded all the necessary means to sustain life. Even if stranded, a significant portion of Franklin's crew may have been able to survive on the natural resources of the region.[5]

Kane described both the dangers and the sublime beauty the Grinnell Expedition had been exposed to while in the Arctic. He invited his audience to picture the scene and to experience its mysteries as if they had been there themselves. He laid out the available evidence and gave his conclusions, then asked the audience to decide for themselves where they thought Franklin had gone. Like the latest detective fiction or unsolved murder—or, for that matter, like the spirit rappers—Kane's presentation appealed to the imagination of his audiences and their desire to take part in the process of discovery. But unlike with the spirit rappers, with Kane there was no taint of deception or self-interest. His goals of finding Franklin and discovering the Open Polar Sea seemed unquestionably noble and virtuous.

His appearances in the Smithsonian lecture hall did not go unrewarded. The *New York Daily Times* reported that "a brilliant assembly of the ladies and gentlemen of Washington" attended Kane's lectures, and that they "manifested their appreciation of his effort in frequent demonstrations of applause."[6] He ended his third and final lecture with a heartfelt call to action that stressed themes of honor and virtue more than it did geography. "The search cannot, will not be abandoned," he was quoted in the *Times*:

> The pride of a heroic nation can never consent to yield up the children she has sent forth to peril without tracing out their pathway of disastrous duty, and at least gathering their bones into a grave. Science that recognizes no nationality less comprehensive than the world it enlightens—Christian philanthropy that has expounded the circle of brotherhood til it includes all who suffer—the chivalry of the age, that assigning the first rank of daring to some, pledges all the rest to follow for support of rescue—manhood itself, responsive to the appeals of a noble spirit and heart-stricken wife—all these reject the dishonor of leaving Sir John Franklin and his companions to perish unremembered, and engage the sternest and most exalted and ennobling of human energies to work out the mysterious problem of their fate.[7]

The Smithsonian was a learned forum for the scientific establishment, a place designed to allow the nation's most prominent men of science to bestow their learning on a large middle- and upper-class audience; but it was also a public institution. Lectures there were geared toward an educated public interested in scientific subjects. Kane's success in lecturing in such a forum was the result not only of his geographic studies, but also of his ability to cloak this learning in the moralism of the day. By describing geographic exploration as a moral crusade, he was able to present his own ambition as humanitarian sacrifice. Unlike the performances of the spirit rappers, Kane's investigations produced unity more than conflict. Or rather, the conflict he invoked was the conflict of heroic men against nature and of knowledge against ignorance. This was a formula Kane would repeat a month later when he delivered a lecture in a more popular arena—the Musical Fund Hall in Philadelphia.

This lecture "was attended by a very large and highly appreciative audience, and was listened to by all with evident feelings of sincere satisfaction, according to the *Philadelphia Evening Bulletin*, which praised Kane's engaging style. His "was a vivid picture drawn with masterly skill, and presenting vividly to all, all the perils, and sufferings, and alarms of the Arctic voyager." Kane again characterized the search for Franklin as a moral imperative. It could be demonstrated, he claimed, that Franklin might still be alive. To find him was a goal nobler even than geographic discovery and more valuable than military or monetary gain. "We have a more sacred duty, but one alike honorable," said Kane. "We have stained the plains of Mexico with blood to obtain more perishable honors, and men shrink and die upon the banks of the Sacramento in pursuit of gold; but good deeds yield brighter laurels than war, and humanity's triumphs are more valued than gold." When the lecture ended, he was met with hearty applause.[8]

In an age of ambiguity, Kane was describing an unambiguous moral crusade. Unlike the morally questionable Mexican War, which was seen by many northern Whigs as an attempt to expand slavery into new territory, and unlike the quest for wealth in a capitalist society, the search for Franklin was manifestly honorable no matter who was judging. It was a quest on behalf of humanity, according to Kane, not of any one faction or selfish interest. This is of particular importance in the context of other events taking place in the 1850s. In the decade of conflict preceding the Civil War, the great issue of the day was the question of expanding the nation, and thus slavery, into the western territories. In the wake of the controversial yet largely successful Mexican War, Congress had with great difficulty formulated a fragile compromise in 1850 that satisfied no one. Northerners, resentful of a "slave power" in the South, found the newly strengthened Fugitive Slave Law abhorrent, as it required them to capture and return into slavery escaped slaves living in free states. And southerners feared the growing influence of the free states in Congress as California's admission to the Union in September of that year upset the balance in the Senate.

Arctic exploration, however, remained above all the political squabbles of the day. In the search for Franklin, North and South and East and West could see eye to eye. Southern slaveholders and northern capitalists could all participate in noble and selfless heroics on behalf of humanity by aiding the quest. Moreover, in this cause America could act as a unified nation in ways that were becoming increasingly difficult at home. Old-fashioned ideals of disinterested American virtue could be expressed through Arctic exploration in a manner that had become difficult, if not impossible, on the battlefields of Mexico and the goldfields of California.

In Kane's success as a popular lecturer after his return from his first Arctic voyage, we see that the culture of curiosity was as much about values as it was about knowledge. Antebellum Americans were not just looking for sensation or for random information about polar bears and icebergs. Rather they wanted to discover things that would support the ideals they held sacred and obscure the conflicts of a changing world. Just as Isaac and Amy Post were attracted to the moral ramifications of communication with the dead, Kane's audiences were attracted to the moral ideal of humanitarian sacrifice that he promoted. Kane was a master of presenting his scientific interests in terms with which his listeners could identify, and he would do so in cities up and down the eastern seaboard in the coming months, as he was bombarded with more invitations to lecture than he could possibly accept.[9]

Kane's success as a lecturer also points to the role of the lecture hall in antebellum culture. Along with the newspaper, it was an important medium for disseminating new ideas. Lectures were tremendously popular, too, because they promoted democracy in an atmosphere of gentility and progress. The quality of democracy, after all, was thought to depend on the quality of the citizenry. If valuable knowledge were disseminated widely throughout the nation, then the nation as a whole would be both morally and intellectually uplifted.[10]

Many of the most prominent men in the United States at this time supplemented their incomes by lecturing. Ralph Waldo Emerson was perhaps the most successful lecturer at this time, but others such as Horace Greeley, George Bancroft, and Henry Ward Beecher all spent a good deal of time behind the podium. Almost any subject could be addressed in a public lecture, so it is not surprising that both the Fox sisters and Elisha Kane would find their way to this medium. Science, history, literature, various social and religious ideas were presented to eager audiences. Moving outward from New England, the lecture system came to predominate anywhere a large audience could be assembled.[11]

Although lecturers were predominantly white men from the upper reaches of society, there were some notable exceptions. Frederick Douglass, probably the most famous black lecturer, was highly popular in the North as an abolitionist speaker. There were also a few female lecturers, such as Mrs. E. Oakes Smith, who generally spoke on topics related to women. A series she gave in New York in the fall of 1852 included one lecture titled "Woman as inferior to Man" and another on the Egyptian queen Cleopatra. The *New York Daily Tribune* noted that Mrs. Smith's lectures betrayed "rare cultivation and the beautiful wisdom of feminine genius."[12] There was also at least one Native American lecturer, George Copway, or "Mr. Kah-ge-ga-gah-bowh," who spoke on Ojibwa culture.[13]

The object of the lecture, according to one reviewer, was "instruction, excitement, and communication between the higher minds of the age, and those of a lower grade."[14] The lecture system, more than mere instruction, was generally seen as a sign of American social progress. When Oliver Wendell Holmes gave a lecture on the topic of lecturing, he commented that the lecture was "the natural product of American civilization" since it allowed people of differing opinions to present their views in a refined atmosphere that promoted social harmony.[15] Another writer commented in a similar way that lectures had a social benefit, since they brought the people of a community together to exchange ideas: "Our division into religious sects tends to alienate and estrange us from each other. The lecture-room must become the Social Exchange—the place where acquaintances are made and friendships cemented."[16]

There was also a financial incentive for lecturing. A speaker could write a single lecture then deliver it repeatedly in different cities and towns around the nation for twenty-five to fifty dollars each night. This brought in more money than simply writing an article that would be published once. Many, if not most, speakers combined careers as writers or editors with careers as lecturers. Of course, this financial side could be a problem as well. A lecturer who was entertaining as well as knowledgeable could bring in more revenue than one who was merely knowledgeable. But what if the desire to bring in ever greater revenue caused the quality of the knowledge to decline? What if entertainment and profit became more important than knowledge? These would be increasingly worrisome issues as the commercial side of popular culture grew in significance.[17]

The lecture system was predominantly a top-down institution that allowed the learned to bestow information on the less learned. Experts in a particular field would be invited to speak on their area of expertise. Great men would bring knowledge to the people. But the lecture system also provided a context for new and radical ideas to be presented and debated. The many reform movements of the antebellum era all utilized the lecture system to disseminate their ideas. As we have already seen, practitioners of new sciences such as phrenology and mesmerism were naturally drawn to the lecture hall. In their local lyceums, people were willing to give new ideas a hearing. The lecture was an open-minded format aptly suited to the culture of curiosity.

WITH HIS interesting subject matter and strong moral message, Kane was typical of lecturers from the upper reaches of society. Less typical was the way the Fox sisters used the popular lecture circuit to further their careers. It was harder for them as women to stand up in front of a large audience and speak. Instead, they used male lecturers, who enabled them to remain in the background. In Corinthian Hall, they had confined themselves to spirit rapping while Eliab Capron delivered the lecture, then in Troy it had been R. P. Ambler who acted as their spokesman. They gave up that format for a time when they went to New York City in favor of private séances in hotel parlors, but they resumed it again as they began their western tour in the summer of 1851, appearing in both hotel parlors and lecture halls. Clearly the lecture system, even when they themselves did not speak, contributed significantly to their fame.

Throughout the spring of 1851, Leah Fish had been receiving appeals from friends and acquaintances to visit Ohio. The citizens of Cleveland especially were growing increasingly interested in the new spiritual phenomena they had been reading about in accounts reprinted from New York papers such as the *Tribune*. John W. Grey, the editor of northern Ohio's largest newspaper, the *Cleveland Daily Plain Dealer*, was very interested in the rappings and, like Horace Greeley at the *Tribune* in New York, gave the sisters a good deal of free newspaper publicity. The stage was set for a profitable tour.[18]

The performances of the Fox sisters on their Ohio tour became linked in the public mind with issues of a scientific and philosophical nature which were being played out in lecture halls and newspapers. Spirit rapping and the debate surrounding it was an excellent vehicle for discussing the nature of the mind and the soul. What was the relationship between mind and body and between matter and spirit? These are, and always have been, important questions discussed by scientists and philosophers, but spirit rapping, like mesmerism and phrenology before it, provided the opportunity to discuss these questions on a popular level. Nowhere was this more apparent than in the events leading up to the Fox sisters' Ohio tour.

The sisters themselves seldom joined in scientific or philosophical debates, but they definitely took advantage of them. In Ohio they allied themselves with a lecturer named Joel Tiffany, who fancied himself something of a spiritualist philosopher. Tiffany had begun speaking on the philosophy of spiritualism in mid-April 1851 in Cleveland. In these popular lectures, many of which were reported in detail in the *Plain Dealer*, he discussed spirit rapping as a means of illustrating the relationships between mind, body, spirit, electricity, and magnetism. He first explained how the mind controls the muscles through will and compared this with the use of an outside source of electricity to contract muscles. He claimed that electricity and magnetism (terms he used almost interchangeably) were the "mediums" by which the will controls the body. Various other "mediums," he said, exist in a hierarchical order between matter and spirit. "Taking nature for one teacher in this respect," argued Tiffany, "we learn that each of the higher mediums hold dominion over the lower ones, thus, that electricity controls matter, vitality controls electricity, sensation controls vitality, and mind or spirit controls sensation, thus the ultimate attenuated spiritual existence controls all lower existences, and, in that respect, is omnipotent." Thus electricity was the agency of the spirit rappings, but electricity itself must be controlled by some higher force, since the rapping demonstrated a higher order of intelligence. He concluded from this that the electricity "excited" during séances must be excited by "individualized spirits."[19]

It is hard to know whether Tiffany's lecture made any more sense to his listeners than to the modern reader, but it was clear, then as now, that the crux of his argument was the primacy of spirit over matter. This was an appealing argument at a time when science was gaining ascendancy, yet the materialist emphasis of modern science had some disturbing ramifications that most people were unwilling to accept. The work of geologists such as Charles Lyell was already threatening the chronology of Scripture, and publication of Darwin's *Origin of Species* was less than a decade away. Although few scientists at this time accepted purely materialistic explanations of the universe, increasingly the role of God and of spirit seemed relegated to the sidelines by scientific inquiry. The lectures of Joel Tiffany and other spiritualists reemphasized the primacy of spirit over matter, but they did so within a scientific framework reminiscent of mainstream natural theology.[20]

Tiffany ended his lectures with a pantheistic call for reconciliation between science and spirit. Reason, he claimed, would ultimately show God's presence in all things: "Reason is the first begotten of God and truth is the first born child of immortality. The Age of Reason will be an age of faith in God, not derived from books of ancient or modern date, but derived from the revelation which God has made of himself in his works, and the divine intuitions of an enlightened and purified soul."[21] Tiffany began his lecture in the guise of a scientist explaining electricity and the contraction of muscles, yet he ended it in the guise of a preacher declaring the Age of Reason to be the new millennium. Tiffany's ideas were novel and radical, but like Kane, he appealed to values such as reason, spirit, and progress that antebellum Americans held sacred. He, like Kane, involved his listeners in an intellectual process that had meaning for them.

WHEN TIFFANY was giving his first lectures in April 1851, the arrival of the Fox sisters in Ohio was still a month away, but he and his audiences were both aware that the one element his lectures lacked was a demonstration of the phenomena he claimed to describe. His theory needed experimental proof.[22] At that time there were some mediums practicing in Ohio, but most worked privately, and were unwilling to perform for the general public as the Fox sisters did. Before the sisters arrived, however, another prominent lecturer made an appearance in Ohio, bringing even greater local attention to the new spiritualist craze.

In the wake of Tiffany's first course of successful lectures, C. Chauncey Burr and his brother Heman descended on Ohio as part of their nationwide antispiritualist crusade. Burr, who was motivated by both a distaste for spiritualism and a love of large audiences for his lectures, was making a profitable business out of denouncing spirit rapping. He claimed to have exposed as frauds all the rappers he had yet witnessed. The *Plain Dealer* first announced that Burr was on his way to Cleveland on April 29. Two days later the paper observed that Leah Fish was also on her way.[23] The buildup could not have been more effective if it had been planned. The citizens of Cleveland would have their chance to judge for themselves now that one of the best-known spirit rappers and one of the best-known antispiritualists were arriving in the city almost simultaneously. "So we are to have both sides of this interesting question presented in its full length and breadth," announced the *Plain Dealer*. "Afraid of no truth, we shall patronize both sides, and report progress to the people."[24]

On Monday, May 5, Burr began his course of lectures. "Rochester Knockings Explained!" announced his advertisement in the *Plain Dealer*, appearing just under another for a performance of Shakespeare's *Richard III*.

> **C. Chauncey Burr** will give his Lectures on Popular Delusion and Spiritual Rappings, at the
>
> MELODEON HALL
>
> on Monday, Tuesday, and Wednesday evenings, May 5th, 6th and 7th. He will be assisted by HEMAN BURR who will exhibit the whole wonderful phenomena of the Rochester Rappings, and who will produce the exact
>
> **"Mysterious Sounds,"**
>
> so loud that they will be distinctly heard by the whole audience.
>
> He will also exhibit the secret of the "*Bewitched Tables,*" and every part of the rapping imposition will be exhibited to the perfect comprehension of the whole audience.
>
> Mr. Burr has spent three months investigating the rappings—he has detected forty seven "Mediums"—he has discovered seventeen different ways by which Mediums in different places, produce the sounds.
>
> Admission 12½ cents. Lecture to commence at 7½ o'clock.[25]

Like Kane and Tiffany, Burr presented knowledge in terms of values. His lectures focused on the moral degradation caused by spiritualism. He presented spirit rapping as mere fraud and delusion which often led believers to insanity or even suicide. It was, he said, a "disastrous influence on the cause of religion and civilization."[26] He also presented himself as the possessor of a rational mind who could see through the deceptive tricks of the mediums. But while he attracted large audiences to his lectures, he did not always convince them. People wondered why, if all mediums were frauds, intelligent men like Horace Greeley and the distinguished guests at the "Post-Mortuum Soiree" had not been able to detect it. Burr seemed to place his own powers of reason and observation arrogantly above those of thousands of others who had also been unable to detect deception. In seeming to deny the people's ability to make reasoned decisions for themselves based on their own observations, he challenged the core of democratic philosophy.

Joel Tiffany recognized these weaknesses in Burr's approach and, soon after Burr's arrival, issued a challenge that was published in the *Plain Dealer*.[27] Tiffany proposed that he and Burr publicly debate the matter before the people of Cleveland so that they could make up their minds themselves. Burr put off the challenge until his own series of three lectures was done, but on May 8 the debate began. The first night attracted such a sizable crowd that the *Plain Dealer* compared it with those flocking to hear the immensely popular Swedish soprano Jenny Lind, then making a triumphant tour of the United States under the skilled management of P. T. Barnum. "There was a tremendous crowd, a full Jenny audience to hear the opening of this discussion last night," read the account the next morning. "The Melodeon, the largest hall in the city, or in the West, was filled to its utmost capacity by the fashion, talent and beauty of the city, and the entertainment was well worthy of their attention."[28] The speakers took turns addressing the audience in thirty-minute intervals. Tiffany, who spoke first, claimed that genuine spiritual manifestations were not like the tricks reproduced by the Burr brothers. Most in the audience had not yet experienced the real thing, claimed Tiffany. He proceeded to give examples from newspaper accounts and from his own experiences that, he said, could not be explained by Burr's theories of toe tapping and trickery.

Burr responded by placing the testimony of witnesses in doubt. "I will show you," he informed the audience, "that there is no limit to mental impressibility."[29] Eyewitnesses could be fooled. They could be led to believe that they were seeing things that were not there. This was a disturbing view, not easily accepted by people with a strong faith in reason and progress. In a comment not well designed to curry the favor of the reporters present, Burr made reference to the expression "He lies like a newspaper," which, he said, was used in some places to cast doubt on a person's veracity. "Newspaper evidence is not always the best kind," he asserted in response to Tiffany's use of testimony recounted in the papers. "If I were to depend upon that alone, I doubt not I could conclusively demonstrate the moon to be made of green cheese."[30] Needless to say, the newspapers did not care for Burr or his argument.

The debate went on for two more nights. Philosophical ideas were intermixed with charges of fraud. Whichever man made the better argument, one thing was clear. Burr lost the battle by coming across as arrogant and unlikable. He presented himself as an authority whose perceptions were superior to all others. He placed no value on people's ability to investigate a phenomenon with their own eyes, ears, and minds. When he and his brother left Cleveland on May 12, the *Plain Dealer* commented: "They came with most pompous pretensions, claiming to cast out devils in every place where evil spirits were known to dwell; and supposing this city was inundated with false mediums, and the people a community of fools, incompetent to detect the tricks of the Rappers, they kindly volunteered to enlighten us at one shilling per lecture or 75 cents for the course."[31]

Burr had entertained but not persuaded the people of Cleveland. He failed to convince the audience that his debate with Tiffany was about the truth or falsehood of spirit rapping. If he had, perhaps he would have won. Instead, Tiffany thwarted Burr by making the debate about the primacy of spirit over matter and about human reason over authority. By framing the issues in this way, Tiffany won. The people of Cleveland chose spirit over charges of trickery and a faith in human reason over expert authority.

TWO DAYS later, Leah Fish came to Cleveland ready to build on this free publicity. She arrived on May 14 with a small contingent including Calvin Brown and her married sister, Maria Smith, but not the two younger Fox sisters. Fish, as usual, did not shy away from confrontation when she reached Cleveland. Hearing that Burr had publicly referred to her as "a woman of notoriously bad character," she promptly sued him for slander, claiming damages of ten thousand dollars.[32] The editors of the *Plain Dealer,* who had grown to dislike Burr, reported this with unabashed glee, adding that Mrs. Fish was now at the Dunham House Hotel, where she would receive visitors twice daily.[33]

In the wake of the excitement generated by the lectures of the previous weeks, Fish did a brisk business in Cleveland. Twelve days after her arrival, the *Plain Dealer* reported increasing crowds at the Dunham House, including "several distinguished gentlemen and their ladies from distant parts of the state."[34] A few days later she was joined by Maggie and Kate Fox, who until recently had been staying at a private residence in New York City. They had come to Cleveland accompanied by a friend from Rochester, Mrs. Kedzie. They had planned to move on to Cincinnati, but instead they stayed for a time in Cleveland. Together the three sisters attracted plenty of attention, but they did not limit themselves to private sittings at the Dunham. They also allied their performances with the efforts of Joel Tiffany. Rather than mounting the podium as speakers themselves, however, they took their seats in the audience. As Tiffany lectured one day at the Prospect Street Church, the crowd was delighted to hear raps responding throughout the church to what was being said. When Tiffany made a point the spirits liked, they reacted with raps of approval.

Performance and philosophy were thus effectively combined, each lending credence to the other. Throughout their Ohio tour, the Fox sisters frequently accompanied Tiffany to towns where he would deliver a learned lecture on spirit and matter while they performed raps to "prove" what he was saying. They maintained the decorum appropriate to genteel young ladies by giving the more controversial public role to Tiffany.[35]

THE FOX SISTERS and their supporters may have won the battle over values in the lecture halls of Cleveland, but by the end of their western tour in late 1851, changes were brewing over the spirit rapping phenomenon that would push the sisters to the sidelines of the movement and reduce Maggie Fox's willingness to take part in it. A growing segment of the American population had made up their minds on the matter, and many were coming around to the view held by Chauncey Burr. Consider, for example, George Templeton Strong of New York, whose journal entry for July 8, 1850, when the sisters first visited the city, was all about the raps. He did not believe they were spiritual, but he found them worth two visits to see and hear the phenomenon, along with a quantity of speculation on the question. By May 1852 he had become a confirmed skeptic and viewed the spiritualist antics with some distaste. He was still interested, but now his interest was in the "human credulity" the rapping demonstrated. He attributed the work of one prominent spiritualist to "a vivid waking dream produced by opium, drink, and mental excitement." Strong continued to believe that the rappings should be investigated, but not because he thought there was any chance of their being of spiritual origin. To an ever-increasing segment of the population, spirit rapping had come to represent the uglier side of life—not human progress but human delusion and degradation.[36]

As spirit rapping was developing a reputation among many nonbelievers as a sign of serious social and moral decline, Maggie and Kate Fox were of course personally affected. This view lent them an increasingly unappealing notoriety. R. Laurence Moore has documented the opposition among Christians to spiritualism, a posture that led Oliver Wendell Holmes to describe Maggie and Kate Fox as the "Nemesis of the pulpit."[37] As time went by, fewer newspaper editors approached spirit rapping as Horace Greeley had—as an opportunity for serious democratic investigation and discussion, or a sign of American progress. Rather, they alternately ignored and condemned the rapping and rappers. Even Greeley began to withdraw from his earlier interest in spirit rapping, although he never wholly rejected it as a fraud.[38]

Two startling new topics emerged in the newspapers after 1851 in connection with spirit rapping: insanity and suicide. In place of the issues of truth and falsehood that dominated early discussion in the papers, now editorials and articles raised questions with ugly moral ramifications. For instance, in March 1853 an editorial in the *Daily National Intelligencer* condemned spirit rapping as a delusion, out of place in an age of progress and reason. "We had resolved never again to burden these columns with the disgusting theme," the editorial read, "but it seems to become a journalist's duty to give 'line upon line and precept upon precept,' since the imposture is still marring domestic happiness and filling our madhouses with its victims."[39] Spiritualism, according to the editorial, preyed on the weak-minded, destroyed families, and sent countless victims to insane asylums. At about the same time, a lecturer speaking in Richmond, Virginia, presented precise figures supporting this view. To date, throughout the United States, he said, 573 people had been sent to asylums because of spirit rapping, while 17 had committed suicide.[40]

In the face of growing public disapproval and ridicule, dedicated spiritualists were consolidating within their own organizations. A growing core of spiritualists had now joined private spiritualist circles that met regularly; they read about spiritualist matters in spiritualist newspapers and went to spiritualist conventions to exchange their views on the new religion. Joel Tiffany would eventually become the editor of his own spiritualist journal. This core of believers would remain strong for another half century, but in the mainstream newspapers and lecture halls where Tiffany and the Fox sisters had once triumphed, spiritualism was losing ground.

To nonbelievers, spiritualism was increasingly seen to bring out the worst in American society. It demonstrated how easily respectable men and women could be guided into delusion. It showed that perhaps the citizens of the United States were not capable after all of making rational decisions or of living outside the control of authority. Spiritualism had entered a milieu dedicated to the rational exchange of ideas, a milieu of newspapers and lecture halls, whose very existence was based on a belief that if citizens were given information and allowed to debate issues freely, then truth and reason would ultimately prevail. Yet in the case of spiritualism, truth and reason were showing no sign of prevailing anytime soon.

Spirit rapping was increasingly making a strong case *against* the idea that a nation could be ruled by reason. To many it therefore represented moral and intellectual decline in an age devoted to progress.

BY THE MIDDLE of 1852 Elisha Kane and Margaret Fox had not yet met, but they already had a great deal in common. They both appealed to American audiences by linking their desire to learn about unknown worlds with their sense of values. Kane's career was taking off, however, while Fox's had reached a plateau. To true believers, her rappings still represented progress toward a new age and a reconciliation between spirit and matter. But unlike Kane, whose reputation would continue to grow, Fox would soon find herself on the fringe, losing the esteem of the American mainstream.

6

Private Lives, Public Curiosity

How disgusting is this life, to be discussed by the papers!
Elisha Kane to Maggie Fox, *The Love-Life of Dr. Kane*

WHEN ELISHA KANE and Margaret Fox finally got to know each other in the autumn of 1852, the values associated with their respective explorations helped define the nature of their private relationship. For Fox, who was aspiring to middle-class status, it was becoming increasingly difficult to reconcile a career as a public celebrity with a respectable private life. Ideals of "domesticity" and the "private sphere" dominated middle-class female life. But Fox did not live in a domestic, private world. She may have mimicked the middle-class domestic scene when she gave séances in hotel parlors, but a parlor in a hotel is a far cry from the parlor of a middle-class home. Maggie Fox was an extremely public woman. That in itself brought a degree of notoriety. Even if spirit rapping had not come increasingly under criticism as a fraud and a delusion by 1852, she would have faced censure for her public life from the more genteel levels of the middle class.

Surprisingly, Kane, too, felt ill at ease with the public aspect of his career. While he actively sought a public reputation, he was uncomfortable about the idea of being observed and talked about by strangers. Disgusted by gossip he read about himself in the penny press, he told Fox, "I need not be so proud, Maggie, for I am no better than the '*rappers*'."[1] Even though Kane took advantage of publicity as best he could, at times the arrogant elitist in him rebelled against this need to appeal to the public with his science. In fact, some of his mentors in the scientific community, such as Alexander Dallas Bache and Joseph Henry, found the idea of taking scientific theories to the public distasteful. Kane, however, was a man who loved the limelight as much as he loved exploration. He was able to mask the crass commercial side of his career with the appeals he made to old-fashioned republican virtue.

The fact was that Kane needed to generate publicity if he wanted to continue with a career as a polar explorer, since the funds for further exploration were dependent on public support. During the winter of 1851–52, when he was not lecturing, Kane worked on his book and corresponded with Lady Franklin and Henry Grinnell about a new Arctic expedition for the summer of 1852. Like Kane, neither had given up hope of locating Sir John Franklin and his crew. In February, Grinnell again offered the navy the use of his two ships and suggested that Congress add a ship equipped with a steam-driven propeller and a store ship manned by naval officers and crew.[2] Grinnell wanted to see a proper government-sponsored expedition, but Congress was not enthusiastic about such schemes and did not act.

Quickly realizing that they could not rely wholly on government support, Kane began to consider a smaller, privately funded venture. He was convinced that Franklin had gone north through Wellington Channel into what was believed to be an Open Polar Sea, but since Wellington Channel was so often blocked by ice all summer, he proposed to take a small group of men to break through to the "Polar Sea" by way of Smith Sound, to the north of Baffin Bay, well east of Wellington Channel. He thought that a small party with boats, sledges, and dogs could make their way north by this route.

In May he was encouraging Henry Grinnell to send for the British whaling captain William Penny, who Kane thought should command the expedition, perhaps in conjunction with himself.[3] Kane's plan for a search differed in significant ways from those conducted in the past. The British tradition was to send large ships on exploring expeditions with large crews under strict naval discipline and laden with years' worth of salted and canned provisions.[4] Kane's idea was to travel with a small party that could partially live off the land. Instead of a navy crew, he wanted to lead a team of enthusiastic comrades without "an artificial discipline." Indeed, "all that is needed," he told Grinnell, "is a crew of proper moral material, controlled by prudence and decision, and made aware beforehand of what they had to endure."[5] He was also advocating a form of travel that mirrored that of the Inuit more than that of the Royal Navy. He planned to eat seal meat, dress in furs, and travel over the ice using sledges and dogs. This was a sensible idea that others would ultimately prove effective, though at this point Kane's limited experience had not yet taught him the necessary skills for prolonged Arctic travel in this manner.

With his busy lecturing schedule and his efforts to get his book on the first expedition to press, any hope for a new expedition during the summer of 1852 fell through. But Kane continued to plan for an expedition, with himself in command, to leave in the spring of 1853. If it was not to be sponsored by the navy, he would have to get support from a variety of sources. He needed to generate enough enthusiasm so that men would volunteer to join the expedition and scientific institutions would lend him instruments. Proceeds from his lectures could go toward buying provisions, and he hoped that if enough public pressure was exerted on the government, it would at least assign some navy men on navy pay to join the expedition. Eventually, with the financial help of Henry Grinnell and an Englishman named George Peabody, a plan seemed to be taking shape, though Kane constantly had to shuttle between these different sources of support to keep the whole thing together. This wore down his already fragile health, so that all through the planning process he suffered through periodic bouts of illness.[6]

MEANWHILE, MAGGIE FOX was becoming increasingly dissatisfied with the course of her spirit rapping career. Despite their great success in Ohio, all was not well within the family. Leah Fish was constantly coming into conflict with her sisters. She wanted to create a new religion with herself in the central role, but Maggie and Kate Fox did not care about such matters. They were teenagers, more interested in enjoying themselves than in propagating a new religion. Nevertheless, even the younger sisters were becoming aware of the social stigma connected with their profession.

Bad blood developed between the sisters which expanded to involve some of their entourage. Mrs. Kedzie, who took Maggie and Kate Fox to Ohio without Fish's prior knowledge, apparently did not get along with Fish. In a letter to Amy Post written at the end of July, Fish complained that Kedzie was making it difficult for her to maintain the proper image: "Mrs. Kedzie's coming out here has caused us much trouble, and the whole affair, i.e., the whole subject of the Spirits was for a time completely sunk—we feared never to arise again. Although she goes to every person she meets and tells them that 'Leah' is not the proper person, a bad manager, extravagant, etc. I believe it is generally allowed by all who know anything about the matter that she is a very improper person, and has no business in the matter except to make a little speculation out of the 'knockings.' "[7]

Maggie and Kate Fox, according to Fish, were little better. Fish felt surrounded by enemies trying to prove her a fraud, and she believed that her sisters were adding to her problems. "Much of my trouble is caused by the girls," she complained to Amy Post, "who are always planning out something and then if they fail in their calculations, they throw the whole thing upon my shoulders. To be frank with you, I do not know how to bear up under my trials." (Besides indicating Fish's conflict with her sisters, her statement seems to acknowledge that Maggie and Kate Fox were engaged in "calculations" in their rappings.) She continued, "I can tell you truly if it had not been for them [her sisters], I should never differ with many, but they are always working so underhandedly that I am tired, tired of Life or in other words of so much deception."[8]

Although this sounds almost like a confession that the rapping was a calculated fraud, it is not. Elsewhere in the same letter Fish told Post that the whole tour of Ohio was a great trial and sacrifice that she was engaging in "for truth's sake."[9] This letter does not indicate that Amy Post was aware that spirit rapping was fraudulent; rather it suggests that even dedicated spiritualists such as Amy Post by this time knew that Maggie and Kate Fox were not always honest or sincere. Post may have believed that the girls often played games with the raps, embellishing what the Posts nevertheless thought was a genuine ability to communicate with the dead.

Spiritualists were always quick to respond to those who condemned the whole movement after discovering a single deception. They often acknowledged that some deception might exist, but argued that this was not proof that it was all deceit.[10] As time went by, and more and more fraud was revealed, spiritualists would respond by admitting to a degree of chicanery. There were a few false mediums, they conceded, but the rest were honest. Or they would acknowledge that even true mediums often felt pressure to impress skeptics when performing by supplementing real manifestations with more sensational fake ones. Some spiritualists disapproved of the whole commercial side of spirit rapping, preferring to attend séances only with noncommercial mediums.

During their western tour there was a growing rift between the sisters caused by their differing priorities. While Fish was trying to promote a new religion, Maggie and Kate Fox were enjoying the opportunity spiritualism offered them to travel, stay in nice hotels, and meet some of the country's most famous people. Unfortunately for them, their own goals often conflicted with the goals of the spiritualists who surrounded them. Sometimes their own personalities would break through, and they would have fun with the rapping. This angered Leah Fish, who was mature enough to realize the price of exposure.

Kate and Maggie Fox's letters to Amy Post during their time in Ohio do not speak of the progress of the movement but rather tell of the famous people they were meeting and their loneliness at being away from home for so long. In an undated letter from Cincinnati, probably sent in the fall of 1851, Maggie Fox wrote Post about Frederick Douglass, who was also in Ohio at the time lecturing on abolition. Douglass, she declared, "is the finest looking gentleman I have seen since I have been in Cincinnati."[11] In another letter Kate Fox boasted about rapping for the renowned Kentucky abolitionist Cassius M. Clay in Cincinnati: "Cassius M. Clay you know is a great man. Of course you know him, he held my feet." She went on with pride, "Cassius Clay is one of our best friends, (but a great flatterer)."[12]

The excitement of meeting all sorts of famous and interesting people was offset by the rootless existence of a traveling performer. "I wish you knew how I felt," wrote Kate Fox to Post. "Oh so homesick. I want to see you Amy. Dear lady, it is raining fast and makes me feel melancholy, it brings up sad recollections. It makes me think of other days, (when I was happy)."[13] The tour through Ohio and other western states, which continued week after week, soon became tiresome to Maggie Fox as well. She wrote to Post, "We are still in Cincinnati, leave for Louisville in two weeks, and as Byron says, I shall leave it without regret, I shall return to it without pleasure."[14]

As the Fox sisters' western tour came to an end, they were getting tired of the way spirit rapping was controlling their lives. They were always away from home. They were always on display. While they enjoyed the opportunity it offered them to meet people and feel important, as they neared adulthood they must have begun to wonder about their future prospects. Their career had afforded them many opportunities, but as negative attention began to solidify, and as newspapers began to blame them for incidents of insanity and suicide, they must have begun to doubt. Spirit rapping had elevated them to the threshold of the middle-class, but the notoriety they had earned also left them just outside the door of gentility. Maggie Fox, at least, was looking for an alternative.

IN THE LATE autumn of 1852, Kane took a break from his efforts organizing his expedition and decided to investigate the "Spiritual Manifestations" that were then being demonstrated daily at Webb's Union Hotel in Philadelphia. Perhaps Kane went to Webb's Hotel that day because he had read in the papers that some spiritualists and clairvoyants in both America and England claimed to know the whereabouts of Sir John Franklin and his crew, but it is doubtful that he put any stock in such reports. Instead, it was probably more as a diversion from work on his book than as a serious investigation that he dropped in to see the "rappers."[15]

Maggie Fox had arrived in Philadelphia in late November and was giving demonstrations in the usual manner in a hotel parlor. The rappings by this time were old news, no longer as great a sensation as they had been in New York and Ohio, though many people were still willing to pay a dollar for a visit with a Fox sister. It had been over two years since Maggie and her sisters had made their first strong impression in Manhattan, and over four and a half since they had begun the rappings, so by this time all the Foxes were quite proficient at holding séances. The three sisters no longer always traveled together, and for this trip to Philadelphia nineteen-year-old Maggie Fox was the sole medium, escorted by her mother.

At about ten o'clock in the morning Elisha Kane looked in on the parlor of Webb's Union Hotel. There were no crowds, an indication that popular interest was not what it once was. Instead, "seeing a very young lady sitting by the window with a book in her hand, he imagined that he had knocked at the wrong door."[16] The young lady, of course, was Maggie Fox, reading her French lessons. Kane was struck, as other witnesses to the spiritual manifestations had been, by her youthful innocence. She did not look like the deceiver that Kane, as a skeptic, assumed her to be. According to one account, Kane fell in love at first sight, and "his determination was formed on this first interview to make Margaret his wife."[17]

Whether or not the thirty-two-year-old Kane really fell in love at first sight with this nineteen-year-old spirit rapper we will never know. The sentimental tendencies of nineteenth-century writers generally dominate descriptions of their relationship, but clearly Kane was smitten with her. Like many men who witnessed the rapping, he was impressed by Maggie Fox's style, but he was not a believer in spirits. He severely disapproved of spirit rapping as an occupation for a young woman of virtuous character, and quite soon, perhaps even at their first meeting, he determined

Daguerreotype of Elisha Kent Kane as a young man. Courtesy of the American Philosophical Society Library.

Portrait of Elisha Kent Kane by James Reid Lambdin, 1857. Oil on canvas, 30 x 25 in.
Courtesy of the American Philosophical Society Library.

Margaret Fox. From *The Love-Life of Dr. Kane*.

Kate Fox. From Emma Hardinge, *Modern American Spiritualism,* 1870.

The Fox sisters. Left to right: Margaret Fox, Kate Fox, Leah Fish.
Lithograph by N. Currier. Courtesy of the University of Rochester, Rush Rhees Library
Department of Rare Books and Special Collections.

Engraving of Elisha Kane at the grave of William Braine of the Franklin Expedition.
From the collection of the author.

Henry Grinnell. From *Arctic Explorations*.

William Godfrey. From *Godfrey's Narrative*.

Sensational cover of *Godfrey's Narrative*.

Hans Hendrik. From *Arctic Explorations*.

The *Advance* in winter. From *Arctic Explorations*.

Scenes of Inuit life from *Arctic Explorations:* "Esquimaux Hut."

Scenes of Inuit life from *Arctic Explorations:* "Catching Auks."

The Lookout from Cape George Russell. From *Arctic Explorations*.

Winter quarters on board the *Advance*. From left to right: Bonsall, Brooks, Kane, Hayes, Morton. From *Arctic Explorations*.

“Walrus Hunt off Pikantlik” showing the Americans and Inuit hunting together.
From *Arctic Explorations*.

THE ARCTIC
ELLESMERE ISLAND
KANE BASIN
GREENLAND
SMITH SOUND
WELLINGTON CHANNEL
MELVILLE SOUND
CORNWALLIS ISLAND
DEVON ISLAND
BAFFIN BAY
BARROW STRAIT
LANCASTER SOUND
PEEL SOUND
SOMERSET ISLAND
PRINCE REGENT INLET
PRINCE OF WALES ISLAND
BAFFIN ISLAND
BOOTHIA PENINSULA
KING WILLIAM ISLAND
GULF OF BOOTHIA
FOXE BASIN

The Arctic.

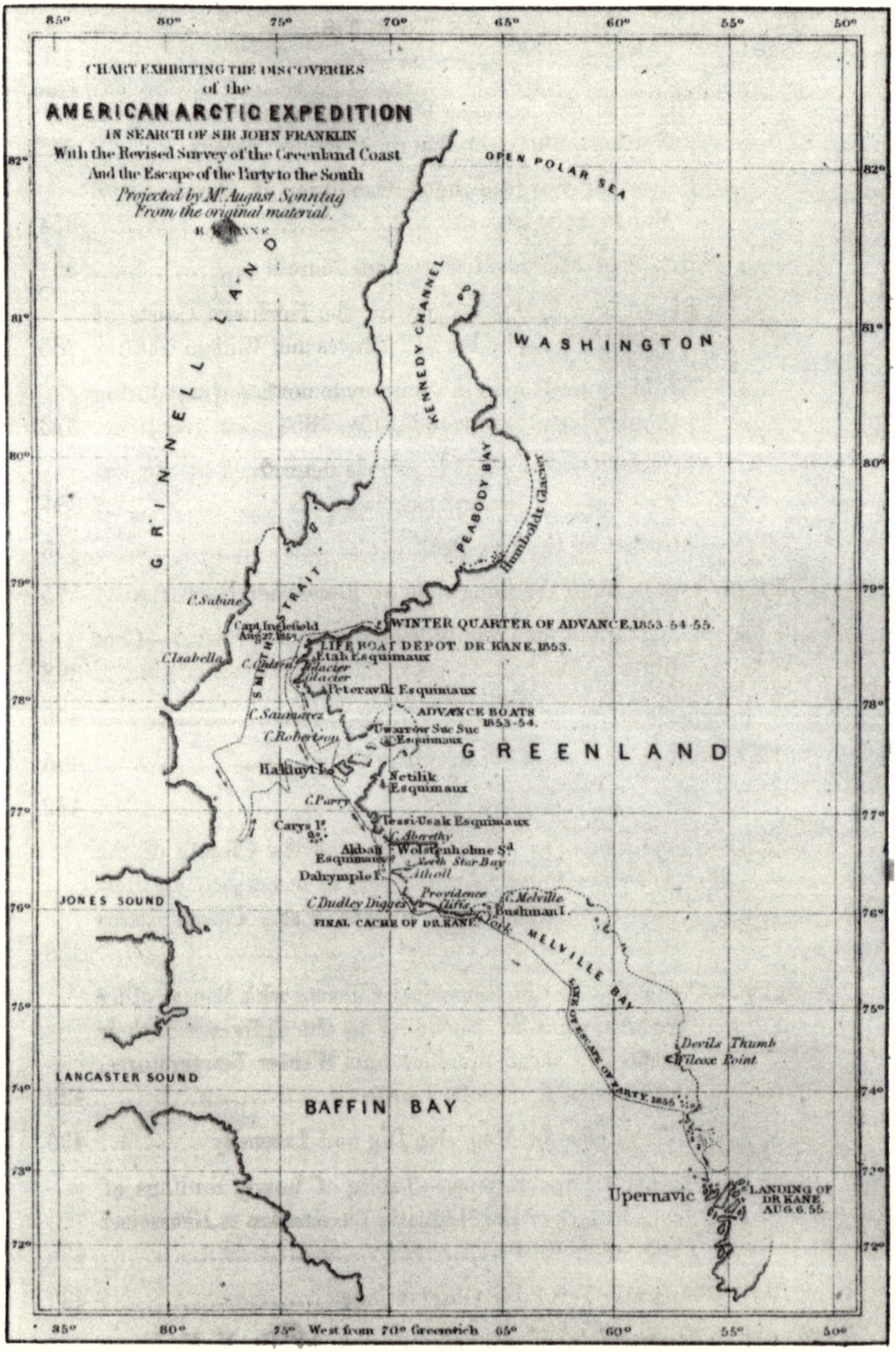

Chart exhibiting the Discoveries of the American Arctic Expedition. From *Arctic Explorations*.

that it was his responsibility to "rescue" this seemingly innocent young woman from such a disreputable profession.

The following day he returned and advised Maggie Fox to give up the rapping and instead get an education. Soon he became a daily visitor to Webb's Hotel. Often during the remainder of her stay in Philadelphia, he invited her to accompany him on carriage rides around town, suitably chaperoned, of course, by Mrs. Fox or one of Kane's aunts. By the middle of December, he was sending expensive gifts and bestowing additional paternal advice.[18]

Most of our knowledge about the courtship that ensued between Maggie Fox and Elisha Kane comes from a little book, published nearly ten years after Kane's death, called *The Love-Life of Doctor Kane*. This book was authorized by Maggie Fox and contains an account of her relationship with Kane, as well as copies of love letters reportedly written by him to her. The authenticity of these letters is, of course, a matter of debate; few originals of the letters printed in *The Love-Life* have been located. Like much of Fox's life, her relationship with Kane is full of controversy and conflicting accounts. During Kane's lifetime, the two were linked by rumor and various claims printed in the newspapers, some of which reported that they were engaged, while others denied that any engagement existed. Despite such rumors, Kane's family always denied that he ever married Fox or that his relationship with her was motivated by anything other than a philanthropic desire to educate her and to save her from a disreputable career. Fox, by contrast, claimed that they were in love, and that, near the end of Kane's life, the two of them were secretly married.

The surviving evidence suggests that Fox's version is closer to the truth. Although the original love letters have not survived, plenty of evidence indicates that they did once exist. Perhaps the most compelling proof is the effort the Kane family made to acquire these letters in order to prevent them from ever being published. There is also ample evidence in Kane's papers indicating that he engaged in a secret correspondence with Fox, often through his friend Cornelius Grinnell, the son of Henry Grinnell, who was financing Kane's expedition.[19] The relationship between Fox and Kane certainly existed, and was clearly romantic, even though her claim that an actual marriage had taken place could be an embellishment. Whether Kane actually married Maggie Fox or intended to marry her, he led her to believe that he would marry her, while at the same time he kept the true nature of the relationship a secret from his family. Fox had little incentive to make the whole thing up. The letters reproduced in *The Love-Life of Dr. Kane* are in Kane's style, and two facsimiles are reproduced in his handwriting. The paternalistic advice and arrogant and often condescending manner expressed in these letters is in keeping with the tone he took with many whom he thought to be his social inferiors, and there is a limited yet significant quantity of independent evidence that supports the account of the relationship given in *The Love-Life*. There were many people, who were in a position to know the truth, who could have renounced *The Love-Life* had it been a complete fraud, but none did, with the exception of the Kane family.[20]

Another convincing bit of evidence in support of the authenticity of *The Love-Life* is that the book was almost certainly compiled by Elizabeth Fries Ellet, a prolific nineteenth-century author best known for her histories of American women. As a historian and biographer Ellet strove for accuracy, even if her style was often sentimental. Although *The Love-Life* was written and edited anonymously, correspondence in the Elisha Kent Kane papers and Robert Patterson Kane papers clearly indicates that Ellet prepared it and was the driving force behind its publication.[21]

FOR SIX MONTHS, between their first encounter in Webb's Union Hotel and Kane's return to the Arctic at the end of May, he and Fox engaged in an unusual courtship as they pursued their respective public careers throughout the eastern United States. Sometimes Kane played the role of the ardent suitor, while at other times he was the stern father lecturing Fox on proper comportment and behavior. During December and January, while Fox and her mother remained in Philadelphia, Kane made frequent visits, sitting in on public séances and taking her on carriage rides. During this time his notes to her are characterized by strict formality. "My Dear Miss Fox," he wrote in one typical note. "The day is so beautiful that I feel tempted to repent my indoor imprisonment. If you will do me the kindness to change your own mind, and take a quiet drive, I will call for you at your own hour."[22] Other invitations were directed to Mrs. Fox, who often accompanied them.

Kane was careful to observe proper decorum. One day Fox invited him into a room at the hotel to see a cake someone had sent her. When he realized that the room had a bed in it, he recoiled and chided her about "the impropriety of inviting a gentleman to pass through a sleeping apartment."[23] She began to call him "The Preacher" for his habit of lecturing to her on morals and etiquette. His goal seemed to be to reclaim the young spirit rapper for a life as a member of the middle class, yet her association with spiritualism made it hard for him to do so. While he desired to lift her up to respectability, he may have worried that his association with her would drag him down into disrepute.

Fox did not, at first, encourage Kane's advances, but she clearly enjoyed his company. Perhaps she was intrigued by this man, who believed her work a fraud yet who seemed interested in knowing her nonetheless. Many who met Fox at this time commented that she possessed unusual self-control, learned from years as a public medium. She was not about to reveal her innermost secrets to Kane the moment he walked in the door and expressed an attraction. Unfortunately we do not have very much of her own account of her initial acquaintance with Kane; the letters in *The Love-Life* are primarily his. In the years leading up to their meeting, Maggie Fox had met many gentlemen, like him, of a class distinctly superior to her own. Most were well behaved, but Fox's position in society was deeply ambiguous. She was a professional woman in an era when such women were virtually unheard of. Her profession catered to the middle class, but she was not of that class herself. In some ways her role as a medium resembled that of an actress, providing an evening's entertainment for a price. The somewhat dubious nature of her profession invited rude and unwelcome flirtations from poorly behaved or drunken men, which she fended off by remaining polite yet distant and aloof during séances. All of the Fox sisters, whether onstage or off, were careful to maintain a very reserved demeanor as a way to deflect attention from themselves.

Kane's advances, however, were neither rude nor overtly flirtatious. Despite his democratic pretensions, Kane had a strong paternalistic streak that showed itself whenever he dealt with those he considered his social inferiors. From the start, Dr. Kane felt free to inform Miss Fox of all her faults, especially the unsuitability of her profession. One day early in their relationship he handed her a note while she was performing a séance. It was a poem that he had written about her rapping:

> Now thy long day's work is o'er,
> Fold thine arms across thy breast;
> Weary! weary is the life
> By cold deceit oppressed.[24]

As he got to know her better, he lectured her about how to dress and behave in a manner becoming to a lady, with the ultimate goal, according to the editor of *The Love-Life of Dr. Kane,* of remaking her into a suitable wife for a young man with great prospects. According to this account, Kane had promised, as early as the middle of January 1853, to marry Fox. But he insisted that first she had to give up the rappings and complete her education. "You must not engage yourself to be my wife unless you can give me all your love—your whole heart; unless you can sacrifice for me all other anticipations and prospects," he told her.[25] Yet Kane seemed to contradict his professions of devotion and demands for concessions on Fox's part by his unwillingness to acknowledge his feelings publicly. His distaste for spirit rapping made him unwilling to introduce Fox to his immediate family or to acknowledge his relationship with her. Kane found it difficult enough to reconcile his own public celebrity with middle-class notions of gentility, but Fox's reputation was, in his eyes, entirely beyond the limits of the acceptable.[26]

Fox had always enjoyed the attentions of famous men, and she was clearly flattered by Kane's interest, yet she gave him little encouragement at first. Elizabeth Ellet, the editor of *The Love-Life,* observed "that she felt as yet none of the impassioned fervor that marked his attachment to her."[27] Understandably, Maggie Fox approached this curious courtship with some hesitation. Kane preached to her and demanded that she give up her livelihood, but his insistence on secrecy undoubtedly put his sincerity into question. Perhaps he was just a wealthy scoundrel toying with her affections. Later in the winter, when Kane was in New England giving lectures and Fox had returned to New York, he responded to her doubts: "Now to you I am nothing but a cute, cunning dissembler; a sort of smart gentleman hypocrite, never really sincere, and merely amusing himself with a pretty face."[28] He blamed her suspicion on the dishonesty inherent in her world of spiritualism, yet, as the historian Christine Stansell has observed of working-class women in New York City at this time, there were plenty of "gentlemen hypocrites" ready to amuse themselves at the expense of young women who lacked any means of protection against mistreatment or sexual exploitation. Fox was right to be cautious.[29]

Kane himself, despite the lip service he paid to propriety, was not unfamiliar with the antebellum world of illicit sexuality. Of Kane's sexual life we know very little, but his biographer George W. Corner noted two letters from 1846 "with scandalous implications," found among Kane's papers, which refer to an unnamed woman, J——, who was pregnant. Kane was apparently trying to arrange for her discreet care during the pregnancy. One of the letters is from a man who assumed that Kane was the lover of the woman in question and the father of the child. This correspondent, who signed himself J.T.L., felt free to tell Kane about a woman, "the surest piece of youthful flesh," whom he had recently encountered while in Richmond. He went on to admonish Kane: "What an ardent fool you must be Elisha—I have heard you generally leave a mark on anything which you touch." Corner did not know what to make of these letters, though he observed that there is no other evidence that Kane had fathered an illegitimate child.[30]

Other letters suggest that Kane, whether or not he fathered an illegitimate child himself, may have been considered by his male friends as the man to turn to when their affairs resulted in unwanted pregnancies. He was, after all, a medical doctor, and he had studied obstetrics while in medical school. It is doubtful that, as a navy surgeon, he practiced much obstetrics, but he would at least have known whom to go to privately for help. There is clear evidence that at least one friend asked him for help in arranging private care for a pregnant lover.[31] Kane may have signed his letters to Fox "The Preacher," but he was not unfamiliar with the seamier aspects of life. Still, though his insistence on secrecy may suggest as much, it is doubtful that Kane simply wanted to make Fox his mistress. He moralizes too much for that.

Whether or not she considered him a "gentleman hypocrite," it is a wonder that Fox responded at all to Kane's advances, since his letters are full of insulting condescension. While in New York trying to publicize his plan for a new Arctic expedition, he wrote to her lovingly: "Maggie dear, you have many traits which lift you above your calling. You are refined and lovable; and, with a different education, would have been innocent and artless"; then, just in case this was too much praise for her, he added, "but you are not worthy of a permanent regard from me. You could never lift yourself up to my thoughts and my objects; I could never bring myself down to yours."[32] Perhaps because of such attitudes, Kane never seemed to reconcile himself to the idea of actually marrying Maggie Fox. Her profession put her too far outside the bounds of respectability. At times he insisted on an engagement, while at others he seems to have been on the verge of breaking off the relationship.

Maggie's interest in Elisha (or "Ly," as she began to call him), despite his arrogance and insults, may have been an indication of her growing dissatisfaction with her life as a spirit rapper. Would she do this for the rest of her life, traveling from city to city and living in hotels? Kane undoubtedly tapped into these concerns. He represented a world apart from spirit rapping—an upper-middle-class alternative to a life of deception and delusion. Kane's voice joined the chorus in the popular press that increasingly condemned the rappings as immoral and dangerous. The relationship between the two became a private reflection of the public debates. Spirit rapping had elevated Maggie, but it had still left her far from the bourgeois respectability she aspired to. Marriage to Kane, by contrast, would offer her solid membership in the most respectable level of society.

IN JANUARY 1853, after a little more than a month in Philadelphia, Maggie Fox and her mother returned to New York City, where her sisters Leah and Kate were living. The year before, soon after returning from Ohio, Leah had rented a brownstone on West Twenty-sixth Street, where she was making a good living holding séances.[33] Leah Fish (now Leah Brown, having married Calvin Brown in September) apparently had little regard for Dr. Kane and his attempts to draw her sister away from spiritualism, so when Kane visited New York, he tried to arrange secret meetings with Fox away from the house and Leah Brown's watchful eye. Brown had done well for herself with spirit rapping in a way her sisters never would. She had the strong personality and will necessary to flout convention and go her own way in a world often hostile to her, and she wished that her younger sisters could do the same.[34] In many ways Brown was wiser than either of her sisters. She had been a child bride, and she had been a single mother. Spirit rapping was the best thing that had ever happened to her, and she was willing to withstand the disapproval of many rather than give it up. Her sisters, however, knew only spirit rapping and did not fully appreciate its value.

While Maggie was staying at her sister's house on West Twenty-sixth Street, Kane was often in New York promoting his plan for a new expedition. Another winter brought another lecture season. In December 1852 he gave an important talk before the American Geographical and Statistical Society in Manhattan, presenting his plans for a renewed search for Franklin; then in January he was back lecturing at the Smithsonian in Washington and the Maryland Institute in Baltimore. Henry Grinnell lived in New York, so Kane was often there to consult with him and look over preparations for the expedition, which was to leave from New York Harbor.

At the beginning of February 1853, he wrote to Fox that he was on his way to New York after his Washington and Baltimore lectures: "Write me how I can see you if I come to New York. How can I meet you, dear Maggie, away from suspicion, away from Mrs. [Brown]. Do you ever walk out alone?" The editor of *The Love-Life* explains Kane's desire for secrecy as a result of his competition with the spiritualists for Fox's time and his wish to conceal his relationship with her from his friends.[35] Around the same time, he set up a rendezvous with both Fox sisters at Satler's Cosmoramas on Broadway, where he hoped they could meet "without exciting the suspicions of—you know who."[36] "You know who" was Leah Brown, whom Kane was now calling "The Tigress."[37] This is an aspect of *The Love-Life of Dr. Kane* that can be confirmed independently. Letters in Kane's personal papers between Kane and Cornelius Grinnell, the son of Henry Grinnell, refer to a private correspondence with Fox conducted without Leah Brown's approval. When he was not in New York, Kane would send the younger Grinnell (who was about Kane's age) to visit the séances conducted at Mrs. Brown's house in order to pass notes surreptitiously to Fox.

Cornelius Grinnell wrote Kane of his first visit to the house. He did not meet Maggie Fox, "but her sister Kate came to the door, and I gave her the letters. She said she would hand them to her sister, *have I done right?*" Later he adds, "I had hard work to deliver the notes, as the old wretch [Brown] kept a sharp look out upon me."[38] Grinnell had some fun attending séances, "in company with several gentlemen," in order to deliver his friend's notes. He found them an entertaining diversion, telling Kane: "I have been several times to Mrs. Brown's 'promiscuous circles' as she terms them, that is, not private. One meets there a most singular collection of individuals, enthusiasts and skeptics, old and young and other like myself, who go there for amusement. I have had some capital fun."[39] He also met Maggie Fox and was impressed. In early February he wrote Kane: "Your last letter for Miss Maggie was safely delivered to her. She is a very interesting girl. Quite out of place where she is now."[40] Kane responded with a letter referring to his interest in Maggie Fox as a temporary weakness and expressing concern that she is "shut up with that Devil of a sister."[41] It is unclear what Kane told Grinnell about his relationship with Fox, but it is clear that he did not suggest he was thinking of marrying her. With Grinnell, the wealthy son of a successful shipping merchant, it was apparently acceptable to play the "gentleman hypocrite."

IN MID-FEBRUARY 1853 Kane went on a lecture trip to New England while Fox, with her mother and Kate, went to perform in Washington. As usual, we do not have much of Fox's side of the correspondence, but it is clear from Kane's letters at this time that he was wrestling with his attraction to a woman he found beneath him intellectually and socially. He advised and scolded her: "How does Washington come on? Many Beaux? Many believers? Many friends? Answer these questions, you wicked little Maggie!" He lectured: "Never venture out in Washington except in the very best company. If you can get a real gentleman, grab him; but have nothing to do with the vulgar members of Congress." Then he moved on to the role of wardrobe consultant: "Wear your undersleeves and spencer always when you have company. I sent a rich ladylike set for morning wear, and another Honiton lace for evening occasions. Do wear them, Maggie, and tell Kate that as soon as I get back to Philadelphia, I will send her a real appliquée."[42]

He also began to accuse her of not loving him as he loved her. At times he affected the role of the wise older brother rather than the suitor, apparently trying to make her appreciate him more. At one point he warned her, "Unless you love me I will soon cease to love you."[43] They had known each other little more than two months, and Fox was still keeping her options open, but Kane's advice often was delivered with threats that he would cut off relations if she did not do as he asked. At some point in late February or March she wrote him a flirtatious letter, encouraging him but not succumbing to his demands for submission to his paternal authority. She recounted a story about getting lost in Washington. When she finally found her way back to her boardinghouse, she met a male acquaintance who "insisted upon it that no young lady could ever lose her way in Washington unless she had some '*affaire du coeur*.'" She teased Kane: "I did not deny the charge. Doctor, there is a rumor—so the General tells me—that you and I are to be married before you go to the Arctic." Knowing Kane's obsession with his reputation and his insistence on secrecy, she must have meant this as a jab at him and as a response to his critiques of her. She then told him of a handsome young French gentleman who flirted with her at a séance.[44] Kane may have been insisting that Fox submit to him, but the few letters of hers printed in *The Love-Life* show that she did not entirely accept his point of view. While he was always ready to tell her how lucky she was to have him and how far above her he was, she in turn made it clear that she had other options.

Yet some of Kane's lectures hit home. If he did not always express himself with the greatest tact, he clearly had what he thought were Fox's best interests at heart. He reminded her that, although spirit rapping would be fun for a time, it would sour with age. In a letter addressed to Kate (perhaps to make Maggie jealous) but clearly intended for Maggie's eyes, he spoke of the often unscrupulous behavior of some mediums, then offered what was probably an accurate assessment of the sisters' position:

> Now, Katy, although you and Maggie never go so far as this, yet circumstances must occur where you have to lacerate the feelings of other people. I know that you have a tender heart; but practice in anything hardens us. You do things now which you would never have dreamed of doing years ago; and there will come a time when you will be worse than—; a hardened woman, gathering around you victims of a delusion. Think of that Katy!
>
> The older you grow the more difficult it will be to liberate yourself from this thing. And can you look forward to a life unblessed by the affections, unsoothed by the consciousness of doing right! For you, no innocence with the blessings of a kindly home is now in store. When your mother leaves this scene can you and my still dear Maggie be content to live that life of constant deceit? Do, dear Katy, think of all this![45]

Dr. Kane may have been right in his diagnosis of the effect that prolonged association with spirit rapping would have on Kate and Maggie Fox, but his prescription was less than satisfying. The alternative to the degradation of spirit rapping, in Kane's eyes, was a return to the traditional role of wife and mother. In Maggie's case this meant submission to his will. If she gave up spirit rapping, if she got an education, if she learned how to dress and behave in a genteel way, if she did everything he told her to do, then he might continue to love her.

Kane was well aware, from his own experience, of the problems of a public life. The constant need to perform for strangers conflicted with accepted notions of virtuous behavior for men as well as women. He found it troublesome, yet bearable, in his own life to be the object of public curiosity, but for a young woman like Maggie Fox it was unacceptable. It would make her unlovable. Kane had struck a nerve. Maggie wrote back with more affection than usual. "Should we never again meet in this world we will in another," she reassured him in the morbid tones of the day. "Then you will know I have loved you, and love you still."[46] But this was not enough for Kane. He would be, he declared, her friend and protector, but not her lover or husband: "I saw that you loved me, but not enough. Dear child, it was not in your nature. You would give me everything when near me, but forget me when away. So I made up my mind, and in a moment you became *my friend*."[47]

This state of affairs was not to last. Soon Kane joined the sisters in Washington, and the relationship was resumed in a more romantic vein. Fox, at this point, seems to have succumbed to Kane's terms. She soon agreed to give up rapping and to be sent to a school to be "improved" while Kane was away on his Arctic expedition. Although there was no public (or even private, in the case of Kane's immediate family) avowal of an engagement, Kane began to inquire among friends about a suitable school in which to place Fox while he was gone, representing himself as a benevolent benefactor rather than a fiancé. Kane was still afraid that his relationship with Fox would reach the public gaze.[48] His actions at this point in the affair begin to appear duplicitous. While he was claiming to be in love with Maggie Fox and intent on marrying her, he sought to insulate himself from any outside criticism or scandal resulting from a romantic association with a notorious woman. He also sought to make sure that his mother, especially, knew nothing of his relationship with Fox.

Among those Kane contacted for advice on an appropriate school for Maggie was Francis Hawks. Hawks was eminently respectable. He was an Episcopal clergyman, a lawyer, and a historian. Months before hearing from Kane he had been offered the post of bishop of Rhode Island but declined the honor. Kane knew Hawks because Hawks was a founder, with Henry Grinnell, of the American Geographical and Statistical Society and currently its vice president.[49] Hawks had been in New York in December when Kane had lectured at the society. Fox also was familiar with Hawks, as he had been a guest at her "Post-Mortuum Soirée" at Rufus Griswold's home in June 1850. The Reverend Dr. Hawks gave Kane advice about schools and gave him the names of some other men to consult, but more important, he lent a respectable public cover to Kane's interest in Maggie Fox. Hawks unwittingly recounted the cover story in a letter introducing Kane to a Reverend Dr. Croswell of New Haven. "Dr. Kane with other gentlemen here have had their sympathies enlisted in behalf of a young woman," he wrote, "whose story I will leave to the Dr. to tell; and are desirous of placing her at a school where her favorable religious tendencies may be cherished."[50] Kane also brought in Cornelius Grinnell as an ally so his actions could be represented as those of a committee of gentlemen snatching a defenseless young girl from the evil clutches of spiritualism, rather than those of a smitten lover. Above all, he wanted his interest to seem paternal, not romantic.[51]

Kane also sought the advice, on behalf of this committee of benevolent gentlemen, of his aunt Eliza Leiper, who lived in the countryside outside Philadelphia. Leiper recommended placing Fox in the home of a Mrs. Susannah Turner in Crookville, Pennsylvania. There she could be tutored by Turner and live a retired life, away from the "bad influences" of spiritualist circles.[52] With the beneficent support of Dr. Kane and his committee, Maggie Fox was to be reclaimed. She would be rescued from the clutches of delusion and fanaticism, perhaps someday to become the wife of a respectable man and mother to a brood of respectable children.

Fox consented because she had tired of spirit rapping. Perhaps she loved Kane, but she did not like his secrecy. At the same time, she had few options and fewer examples to follow. She had been propelled far outside the mainstream at an early age. Now she wanted back in, and Kane offered that chance. She wrote to him, "What have I ever done that I should be denied the pleasure of a quiet home, the blessings of love, the reward of virtue?"[53] These middle-class prizes now appealed to her more than the excitement of public celebrity.

In late May 1853, as Elisha Kane made final preparations to embark on the most ambitious adventure of his life, Maggie Fox found her own adventures seemingly at an end. By her own consent, she was secluded in the Pennsylvania countryside to be remolded as a lady. Kane and his committee of gentlemen had done to Maggie Fox what many wished they could do to the entire spiritualist movement. They had contained her within the confines of gentility. She started out a willing captive, but she would not remain a contented one.

7

Departure

The Second Grinnell Expedition

I was led, by a romantic taste for whatever is strange and marvelous, to visit a region which seemed to be enshrouded in mystery, and which was supposed to contain many scenes and objects that have no counterparts in any other quarter of the world.

William C. Godfrey, *Godfrey's Narrative of the Last Grinnell Arctic Exploring Expedition*

IN THE SPRING of 1853, William C. Godfrey, an East River boatman from New York City, engaged himself as a common sailor on board the brig *Advance* bound for the Arctic regions. By his own account, Godfrey's motive for signing on to the latest American Arctic expedition, led by the renowned Dr. Kane, was personal rather than financial. The eighteen dollars a month pay he would receive for the voyage was only a fraction of what he was accustomed to earning at home, but Godfrey had a love of adventure and a desire to see the world. He had heard of the wonders of the Arctic regions and was determined to see them with his own eyes.[1]

Godfrey knew that service on board the *Advance* would not be easy. Most likely he had heard tales of the extreme cold and the constant danger from the polar ice, but he had a strong faith in his ability to endure whatever hardship might lie ahead. He had never before been to sea, but he was tall and strong in his early twenties with a young man's arrogance. Later he would admit "that there was something of youthful audacity, somewhat of a restless craving after novelty and change," that led him into this dangerous enterprise.[2]

When Godfrey signed on to the second Grinnell Expedition, he put himself under the authority of Elisha Kane—a decision that he would later come to regret. Godfrey and Kane were not so very different, despite occupying unequal social positions. The small, high-strung doctor and the big, arrogant workingman were both influenced by a mass culture that promoted inquiry into the mysteries of the universe, and they shared a common desire to travel the world and experience its wonders. They were young and free Americans who saw themselves as citizens of a new nation based on progress, equality, and liberty. Having ambition and a thirst for adventure, they saw no limits to what they and their country could do. But Godfrey and Kane would come into conflict when they learned that, despite their similarities, they had very different ideas about the nature of American freedom and the meaning of authority, class, and status in a democratic nation. Kane would find it much more difficult to persuade William Godfrey to conform to his authority than it had been to persuade Maggie Fox.

Kane and Godfrey and a small band of men set out with unbridled enthusiasm and camaraderie to explore the unknown regions of the world. In the end, they were torn apart by the differences and unresolved questions that divided them and their society. While they were soon to depart the physical shores of antebellum America, they never truly left behind its social and cultural landscape.

WHEN KANE, Godfrey, and the fifteen other members of the expedition stepped on board the *Advance* in New York Harbor, most were meeting one another for the first time. All were young men, on average in their mid-twenties. Each one encountered other men who, like himself, were enthusiastically looking forward to the upcoming journey and enjoying the respect and acclaim of their fellow citizens as the expedition prepared for departure. Many of them were immigrants to the United States, as were many residents of the country at the time. Ordinary seamen George Riley and George Stephenson, and Kane's personal steward and first Grinnell Expedition veteran William Morton, were all born in Ireland. Ordinary seaman George Whipple was English, and the cook, Pierre Schubert, was French. Only three of the seamen, including Godfrey, Jefferson Baker, and John Blake (alias William Hussey), were native-born Americans.[3]

Among the officers, only half were experienced sailors; the rest joined the expedition in scientific capacities. Henry Brooks, who served as first officer, was a skilled navy boatswain who had been on the first Grinnell Expedition with Kane. Executive officer James McGary was an experienced whaler out of New London, used to sailing in Arctic waters, and sailing master John Wilson had served for many years on merchant ships in the Indian Ocean. The carpenter, Christian Ohlsen, was a Dane with plenty of experience at sea. The other officers were landsmen of the type considered "gentlemen." They were chosen by Kane either for their scientific knowledge or because they were personal acquaintances. Isaac Hayes, who hailed from the Philadelphia area, was the expedition's surgeon and naturalist; August Sonntag was a German astronomer; Amos Bonsall, a relative of Kane's, was to be the expedition's photographer and part-time naturalist; last of all, Henry Goodfellow, a young friend of Kane's from Philadelphia, came along in an unspecified capacity, at times filling the role of an officer and at other times that of a "gentleman passenger."[4]

The makeup of the crew of the *Advance* had a great impact on the progress of the expedition. Although they shared a common thirst for novelty and adventure, the small group of amateur scientists and the mix of seasoned and green sailors came from diverse social and economic backgrounds. The potential was there from the start for problems, especially in the area of discipline. Some, like the seafaring officers Brooks, McGary, Ohlsen, and Wilson, were used to the discipline and routine of navy, merchant, or whaling ships. Others, including Godfrey, were unused to the discipline of shipboard life and preferred to consider themselves free American workingmen. Influenced by the growing democratic trends of the day, they would do their jobs but show no undue deference to their superiors. The young gentlemen, scientists, and friends of Kane's on board most likely assumed that camaraderie, rather than authority, would hold the band of adventurers together.

Kane's idea at the start of the voyage was that little in the way of harsh discipline would be required. He was one of the growing number of Americans who rejected corporal forms of discipline and punishment at sea. Rather, he expected that he would guide the small band of adventurers like a family, with himself as the benevolent, yet if need be severe, paternal figure. Shortly into the journey, in a letter to his parents, he claimed, "Thus far we have all the characteristics of a family." Six weeks later he wrote to Cornelius Grinnell "a word about our little family on board ship, for family is the word which I strive to apply to them."[5] He approached his leadership of these men as he did his relationship with Maggie Fox: he expected to be obeyed because he felt himself to be superior. Yet he did little to prove himself superior. While at home he had been able to convince Maggie Fox to accept his authority; he would have a much harder time with this group of men, especially William Godfrey.

At first, camaraderie and enthusiasm for the goals of the expedition did hold the crew together. In May 1853, as the young men met on board the *Advance,* all was excitement. "It was an exhilarating moment for all on board," recalled Godfrey. "Every man of our company, from the commander down to Mons. Schubert, French cook, must have experienced a feeling of expansion for the time being, as though we had all been suddenly enlarged to heroic dimensions."[6] On May 31, when the expedition departed, friends and spectators came out in small boats, and crowds gathered at the Battery to see the expedition off. As the *Advance* left the harbor, "every vessel passed in the Bay gave her a parting cheer, a ringing salute, and shouted good wishes."[7] Despite the diverse social, economic, and even national backgrounds of the little crew, this was an American expedition. The crowd on shore as well as the crew on board felt national pride in the glory of their projected endeavor in distant lands.

Aboard the brig, excitement soon was put aside in order to face the hard realities of sailing into headwinds on the North Atlantic. Some of the men who, like Godfrey, were not experienced sailors had to be taught their jobs. But more important, "Captain Kane" had to learn how to command a ship. While he had been in the navy for almost ten years, Kane had never before been in a position of command. It was not a position he took to naturally, although he claimed as much in a letter home little more than a week into the journey, telling his parents, "This *trade* of *authority* sits so easily upon me that I feel as if to be toadied was a natural and inevitable province of my particular self."[8] Still, the power he held as commander troubled him. He, after all, claimed to be a firm believer in democratic and egalitarian principles, and for much of his life he had resisted most arbitrary forms of authority. This was the man who had scoffed at the aristocratic pretensions of the emperor of Brazil and looked in disgust on the servility of the Brazilian laboring classes. As a child, Kane had always been quick to rebel against any schoolmaster who seemed to him unfair, and even in the navy he had been critical of excessive displays of power by his superiors or harsh forms of discipline.[9] He thought that the corporal punishment so often dished out on board navy vessels was a brutal relic of a less democratic era in the past. Now, as a commander, Kane admitted to his loved ones at home: "I find myself rebelling against the exercise of an artificial power—a disgust at even the necessary despotism of authority—and while a conviction of their necessity comes over me as a sort of sober puzzle—I try every means in my power to diminish and soften down their exercise."[10]

What this meant, in some of his officers' eyes, was that he seriously curtailed their control over the crew. He demanded that the officers treat the men civilly, and forbade the use of physical violence against them.[11] He was not willing to give up on the notion of authority altogether. Rather, Kane resolved that his own authority on board the *Advance* would be benevolent and paternalistic. Again, he wanted to be seen as the kindly father figure whose control stemmed from his own superior knowledge and abilities rather than from his rank, and he expected the men willingly to show him respect and deference.

Unfortunately for Kane, this theory did not always work well in practice. Since he expected respect and submission from his subordinates without demanding it, he eventually came to be seen by them as inconsistent and moody. Sometimes he adopted the severe tone of a navy captain, while at other times he acted like a friend and colleague. While this problem would not surface until later in the voyage, it was inherent in the approach he took from the first week of the journey. It surfaces even in his own description of how he exercised his command: "On deck I am as curt and unbearable as my worst enemy could desire, but if I do see a man or men in a state of reasonable *sunshininess* I strive hard not to cloud him, and with every one—when I can find the luxury of finding *one* off duty—I am as free and easy as if on shore—shame to me that I should make a merit of such a confession. So we wear into the harness and so *the harness wears into us*."[12] Although Kane sought to be the benevolent head of what he referred to as his "family," he never succeeded in attaining that status with all the men on board. This was not surprising, given the declining acceptance of paternalistic authority in general by American workingmen at this time.

William Godfrey, like Kane, was critical of the exercise of arbitrary power, but his position as a common sailor on board was entirely different from Kane's. By his own admission, he possessed what he called "a certain inflexibility of disposition, for which Yankees, in all situations, are more or less remarkable."[13] By this he meant that, as a working-class American citizen with egalitarian principles, he rejected the notion of paternalism and refused to show undue submission to what he called the "aristocracy of the brig," who, according to him, expected "as much homage from the sailors as a king could expect to receive from his subjects."[14] Godfrey did what he considered to be his duty on board ship, but refused to be any more humble, submissive, or deferential than he "supposed the exigencies of the service to require."[15] To him, his position on board was defined by a contract. He would receive eighteen dollars a month; in return he would do his job as a sailor. Elisha Kane was his employer, not his master. While both Kane and Godfrey would have described themselves as believers in democracy, in truth their views of what that meant differed greatly. This reflected the American political landscape at the time, where democratic ideals were still being worked out in practice.

As this potential discord fermented on board the *Advance*, the brig sailed north to St. John's, Newfoundland, its first port of call. Here another Irishman, Thomas Hickey, joined the crew as cabin boy, bringing the total number on the expedition to eighteen.[16] At St. John's, they picked up supplies and tried to make up any deficiencies in the stores, adding fresh meat, as well as a pack of dogs, to their outfit. Kane intended to use these dogs to haul sledges on the journeys he planned to make over the northern ice as far as the "Open Polar Sea."

After Newfoundland, the next port of call was the small community of Fiskernaes in Danish Greenland. The Norse had colonized this part of southwestern Greenland in the ninth or tenth century, but their settlements died out in the fifteenth century because of a cooling climate. The Norse were replaced by the Inuit, a hunting culture that had first appeared in northern Greenland around 1100 and migrated south toward the Norse settlements as the climate cooled. After the Norse left, the Inuit remained in control of Greenland until colonists from Denmark arrived again in 1721. The Danes set up trading posts and brought Lutheran missions to convert the Inuit to Christianity. When Kane and his crew arrived, southwestern Greenland was in the hands of Denmark, but most of the Native Greenlanders living there were descended from Inuit though practicing Christianity.

Here Kane inquired of the superintendent of the Danish Company, a Mr. Lassen, about acquiring a Native Greenlander to join the expedition as a hunter to supply the dogs and men with fresh meat.[17] Lassen recommended a nineteen-year-old Inuit named Hans Christian Hendrik, who, he said, was "an expert with the kayak and javelin."[18] Hendrik joined the expedition in exchange for a supply of provisions, which he left with his mother.[19] He would prove to be one of the expedition's most valuable members.

Also at Fiskernaes, Kane and Godfrey came into open conflict for the first time. Godfrey and his new friend John Blake, according to Kane, "insulted, by what sailors call 'Jaw,' a couple of the deck officers." In reaction to this slight, Kane felt he needed to teach the disrespectful sailors their place. The other officers, especially Wilson, would have liked to teach that lesson with violence, but Kane decided instead to isolate Godfrey and Blake in a way that would make them think about their misdeeds. So he "tied them hand and foot, covered them up with warm buffalo robes, and nailed them under the booby hatch."[20] Blake and Godfrey were not too quick to submit, however. According to Thomas Hickey, while under the booby hatch the two miscreants tapped "a barrel of whiskey, and [passed] the liquor down their throats by means of a straw."[21] Kane reported, however, that after four days on bread and water, the two "promised to be good boys, and have been since two of our best men."[22]

The *Advance* sailed up the coast of Greenland, stopping at more settlements to pick up additional supplies, especially furs and fresh provisions. Eventually they reached Upernavik, the northernmost Danish settlement on the west coast of Greenland. Here they picked up the final member of their crew, Carl Petersen, who would be the expedition's interpreter, serving as an officer for thirty dollars a month. Petersen was a Dane who had resided in Greenland for many years and spoke the language of the Native Greenlanders. As a man in his late thirties or perhaps early forties, he was older and more experienced than any other member of the expedition, including Kane. He was also a veteran Arctic explorer, having been interpreter on board a British expedition led by Captain William Penny.[23] Perhaps because of this experience, Petersen was critical of his new comrades and the expedition in general. Soon after consenting to join, he noted several deficiencies. The ship's provisions, he thought, contained too much salted and not enough boiled meat. The crew, he felt, was too small and not experienced enough, and the commander inexperienced, yet unwilling to take the advice of his more knowledgeable subordinates. Petersen, as a Dane, found the nationalistic pride and bonhomie that Kane tried to instill in the crew distasteful. Nor did he put much stock in the belief in an "Open Polar Sea" which guided the expedition. Indeed, it is surprising that Petersen consented to join the expedition at all. As it was, he contributed some important skills and experience to the small band of explorers, but he never accepted, and at times undermined, Kane's authority as the expedition's leader. Petersen's presence eventually helped bring to the surface many of the latent divisions in the crew.[24]

With the expedition's crew and stores now complete, the *Advance* sailed north once again. Kane's plan was to drive north to find a passage through Smith Sound and force a way past all of the ice to the open water he imagined lay beyond. If the brig could not get through, he intended to find a suitable harbor and allow the *Advance* to become frozen into the ice for the winter. The crew could then use the dogs and sledges to reconnoiter to the north, map the coastline, and make astronomical and other scientific observations before completing a passage through to the supposed Open Polar Sea the following spring. This is exactly what he proceeded to do, the only major flaw in his plan being that the intended destination they were risking everything to reach did not in fact exist. Instead of breaking through the barrier of ice to warmer seas beyond, they found that their surroundings just kept getting colder and icier.

BY THE END of July, Kane and his crew were in Melville Bay, heading north toward Smith Sound. Navigation was a matter of finding a route through shifting fields of ice without getting crushed between them. When the weather turned rough, they often fastened the *Advance* to icebergs for a tenuous form of security, using these huge floating islands as protection from the churning sea of pack ice around them. Often, when the pack ice drifted south toward the Atlantic, the icebergs, whose massive submerged portions reacted to currents well below the surface, remained stationary or even drifted north. Attaching a small brig to an iceberg, however, could prove dangerous, as they discovered on July 29, when the one they were moored to split apart. Kane recalled, "We had barely time to cast off before the face of the berg fell in ruins, crashing like near artillery."[25]

At other times the wind died, and the boats would be lowered to tow the brig. This was hard work that resulted in little progress, and the men did not enjoy it. According to cabin boy Thomas Hickey, at one point while towing the brig in this manner, "Mr. Godfrey, becoming somewhat disgusted with the exercise of rowing, gave an exhibition of his talents as a pugilist. He made an assault upon Mr. Wilson, but was arrested before much blood had been spilt."[26] As a result Godfrey once again found himself under the booby hatch reflecting on his sins. Godfrey was quickly proving himself a troublemaker, but perhaps he had some provocation, as his superiors had yet to impress him with their superiority.

The victim of Godfrey's violent outburst, John Wilson, originally hired as second in command, was apparently turning out to be a disappointment as an officer to his superiors and inferiors alike. Kane had observed in a letter to his friend Cornelius Grinnell just days before that Wilson "had no control over the men, and was deficient in seamanship as a deck officer."[27] Wilson could not win the respect of a man like Godfrey, who was intensely proud of his own abilities and not likely to suffer humbly the incompetence of a superior. Nor did he win the respect of Kane, who reduced Wilson's position on board the brig and relied more on the superior seamanship of Brooks, McGary, and Ohlsen. Wilson was not the only officer who presented a problem. Kane's friend Goodfellow was totally incompetent when it came to just about anything, and was considered an officer only because he was a "gentleman." To make matters worse, he was proving to be clumsy and a slow learner, even though the more experienced Brooks patiently tried to teach him.[28] Although Kane liked to think that his own authority and that of the officers on board was based on merit, it must have been clear to Godfrey and the rest of the men that this was no meritocracy.

By the beginning of August the expedition had made its way through to the "North Water," the ice-free region at the north end of Baffin Bay, and on August 6 they sighted the entrance to Smith Sound. No previous expedition had ever sailed very far into Smith Sound, and whalers never ventured there from their cruising grounds in Baffin Bay. The previous summer Captain Inglefield of the Royal Navy had noted open water as far as he could see in Smith Sound, but he had little time and explored only a short distance into it, reaching a northern latitude of 78° 28' 21".[29] Now Kane pointed his brig north and attempted to sail where no other American or European had ever penetrated before. To the east the coast of Greenland rose in cliffs over a thousand feet high. To Kane, these cliffs "looked down on us as if they challenged our right to pass."[30]

Kane may have been correct in this, for he soon discovered that Smith Sound was not as ice-free as it had been the previous summer when Inglefield was there. The expedition had not gone far before they began to encounter ice, which soon clogged the narrow passage they hoped to travel. Determined to proceed, Kane decided to leave a cache of supplies on nearby Littleton Island as a fallback position in case of emergency.

Soon after, the ice turned so thick that sailing became impossible, so Kane ordered that the brig be "warped" down narrow leads of open water along the shallow Greenland coast. This meant that the brig would be pulled forward by means of a capstan and a rope. At low tide the brig was often grounded on the shallow bottom near shore, only to be pulled forward as the tide rose again. At other times, when the ice was spaced farther apart, they "tracked," meaning that the men put on harnesses and pulled the brig along the edge of an ice field with ropes, like mules pulling a barge on a canal. This physically strenuous and discouraging job fell to the crew. Godfrey recollected that days were thus spent with very little progress, and he grew resentful that so much of the heavy work fell to him as one of the stronger members of the expedition.[31] He had signed on for adventure, but he was quickly finding out that hard labor and constant submission to the will of the officers was the order of the day. In addition to hard physical labor, the crew was also subjected to danger from storms that periodically blew in from the north, setting the ice in motion and threatening to crush the little brig. No doubt this constant peril raised some questions in the men's minds about the wisdom of Dr. Kane and his plans.

As the hardship and danger of the expedition increased, some members of the crew began to have their doubts about the whole endeavor. It was beginning to look like suicide. Petersen, critical of the expedition's goals from the start, repeatedly recommended that the *Advance* be turned southward to find a place to winter at a lower latitude.[32] Godfrey and most of the officers except Brooks also began to advocate turning back.[33] But for Kane to turn back at such an early stage would have been an admission of defeat. To find the Open Polar Sea, he felt, every mile farther north was important. Even if they did not reach the open sea, Kane knew that his reputation would be well served if he attained a new "highest north" record.

On August 23 Kane checked the latitude, which he determined to be 78° 41' north. Ever mindful of his honor and reputation, he observed with satisfaction: "We are farther north, therefore, than any of our predecessors, except Parry on his Spitzbergen foot-tramp. There are those with whom, no matter how insuperable the obstacle, failure involves disgrace: we are safe at least from their censure."[34]

Because of their high latitude and the approaching end of the short Arctic summer, the mean temperature was now dropping below the freezing point. Kane wanted to push still farther north, but he was beginning to realize that such a goal was unrealistic.[35] As some of the crew warped and tracked the *Advance* into a nearby bay, Kane, accompanied by seven others, set out to reconnoiter ahead. After a few days' search he found that further progress was impossible because of the ice. Scanning the terrain, he realized that he had "seen no place combining so many of the requisites of a good winter harbor as the bay in which we left the Advance." Putting a positive spin on the situation, he observed that the streams flowing into the bay from shore would cause the ice to break up early in the spring and that "lofty headlands walled it in beautifully to seaward, enclosing an anchorage with a moderate depth of water; yet it was open to the meridian sunlight, and guarded from winds, eddies, and drift."[36] He named the bay Rensselaer Harbor and informed the crew that this was where they would spend the winter.

WHEN THE second Grinnell Expedition set off for the Arctic, Maggie Fox was safely deposited at Crookville, Pennsylvania. There Elisha Kane expected her to study her lessons and cultivate her sensibility to the point where she could pass as a suitable mate for a gentleman like himself. The plan must have sounded fine coming from Kane. Fox would forgo the deception of spiritualism. She would become genteel. Separated from the evil influences of her sister Leah Brown, she would develop self-respect and learn the role of an upper-middle-class wife who could occupy an honorable place in society. Yet once Kane was out of the picture, Maggie Fox had time to take stock of her situation. For five years she had led an interesting and stimulating, if not altogether honest, life. She had seen much of the country. She had met the nation's most famous men and women. She had had fun, and she had made friends. Now all that was gone. She had promised Kane never again to take part in the rappings. Although Susannah Turner and her husband, with whom she was staying, were pleasant country people, they could hardly provide the stimulation that her former life had given her.

Fox's confinement in Crookville was made even more difficult by the ambiguous nature of her position. She had submitted to Elisha Kane's wishes, but he was thousands of miles away. By default she fell under the informal authority of her keepers, Susannah Turner and Cornelius Grinnell. Turner acted as Fox's governess. For ten dollars a week, she provided a place for Fox in her and her husband's rural home and took charge of the young woman's education. Fox took French lessons, practiced the piano, and did everything she could to cultivate the skills necessary for her to take her place one day in society as Dr. Kane's wife.

Cornelius Grinnell meanwhile held the purse strings. Kane had left money with his friend, making him into a sort of trustee for Maggie Fox. Every time Turner needed to be paid, or Fox needed money for anything at all, Fox had to write Grinnell to get a portion of what Kane had left for her benefit and support. This sort of dependence was a new situation for her. As a spirit rapper Maggie Fox had earned a good living by her own labor. It is not clear who controlled the money she had earned—most likely her mother—but it is clear that, while she remained active, Maggie had been left with a good deal to spend on herself. She had occupied the unusual position of being financially independent as a teenager, and her spending habits had formed accordingly. Now that was no longer the case. To become a genteel lady, she had to be cast back into the traditional role of a dependent.

By autumn 1853, as the Grinnell Expedition was settling into its first winter quarters, Maggie Fox was already tiring of Crookville. She wanted to go to New York City to visit her friends. She had become particularly close to Ellen Walter, who lived on Clinton Place in Manhattan. We know little of Ellen Walter other than what Elizabeth Ellet wrote of her in *The Love-Life of Dr. Kane*. Ellet identified Walter as the sister of John Cochrane, a prominent New York lawyer, who would later be active in local and national politics.[37] Walter was a member of respectable middle-class New York society, and their friendship suggests that Maggie Fox, despite her new position of dependence, was not just a poor, unconnected girl relying on Kane as her sole benefactor.

Walter invited Fox to take a break from her studies and stay with her in New York for a time, but first, twenty-year-old Maggie felt it necessary to ask permission of her keepers. While Cornelius Grinnell and Susannah Turner had no legal authority over her, Fox soon learned that respectability demanded that she conform to their wishes and consent to their control. Her letter to Grinnell, in which she asks permission to go, clearly indicates her standing at the time. "My dear Sir, I am very lonely and should love very much to go and spend a few days with my friend Mrs. Walter," wrote Fox. "Will you please do me the kindness to write to Mrs. Turner and tell her to let me spend say one week with Mrs. Walter," she continued, sounding disturbingly like a child begging her parents for permission. "Mrs. Turner knows very well who Mrs. Walter is and would be very happy to let me go, but says she is afraid it might not please all my friends if I should leave my studies. Will you please have the kindness to say to her that Mrs. Walter will see that I return in one week." In a postscript Fox apologized for bothering Grinnell and closed in a pleading tone, "Mrs. Turner dislikes very much to have me leave my French for a week, but I will take my French books and study an hour every day."[38]

The deference expressed in this and other letters like it is remarkable. Neither Turner nor Grinnell should have been in a position to tell her what to do. Even Kane, before he departed on his expedition, had promised Fox that she would be in control of her own life. At Turner's, he told her, "you will be a lady; your own mistress, and a person regarded with respect by the whole house. It shall be distinctly understood that you go or stay just as you please;—for I am not going to turn 'preacher' and bind up my little Maggie by a set of rules."[39] In practice, however, age, class, and gender served to keep Fox in a subordinate position. But most of all, Fox's dependence had to do with money. In her letters to Grinnell, she tried vainly to come up with an appropriate way to ask for money from a man who was essentially a stranger. "Will you also please send me 80 dollars by return of mail? Pardon me for giving you so much trouble," she asked in one letter.[40] The following week she wrote: "I sent you a letter some five or six days since in which I requested you to send me eighty dollars, but if you have not yet attended to my request I should prefer one hundred. Will you please send this at your earliest convenience."[41] Another note read: "Will you please send me one hundred and ninety dollars. I would like to have you send it in bills if it will not incommode you."[42]

Fox was aware that she was becoming increasingly beholden to Grinnell. In an undated letter she acknowledged the receipt of $120, part of which would be spent, according to Fox, "to liquidate some necessary expenses which I have incurred." She then asked for sixteen dollars more by return mail. She added a postscript, "I hope I shall not have to send for any more money."[43] The line "Pardon me for giving you so much trouble," or close variations of it, appears repeatedly in Fox's letters to Grinnell.[44] She clearly felt awkward to be dependent on a man she hardly knew, but she was motivated by her desire to fulfill her promise to Kane and find a way out of spirit rapping. She wanted to earn the good opinion of polite society, despite her colorful past.

Her uneasiness at having to ask constantly for money did not hold her back entirely. She maintained social connections with her friends in New York. She went to visit Ellen Walter, and stayed more than a week, apparently because she became ill and her doctor, Edward Bayard, feared having her travel back to Crookville.[45] Her mother and two sisters were also living in New York City by this time. Although Fox stayed away from Leah Brown, she maintained a close relationship with her mother and with Kate, even though Kate was still a practicing spirit rapper.

Fox also spent money in startling quantities. In many of her appeals to Grinnell she asked for between one and two hundred dollars—significant sums for the 1850s.[46] Perhaps because her rapping career had been so lucrative, she had developed little notion of the value of money. She and her sisters could earn fifty dollars or more in a single day as spirit rappers. That was almost as much as Kane earned in an entire month as a navy surgeon. While Kane would get twenty-five dollars for a single lecture, the Fox sisters could hold three "promiscuous circles" a day, with each participant paying a dollar.[47] Undoubtedly, this money added up, but there is little indication that anybody but Leah Brown saved much of it. Ironically, while Fox's association with Kane had the potential to elevate her social status, it also reduced her spending power—evidence that class in antebellum America was not just a matter of wealth.

Turner and Grinnell soon came to consider Fox irresponsible with money, but she was not as much of a spendthrift as she may at first appear. Much of the money she asked Grinnell for was to pay Susannah Turner, who charged ten dollars a week for her room and board, or to pay for such things as French lessons. These are expenses that Kane had agreed to cover in order to achieve his own paternalistic goals of persuading Maggie Fox to give up spiritualism and be placed in a school. Fox was trying to live up to Kane's expectations, but he had not left her the resources to do so. In many ways it was Kane who was the spendthrift. By playing the great man in order to woo Fox away from spiritualism, he had committed himself to expenses he could not really afford, just as he was making promises he would find difficult to keep.

As Grinnell doled out hundreds of dollars to Maggie Fox, he wondered if he was sending her too much. In a short time, all the money Kane had left with him was gone. In February 1854, when Kane had been gone a little over eight months, Grinnell wrote to Elisha Kane's younger brother Robert Patterson Kane, who was a lawyer, and asked his advice. "I am desirous of doing everything in my power to carry out your brother's wishes," Grinnell wrote, "and at the same time to promote his happiness, and unless you should deem it in all respects advisable to inform her that her funds are exhausted, I will forward the amount she requests without delay."[48]

Robert Kane wrote back to Grinnell telling him to send the money, but that it should come out of his own pocket rather than Grinnell's. Robert Kane, who disapproved of his brother's involvement with a spirit rapper, also took the opportunity to spell out exactly how he wanted his brother's relationship with Fox presented. He felt that Grinnell should take advantage of Fox's need for money to let her know where she stood:

> It does strike me that the opportunity presented of letting the young lady know your own impression of her position which she bears to the doctor, should not be lost. We know her only as a dependent, as one to whom the doctor bears the relation of a kind hearted friend whose interest in the young lady shows itself by furnishing her with the means of leading an honest life and resisting the temptations which beset a poor girl with a pretty face and an already disreputable association. My dear brother resembles our very lovable Don Quixote; but then this resemblance must not be construed into anything affecting his reputation. Etc. Etc.
>
> The funds in your hands are exhausted. The trustee reports accordingly. The Doctor is your friend; but [Fox] is not his mistress and holds to him no other relation than that of the recipient of his charity and to you no other than that of a purely business correspondent.
>
> Do you take my drift! I am in such haste that I fear I am not writing intelligibly.

Kane reminded Grinnell that the two of them had a higher goal than simply saving money, that of saving "that which we both of us value much more." presumably referring to Elisha's reputation. He ended by instructing Grinnell, "Burn this."[49]

His "Do you take my drift" at the end of his careful delineation of Fox's position in relation to his brother, clearly gives a wink and a nod to Grinnell. Robert Kane certainly did not think that Fox and his brother would ever marry, but he also realized that the official story he was so painfully spelling out was not the truth. He must have believed that Elisha was simply engaged in a brief and impetuous romantic infatuation, or perhaps even a sexual affair, with Maggie Fox. His job, as he saw it, was to humor his reckless brother until his fascination with the spirit rapper passed. Moreover, he thought that Maggie Fox could only benefit from the interest of a man like Kane, even if that interest was just temporary. Elisha Kane may even have encouraged his brother to think along these lines. The story Elisha told him was definitely not the same one he told Maggie Fox, though it is unclear exactly what he did tell his brother.

Cornelius Grinnell, like Robert Patterson Kane, seemed to think that Fox was simply a temporary diversion, which Elisha would soon get over. Grinnell knew that the story of a "committee of benevolent gentlemen" acting in Fox's best interest had been largely fabricated by Kane for appearance's sake. He knew that the two were engaged in a secret correspondence, since he had at various times acted as messenger between them. Although his earlier exchange with Robert Patterson Kane left some ambiguity as to what he thought, there are clear indications that he did not think of Fox as Kane's fiancée.[50] In a letter to Elisha Kane sent a year and a half later, Grinnell would refer to rumors circulating about an engagement, calling the rumors ridiculous and blaming Leah Brown for them: "She [Brown] has endeavored to spread about a report that you are educating Miss F with the intention of marrying her on your return. I have done everything in my power to contradict such insinuations, and as I have heard nothing of them of late I trust they have 'died out.'"[51] Since he did not believe that the two planned to marry, and he knew that the "benevolent gentleman" story was a fabrication, it is not unlikely that Grinnell assumed Fox was Kane's mistress. He certainly knew that the amount of money Kane was spending on her exceeded mere paternal benevolence.

Regardless of what he suspected, by April 1854 Grinnell was increasingly concerned about how much money Maggie Fox was spending. He asked her to account for all the money he had sent her. This letter no longer exists, but Fox's reply does. "I cannot for the love of my life tell how much money I have had from you since Dr. Kane left. I thought of course you kept an account," she wrote. She then recalled her expenses: nine months at Turner's at forty dollars a month, thirteen dollars for French books and drawing materials, twenty dollars for clothes, ten dollars for the doctor, fifty dollars for travel expenses. She concluded, "I fear yourself and Dr. Kane will both think I have been very thoughtless."[52] Eventually Grinnell began to deal directly with Susannah Turner for most of Fox's financial affairs, which further removed the young woman from control of her situation.[53]

Fox's lifestyle remained essentially the same for over two years while Kane was away on his expedition. Now largely out of the public eye, she spent most of her time in the domestic surroundings of Turner's Crookville home. As the months went by, she frequently made extended visits to stay with Ellen Walter in New York City, where she enjoyed a more social and sophisticated atmosphere. No longer a spirit rapper, but not formally recognized as Kane's fiancée, she occupied an ambiguous social position. In *The Love-Life of Dr. Kane,* Ellet asserts that Cornelius Grinnell, Susannah Turner, and Ellen Walter all considered Fox Kane's bride-to-be. As we have seen, this was not entirely the case, but Ellet may have been correct in regard to Mrs. Walter and her circle (most likely Ellet and Walter knew each other). Ellen Walter and her friends were respectable upper-middle-class women and men who knew Maggie Fox and liked her. They would have seen nothing wrong in a match between her and Kane. Turner may also have assumed that Kane was paying for Fox's education because he planned to marry her. But as there had been no formal announcement of an engagement, few would have thought it their business to pry. If Turner and Walter believed it was Kane's intention to marry Fox, theirs was probably an unspoken assumption. The only other key player was Eliza Leiper, Kane's aunt, who had first recommended Susannah Turner to her nephew. Leiper lived nearby, and she met Fox a few times while she was at Crookville, but it is not clear what she thought of Fox's status. Unlike Robert Kane and Cornelius Grinnell, Leiper must have trusted that her nephew's intentions, whatever they were, were honorable.

BACK ON THE *Advance* in the fall of 1853, the men of the second Grinnell Expedition commenced converting the brig from a sailing vessel into winter quarters, which entailed unloading and changing the layout of the hold and building an enclosed house on the deck. They also built a storehouse on an island in the bay and transferred the contents of the brig's hold into it. Then they built a kennel for the dogs and a stone observatory where Sonntag could take regular astronomical observations. By the middle of September, as they settled into their new home and the water around the brig froze solid, Kane began to send out expeditions to reconnoiter and deposit caches of supplies in preparation for springtime sledge journeys to the north. All this was part of Kane's well-thought-out master plan of exploration: "My plans of future search were directly dependent upon the success of these operations of the fall. With a chain of provision-depôts along the coast of Greenland, I could readily extend my travel by dogs . . . with relays of provisions I could start empty, and fill up at our final station."[54]

They made some progress laying out cache depots during the short fall season; McGary and Bonsall, accompanied by Godfrey and three others, made a particularly long trip up the coast that lasted twenty-seven days. They got as far as a mammoth glacier that flowed into the sea from deep in the interior of Greenland. Its face, which dropped massive icebergs into the Arctic waters, was miles wide and blocked any further progress to the north. This glacier, which proved to be the largest on earth, Kane named the Great Glacier of Humboldt after Alexander von Humboldt.

Soon, as winter set in, the days shortened and the cold intensified, bringing an end to such journeys.[55] By November their long winter's confinement had commenced. Since the small group of men would be holed up together for many months, it was important that everyone keep occupied, and, in Kane's words, they developed "schemes innumerable to cheat the monotonous solitude of our winter."[56] These entertainments and diversions mirrored those of the world they had left behind. They published a small newspaper, which they called the *Ice-Blink*, containing articles written by everyone on board. Kane also organized games, such as the "Fox chase," which Godfrey won, and the men put on plays and gave lyceum-type lectures for one another's amusement and education. They even had a fancy dress ball at Christmas.[57] Godfrey, who had a penchant for the racist comedy of minstrel songs, often blackened his face with charcoal and entertained the crew.[58]

There was also the routine of work to be accomplished. Kane spent much of his time training the dogs to pull a sledge. He hoped that by springtime he and the dogs would be skilled enough to make the journey to the Open Polar Sea. There was also the routine of making regular observations of a number of natural phenomena, such as tides, magnetic variation, and temperature, for the advancement of Humboldtean science. This duty fell to the scientific officers, Sonntag, Hayes, Bonsall, and Kane. Kane described the often difficult process in his narrative of the expedition, *Arctic Explorations*:

> The observer, if he were only at home, would be the "observed of all observers." He is clad in a pair of seal-skin pants, a dog-skin cap, a reindeer

> jumper, and walrus boots. He sits upon a box that once held a transit instrument. A stove, glowing with at least a bucketful of anthracite, represents pictorally a heating apparatus, and reduces the thermometer as near as may be to ten degrees below zero. One hand holds a chronometer, and is left bare to warm it: the other luxuriates in a fox-skin mitten. The right hand and the left take it "watch and watch about." As one burns with cold, the chronometer shifts to the other, and the mitten takes its place.
>
> Perched on a pedestal of frozen gravel is a magnetometer; stretching out from it, a telescope: and, bending down to this, an abject human eye. Every six minutes, said eye takes cognizance of a finely-divided arc, and notes the result in a cold memorandum book. This process continues for twenty-four hours, two sets of eyes taking it by turns; and, when twenty-four hours are over, term-day is over too.[59]

Kane went on to note, " 'A grateful country' will of course appreciate the value of these labors, and, as it cons over hereafter the four hundred and eighty results which go to make up our record for each week, will never think of asking '*Cui bono* all this?' "[60]

As winter progressed, the intense cold and dark began to take their toll, both physically and mentally. From the end of November until the end of January the darkness was complete, without even the faintest glow of the sun at the horizon. Godfrey described the scene as one of sublime gloom: "Outside of our vessel nothing was seen but ice, snow, and naked rocks; unless we turned our eyes upward to behold a sky which could not be seen without a thrill of horror, so repulsively unnatural was its appearance. The Arctic heavens, after the disappearance of the sun, resemble a vast arch or dome of granite, almost forcing the beholder to imagine himself in one of 'the profoundest caves of gloomy Dis,' or in one of those central caverns of the earth which, (according to the theory of Captain Simmes,) have their entrance near the Pole."[61]

Not until late February did the rays of the sun once again shine on Rensselaer Harbor. In March daylight returned, but the mean temperature for the month, recorded at −38.09°F, was the coldest yet.[62] These conditions, in combination with a diet short on fresh meat and vegetables, resulted in symptoms of scurvy in the crew. The dogs fared even worse; they began to die off of an unknown malady, and by the end of the winter only a handful were left.

Despite the prevalence of sickness and the severe temperatures, Kane decided in March that it was time to recommence laying out provision depots for his planned trek to the north. Petersen claimed that Kane was determined to send out an expedition so early out of a nationalistic desire to outdo the British, who usually waited until April before sending out sledging expeditions. Petersen and Ohlsen objected to sending men out while it was still so cold, but Kane was impatient and insisted.[63]

The expedition was put under the command of Brooks, who was to be accompanied by Petersen, Ohlsen, Sonntag, Wilson, Hickey, Baker, and Schubert. On March 19 they began dragging the sledge over the ice. The mean temperature that day was −42.31°F.[64] As Kane described it, they left in good spirits, giving three cheers, but according to the accounts by Godfrey and Petersen, the mood was less spirited.[65] The men made very slow progress and were in constant danger of getting frostbite on their faces and toes. They soon found that the runners of the sledge were too narrow, causing them to sink into the snow. Kane sent them a different sledge with wider runners, but still they made slow progress. The first day they traveled only five miles. In the days that followed they took a circuitous route north through the icebergs and hummocks, trying to make their way to the western coast of Smith Sound about forty miles away. The men discovered that they had to travel much farther than planned because of the constant need to change course to get around hummocks and icebergs. On the second day they walked five miles but made only two and a half miles' progress. The third day they advanced only a mile and a half, although they dragged the sledge for five miles around icy obstacles. This discouragingly slow pace continued until March 29, when they decided to turn back, their journey having been largely a failure. The next morning, however, they awoke to find that four of their party, Brooks, Wilson, Schubert, and Baker, had got severe frostbite on their feet and were unable to walk. Brooks sent Petersen, Sonntag, and Ohlsen back to the brig to fetch help, while Thomas Hickey stayed to tend to the four injured men.[66]

Petersen, Sonntag, and Ohlsen arrived unexpectedly back at the brig around midnight in a state of total exhaustion. Godfrey recalled: "Their faces were absolutely black. Ohlsen's toes were frozen; Sonntag was stupefied, and appeared to be unconscious of his situation; Petersen was in a similar condition."[67] Ohlsen, who was the only one still coherent, reported on the condition of the men they had left in the tent. Kane began to organize a rescue mission.

As soon as morning came, Kane departed with a party of men to retrieve their five companions. Ohlsen, whose toes had been amputated the night before by Hayes on account of the frostbite, was wrapped in robes and strapped to the sledge to guide the rescue party. After a twenty-hour trek, during which Kane often fainted and had to be helped by the others, and Ohlsen, with his toes just recently amputated, often had to walk, they finally arrived at the little tent pitched in the snow, expecting to find their friends dead from exposure. Godfrey was first on the scene. "The death-scene I had imagined appeared to be realized when we reached the door of the tent," he recalled. "Four bodies, apparently lifeless, each one enclosed in a sleeping bag, were lying closely together in the little enclosure."[68] Godfrey, Kane, and the others examined the men and found that they were still alive, though in serious danger. They did what they could for them, fed them broth to warm them, and, after a short rest, loaded them onto the sledge for the trip back to the brig.

The journey back was even more grueling than the one out. Now the sledge had the weight of five men on it. Soon the men became so tired that they no longer had any concern for their own lives, and they begged Kane to be allowed to fall asleep on the ice, which would have meant freezing to death. Finally they would go no farther, so they pitched a tent to rest. All could not fit in the one tent, however, so Kane put McGary in charge with orders to proceed in four hours, and continued on with Godfrey another nine miles to the place where they had left their other tent and some provisions. Kane's and Godfrey's accounts of the journey they made together tell of hardship that descended into delirium. Kane recalled a polar bear, "who walked leisurely before us and tore up as he went a jumper that McGary had improvidently thrown off the day before. He tore it into shreds and rolled it into a ball, but never offered to interfere with our progress."[69] According to Godfrey, however, "this bear, in fact, was a creation of the Doctor's fancy. He spoke of it at the time when he supposed that he saw it; but, although my eyesight was much better than his, I saw nothing of the kind."[70] Godfrey observed that Kane was delirious and incoherent during most of their journey together, and what is more, "when he swooned away, as he did two or three times, I carried him on my shoulder."[71] Godfrey's account here is more likely the truth, for even Kane noted that Godfrey's role on that march "may atone for many faults of a later time," though Kane did not admit that Godfrey carried him much of the way, saving his life.[72]

Kane and Godfrey finally got to the tent and went to sleep. When they awoke, they heated water for soup and waited for the others to arrive, which they soon did. Then the party proceeded together to the brig. By the time they reached it, all were exhausted and delirious. There they were cared for by Dr. Hayes, who had remained behind. The four men who had been rescued were alive, but their condition was deplorable. Brooks never fully recovered, and Wilson was significantly weakened. The other two fared even worse. Baker died on April 8, a few days after their return. Schubert lingered a bit longer, but was dead by the middle of May. Both were, in Godfrey's words, "unhonored victims of the exploring mania."[73]

THE DISASTER of this first spring exploring party, needless to say, did much to dampen the spirit of adventure in the remaining members of the second Grinnell Expedition. Two men were dead, and most of the rest had suffered the severe hardships posed by this type of Arctic travel. Many had lost flesh to frostbite. Kane, however, had not given up his ambition to advance farther north, and planning for future sledge journeys continued.

Despite Kane's undiminished ambition, the expedition was in sorry shape; the men were not healthy, and they were running low on fresh provisions. They had plenty of salted meats, but this was the cause of their scurvy. They needed fresh food badly. What made matters worse was the condition of the ice surrounding their brig. It showed no signs of melting, even as the weather was beginning to warm. Of course, this was not yet a matter of great concern. It was to be expected that the brig might not be freed from its icy harbor until July or August, but earlier than this some of the men started to wonder what would happen to them if the brig was not freed at all that summer.

With this prospect still well in the future, a fortuitous event occurred. A party of Inuit from a community called Etah, about ninety miles to the south, showed up unexpectedly at the brig. For hundreds of years, people had lived and raised families in the seemingly inhospitable environs of Smith Sound.[74] The Polar Inuit of this region had long ago learned how to survive in a far northern climate, but they had little contact with people to the south, and none with the Danes or Christianized Inuit of southern Greenland, as they were cut off from them by a region around Melville Bay where travel was hard and game was scarce.[75]

The Polar Inuit of Smith Sound had had no contact with people from Europe until 1818, when John Ross met a group of them off Cape York, calling them "Arctic Highlanders." After that they may have encountered the occasional whaling vessel or exploring expedition passing by the mouth of Smith Sound, but it was not until the arrival of the second Grinnell Expedition that they had any extended contact with southlanders. Living farther north than any other people on earth, the Polar Inuit survived by hunting marine mammals, caribou, and smaller land mammals such as foxes and hares; they collected eggs and caught migrating birds. They lived in stone huts heated and lighted with the blubber of marine mammals, resorting to the snow igloo when traveling. They used tools made from stone and bone. Although no trees grow this far north, the Polar Inuit collected wood that drifted to the northwest shores of Greenland from the forests of northern Siberia to use as rafters for their huts and as parts for their sleds. Their dress consisted of thick fur outer garments with softer underclothes made from feathers. While this technology seemed primitive to outsiders, it was well suited to life in the Arctic, and explorers had much to learn from the Inuit about how to survive in such a region.

The Inuit of Etah had the skills necessary to help the explorers. They knew the habits of the game in the region and could supply the "Kabloonah," or white men, with the fresh meat they so desperately needed. In return, Kane and his companions had many things that these Inuit wanted, such as steel knives, needles, and wood. Kane, unlike many explorers in the nineteenth century, understood this. Unlike many of the British explorers in the Arctic, who did their best to insulate themselves from the environment and people outside their ships, Kane had hoped to encounter and learn from the people of the region. This is not to say that he considered them his equals. None of the members of the expedition did. In his first description of them Kane observed that they were "wild and uncouth, but evidently human beings."[76] Godfrey, too, found himself "much amused by the jovial and eccentric behavior of these savages."[77] To all the Americans, the "Esquimaux" were rather humorous and potentially dangerous, but all recognized that they were indispensable to them for their skills as hunters.

Soon the two groups entered into negotiations, with Petersen acting as interpreter. Despite Kane's marked inferiority in this context, his approach was to attempt to impress the people from Etah with his own superiority. He invited the visitors into the brig. Here, with behavior reminiscent of his treatment of Maggie Fox as well as of his own crew on board the *Advance*, Kane "tried to make them understand what a powerful Prospero they had for a host, and how beneficent he would prove himself so long as they did his bidding."[78] He then traded some needles, beads, and pieces of metal for all the walrus meat the Inuit had.

Kane's interpretation of his encounter with the "savages" notwithstanding, it is doubtful that the people from Etah considered themselves to be doing Kane's bidding when they agreed to trade with him. The men of the expedition were in poor condition, and it seems unlikely that their visitors did not realize as much. It was all Kane could do to prevent them from seeing Baker's corpse, which had not yet been buried since his death the day before. Schubert was still lingering near death, and the others were in bad shape as well. Most likely the Americans were something of a novelty to the Inuit, who were interested to see what these newcomers were all about. They were quite willing to engage in trade, since the Americans had some items that the Inuit realized could be very useful, but it is hardly likely that they accepted the subordinate position Kane assigned to them. During the remainder of their time in the Arctic, Kane and the members of the expedition got to know the men and women of Etah very well, and it was the cooperative relationship that developed between the two groups that allowed the expedition to survive another year.

AS THE WARMER weather of late spring and early summer arrived, Kane once again began to send out sledging parties. Despite the disaster of the first sledge expedition, he had not yet given up hope of finding the Open Polar Sea. Kane attempted one trip with Godfrey and McGary, but did not get far before turning back. His persistent poor health always kept him from getting very far himself, but he would send others in his place. One of the most successful trips was made by Hayes and Godfrey, who made it to the west coast of Smith Sound and explored a good distance to the north, reaching a latitude of 79° 45'. Finally, in late June and early July, using the few remaining dogs to haul their supplies, William Morton and Hans Hendrik made a successful trek north along the Greenland coast, past the great glacier that Kane had named for Humboldt. When they returned on July 3, Morton reported to Kane that he and Hendrik had come to a steep headland at 81° 22' north. From that vantage point, looking out over the sea to the north he could see no ice. This was the highest latitude that any member of the expedition would reach, and Morton's report seemed to prove Kane's theory of an Open Polar Sea. Or at least it did to Kane. Some other members of the crew were more skeptical; Godfrey did not believe that Morton had seen the Open Polar Sea, and Petersen thought that he had probably just seen a patch of summer open water, but to Kane, Morton and Hendrik's sighting was the crowning achievement of the expedition. He happily reported in his journal that "now in spite of the lockjawed Dogs and the dead and the crippled and the stiff limbed scorbutic—I can say that I have led an expedition whose results will be remembered for all time." The "Open Polar Sea" had at last been found.[79]

8

Homeward Bound

God in Heaven! It makes my blood boil to think that men who so leaned on me, trusted me, and like little children been taught by me their very walk, should at last in the midst of a coming winter, set up their puerile opinions, against my own drearily earned judgment of Arctic Ice.

Elisha Kent Kane, "Journal of the brig *Advance*"

AS THE END of the Arctic summer neared and there was no sign of melting in the ice around the brig, Kane had to decide what to do. Since early June he had been observing the ice and had realized that the season was late. At that time he was convinced that spending a second winter in the ice would be impossible because the supply of coal and fresh food was low, and he began to consider abandoning the ship to return home by open boat.[1] After Morton and Hendrick returned from their successful journey north along the coast, Kane traveled south to inspect the condition of the ice, and what he saw was not encouraging. The season was still late; but he also knew that when the ice finally did break up, it could do so very quickly, so he continued to hope for an August, or even September, liberation from the frozen bay.

Although Kane realized that this liberation might never occur, and that it would be difficult for him and his men to survive another winter, in the past month he had changed his views on abandoning the brig. He decided that it would not be honorable to leave the *Advance* when there was still a chance it could be liberated late in the season. But he also knew that if the men were to head south by open boat, it had to be done early while there was still time to make the journey to Upernavik before winter set in. By late August or early September it would be too late. He mused on this paradox in his journal: "Now to desert the brig, to abandon my trust and the dearly earned discoveries and material of the cruise is clearly impossible as long as a chance remains of saving them. This matter I settle at once in my mind and by my own dictum, I wont leave the *Advance* until September, *and after September—we cannot leave!*"[2]

Instead of making a firm decision to stay if necessary and preparing for that contingency, Kane came up with an alternative plan to travel with five others in a small boat to Beechey Island, where he hoped to meet up with a British expedition commanded by Captain Edward Belcher and obtain stores from them or perhaps even a launch in which he could return to deliver the rest of his men.[3] This plan was ill conceived at best. Beechey Island is in Lancaster Sound, in the middle of the Canadian archipelago about six hundred miles from Smith Sound. There was no way of knowing if Belcher's squadron was actually there (it was not), and it was almost as likely to be frozen over by the time Kane reached it as was Smith Sound or Baffin Bay. If conditions were clear enough to get to Beechey Island, why not just go to Upernavik, where the men were sure of getting the food and shelter they needed? The only advantage of the Beechey Island plan was that, if by some miracle it worked, it would enable Kane to desert his ship in September rather than July, which in his mind would preserve his honor.[4]

This mission failed, however, as it was bound to do. Kane found pack ice blocking the route to Baffin Bay, which made a boat journey to either Beechey Island or Upernavik impossible, so, after a three-week journey, he returned to the brig with the news. This unwelcome but not unexpected report brought to the surface much of the hostility that had been fermenting. There were distinct factions emerging, some of which were not supportive of Kane's authority. Among the crew, Godfrey and Blake had persistently resisted the authority of the officers, but their hostility seemed aimed toward the officer class in general rather than Kane in particular. The real threat to Kane's authority came from Petersen and Ohlsen, the two experienced Danish officers who had grown to despise Kane and the whole premise of the expedition, especially after the disastrous March trip. Petersen believed that Kane was utterly incompetent. Other members of the crew, however, remained faithful supporters of Kane. Brooks owed his position on board the brig to Kane, and his advancement in the navy was dependent on Kane's good graces. William Morton, Kane's personal steward, also a loyal follower, greatly admired Kane, as did Thomas Hickey, the second steward. Others fell somewhere in between. Hayes, Sonntag, McGary, and Bonsall all shared Kane's enthusiasm for exploration, but perhaps were not willing to be part of his "family" or to show him the deference he wanted or to follow him blindly. Then there was John Wilson, the demoted first officer, whose diary at this time, and throughout the voyage, was filled with the most bitter denunciations of his commander.[5] It was thus with these varying degrees of loyalty to Kane and the expedition that they faced a second winter.

Kane's plan, which he now presented to the others, was for the crew to remain with the brig over the winter and, in the spring, to abandon it and return south to Upernavik by sledge and open boat. Others, however, especially Petersen and Ohlsen, disagreed with Kane's plan. They thought they would have a better chance if they abandoned the brig right away and headed south before winter set in. Kane thought this a foolish idea that would result in the party's getting stranded halfway by the onset of winter, so he made the decision to stay. Yet grumbling persisted, and Kane came to fear an open break.

In hopes of putting an end to such dissension, Kane called the crew together and explained his reasons for wanting to remain with the brig and his conviction that any attempt to travel south that fall would be foolhardy. Most likely he thought that his superior knowledge and reasoning would convince the men of the error of their ways, but just in case some still wanted to make the attempt, he gave his permission to anyone who wished to leave to do so under the command of officers. He asked them all to consider the matter carefully and to state the next day at noon whether they chose to stay or go.[6]

In *Arctic Explorations,* Kane claimed that he made this offer because he did not feel his authority as commander went so far as to demand that the men all stay with the expedition against their will; he pointed out the custom on whaling ships, when they were beset by ice, to allow whoever so wished among the crew to leave the ship. But Kane's decision was more the result of his own views of authority. Kane wanted to be obeyed without question, but he wanted that obedience to be voluntary. His command of the *Advance* was plagued from the start by his desire that his authority be based not solely on his power as commander, but instead on superior capabilities that he nevertheless failed to demonstrate adequately. By giving the crew the choice whether to stay or go, he was allowing them either to accept or to reject his leadership.

Kane expected some, such as Petersen and Godfrey, to take him up on his offer and leave the brig, but he thought that most would choose to stay with him. In a consultation with Sonntag before he made the offer, the astronomer had seemed to concur with Kane that it would be unwise to leave the brig so late in the season, and had assured his commander that he thought few would wish to go.[7] A decision by most of the men to stay would thus be a ringing endorsement of Kane's command; a decision to leave would be a cruel rejection.

At noon the day after Kane's speech the men gathered together to state their choices; each man's name was called, and he responded with either "yes" to leave or "no" to stay. One after another the men answered "yes." Out of the entire crew, only five men responded "no." Kane was surprised, angered, and hurt by how few wanted to remain with him. Brooks was an invalid and had no choice but to remain on the brig. Besides him only William Morton and Thomas Hickey, dedicated followers of Kane, and Henry Goodfellow, his friend from Philadelphia, initially chose to remain. Hans Hendrik also agreed to stay, though there is some indication that the young Inuit hunter may not have been offered the same choice as the rest. To this small group McGary added his name that night and Wilson the next day, after reconsidering their initial decisions.[8]

Of those who chose to go, many came as no surprise. Some, such as Petersen, Blake, and Godfrey, had never submitted to Kane's authority, and perhaps he was glad at the prospect of being rid of them; but the defection of some of the others deeply wounded his pride. Hayes and Sonntag were both gentlemen and scientists whom Kane was distressed to see join the withdrawal party, but perhaps most shocking to him was Amos Bonsall, who was both a friend and a relation by marriage. Kane had especially advised Bonsall to stay with the brig and its commander: "I stated his dangers ahead, my own personal interest in his well being, and his certain loss of reputation and respect at home, he listened with tears in his eyes, but kept to his selfish fears."[9]

Contrary to the published accounts, the journal that Kane kept while the expedition was under way gives a clear picture of the commander's sense of betrayal by the men who withdrew from his expedition that autumn.[10] To Kane, it was the greatest of insults to have his judgment and leadership rejected. He spit venom onto the pages of his journal. He was especially bitter about the officers who chose to go. "The conduct of Mr. Sonntag is perhaps of all this party the most difficult to palliate," he wrote. "His conduct has been such as to prohibit between us any future associations of respect. I regret this for his own sake, as I could have aided him much at home."[11] He decided that the character of the men who chose to go was fatally flawed while all the virtue lay with those who stayed. "Bonsall, Hayes, and Sonntag had never the associative gallantry and right mindedness of Goodfellow or the whaler McGeary, or the man of war's man Brooks. Petersen was always a cold blooded sneak—Ohlsen double faced fawning and insincere their associates number all the crew except Morton and the Irish cabin boy Hickey. These two stand out as natural gentlemen when compared with any of the officers or men who are leaving their post."[12]

Despite the permission he had granted them to leave, he considered all these men deserters. While outwardly he assisted them in their preparations for their long journey south, inwardly he fumed, as when he addressed himself in his journal to his younger brother John: "If I ever live to get home—Home! and should meet Dr. Hayes or Mr. Bonsall or Mr. Sonntag—let them look out for their skins. If I dont live to thrash them—which I'll try very hard to do, (to live I mean) why then dear brother John seek a solitary orchard and maull them for me. Dont honour them with a bullet and let the mauling be solitary—save to the principals—It would hurt your character to be wrestling with such low minded sneaks."[13]

Kane insisted that those who had decided to leave the brig were forever severing themselves from the expedition and absolving him of all responsibility. He insisted that the officers sign a paper to this effect before they left. Christian Ohlsen, however, refused to do so. Petersen's view was that Kane, by making them sign such a document, was pressuring Ohlsen and the other officers to stay, "partly by persuasion and not without some menace, as it seems to me."[14] Clearly Kane wanted as many skilled men, such as Ohlsen, to stay as possible, and he told Ohlsen if he did not sign his withdrawal would be considered desertion. Eventually Ohlsen, despite having been elected commander of the withdrawal party, decided to stay rather than sign.[15]

THE TWO factions now divided the ship's supplies, and on August 26 the withdrawal party, commanded now by Petersen, began to drag their boat and provisions south by sledge. Within a few days they were out of communication with the brig. One of the party, Riley, soon changed his mind and returned to the brig, but the rest continued on.[16] Those who stayed prepared for another long winter. Kane was wise enough to realize that their best chance of survival was to cultivate good relations with the Inuit at Etah and at least partially emulate their way of life. With his customary mix of admiration and contempt for the people of Etah, he resolved "to practice on the lessons we had learned from the Esquimaux. I had studied them carefully, and determined that their form of habitations and their peculiarities of diet, without their unthrift and filth, were the safest and best to which the necessity of our circumstances invited us."[17]

The first priority was to secure fresh meat. The ship's stores were plentiful, but the persistent vitamin deficiency had caused the crew to become ill and weak with scurvy. Only emulating the native diet of fresh meat could prevent them all from dying, so Kane did his best to hunt seals and other game, but in this he was not very successful. He was more successful in getting fresh meat in trade from the skilled hunters at Etah.

The relationship with the Inuit was not easy to maintain. Shortly after the withdrawal party departed, those who remained with the brig were visited by three Inuit from Etah. After offering them every hospitality, Kane was distressed to discover in the morning that their guests had "repaid my liberality by stealing not only the lamp, boiler, and cooking-pot they had used for the feast, but Nannook also, my best dog." They took some buffalo robes and some India-rubber cloth as well.[18] Kane felt that to put up with such theft would be an admission of weakness, so he sent out Morton and Riley to apprehend the miscreants. This they did. After a difficult forced march of thirty miles each way, they brought the suspected culprits back to the brig with the stolen goods. Kane was evidently satisfied with the impression this made of strength. "It was hardly twenty-four hours since they left the brig with their booty," he wrote, "before they were prisoners in the hold, with a dreadful white man for keeper, who never addressed to them a word that had not all the terrors of an unintelligible reproof, and whose scowl, I flatter myself, exhibited a well-arranged variety of menacing and demoniacal expressions."[19]

To Kane this display of strength must have "confirmed them in the faith that the whites are and of right ought to be everywhere the dominant tribe."[20] This was Kane's impression, but perhaps the Inuit were simply convinced that Kane and his crew were insane. The Canadian observer of Inuit life, Farley Mowat, has remarked that "Kane and his men certainly gave the Eskimos sufficient reason to suspect that they were a band of dangerous lunatics."[21] In any case, the result of this conflict was a treaty between the two groups, made, presumably, with Hans Hendrik's help as interpreter now that Petersen was gone. According to Kane, the Inuit of

Etah promised not to steal, to provide the expedition with fresh meat and dogs, and to accompany them in the hunt. In turn, Kane's men promised not to harass the Inuit with sorcery, to help them in the hunt with their guns, to welcome them at the brig, and to give them "presents of needles, pins, two kinds of knife, a hoop, three bits of hard wood, some fat, an awl, and some sewing thread."[22] However it was understood by the people of Etah, this treaty established good relations between the two groups, which lasted for the remainder of the expedition. For much of the remaining autumn the two groups hunted together, and the Americans learned a great deal about living in the Arctic.

As the darkness of December set in, the men on the brig were surprised one morning by the approach of five sledges. Kane recalled: "The strangers proved to be a party who had escorted to our lonely harbour, two of our absentees. These wretched men were Bonsall and Petersen, who had reaped the bitter fruit of want of faith and were now the bearers of a frightful tale."[23] A few days later the remaining members of the withdrawal party arrived. It was not without some degree of satisfaction that Kane reported their return to the brig. The group had traveled close to three hundred miles to the south before being stopped by the onset of winter, just as Kane had predicted. They had built a small hut for themselves and tried to survive by hunting, but it was not long before they began to starve. They had tried to obtain food from the local band of Inuit but were not very successful. Eventually they were forced to admit defeat and return to the brig.[24]

The return of these men was, for Kane, a vindication, and he made a great show of welcoming these prodigal crew members back into the fold, but he was not about to let them forget their sins. He shared provisions equally with the returning deserters but had them mess separately and did not recognize them as officially rejoining the expedition, for this would have been "an injury to the brave men who had abided to their trust."[25] The "truant and the faithful" would thus form two separate groups on board, with the further distinction of Blake and Godfrey, who, "being outlawed by their late associates have to eat by themselves."[26] Apparently these two had been even less willing to submit to the authority of the withdrawal party officers than they had been to submit to Kane's.

In such a state of division the second Grinnell Expedition spent its second winter. The men were constantly hungry, cold, and sick. Most had scurvy, and Kane's sick list usually included a majority of the crew. Uncharacteristically, Kane was among the healthiest of them all, since he supplemented his diet by eating rats, while the others refrained from this delicacy. Needless to say, they were not the happy family bound together by camaraderie and national pride in discovery that Kane had envisioned at the start of the voyage. They barely tolerated one another. Back in November, Goodfellow had ceased to be on speaking terms with any other officer, and throughout the winter Wilson lay in his bunk with swollen legs, venting his anger at Kane and the others into his private journal.[27]

According to Petersen, during that final winter "Dr. Kane was often out of humour and unkind in his treatment."[28] He had lost many of his qualms against corporal punishment and resorted to striking Godfrey and Blake with a belaying pin to keep them in line.[29] He also threatened to shoot Hans Hendrik if he did not obey orders, according to Petersen.[30] Kane's most drastic resort to corporal punishment, however, came in his dealings with William Godfrey, who remained healthy and strong. In the middle of March, while Hendrik was on a journey to Etah, ninety miles to the south, in his increasingly paranoid mind Kane became convinced that Blake and Godfrey were planning to escape from the brig, waylay Hendrik, steal the few remaining dogs, and go off to live with the Inuit. It is unclear what evidence he had for this suspicion, but he began to keep a close eye on them. On the nineteenth of March, Kane claims to have discovered the two of them trying to leave the brig. He confronted them and confined them to the brig, yet despite this, Godfrey soon escaped. "His intention," wrote Kane, "undoubtedly is to reach Etah Bay, and, robbing Hans of sledge and dogs, proceed south to Netlik."[31]

Godfrey's account of what happened is quite different. He claimed that he had become aware that Hans Hendrik was romantically involved with a woman named Choolakee at Etah: "Hans entrusted to me the secret of his love, and declared his intention to elope from the brig at the first opportunity."[32] Godfrey was not willing to inform on Hendrik, yet he became concerned when Hendrik left for Etah with the dogs and sledge for much-needed meat. Godfrey began to fear that Hendrik was not planning to come back, so he left the brig for Etah to persuade him to return and to try to get some provisions.[33]

Godfrey's version of events is supported in part by his subsequent actions. After a difficult ninety-mile trek on foot, he found Hendrik at Etah claiming to be sick. Instead of stealing the dogs and running off to Netlik, as Kane thought he would do, Godfrey secured a sledgeload of meat from the people of Etah and returned to the brig with the dogs. Kane's and Godfrey's accounts of what happened next do not vary significantly, except in the motive attributed to Godfrey's actions. Returning with the sledge, he stopped about fifty yards from the *Advance,* where he was greeted by Bonsall. The seaman claimed he was not prepared to go on board until he "was assured of meeting with friendly treatment."[34] Kane and Bonsall went out to meet Godfrey on the ice. Godfrey offered up the meat and said he would then return to Etah. Kane claimed that Godfrey was returning to live at Etah, while Godfrey claimed that he was only going back for more provisions. Kane, who was holding his pistol, demanded that the sailor return to the brig, but he refused. At this point Kane handed his pistol to Bonsall and went back to the brig for irons in which to confine the supposed deserter. Godfrey, however, was not willing to be treated as a prisoner, so, leaving the sledge, meat, and dogs with Bonsall, he turned to leave on foot despite Bonsall's threats to shoot. As Godfrey ran off, Bonsall fired, but the pistol "failed at the cap." Kane, then on the deck of the brig, "jumped at once to the gun-stand; but my first rifle, affected by the cold, went off in the act of cocking, and a second, aimed in haste a long but practicable distance, missed the fugitive. He made good his escape before we could lay hold of another weapon."[35]

To Kane, his unsuccessful attempt to shoot one of his men was a justifiable action by a commander to discipline a mutinous and dangerous crew member, while to Godfrey it was attempted murder. He was acting entirely outside of Kane's authority, but there is no credible evidence that he planned to harm Hendrik and steal the dogs as Kane believed. Godfrey was refusing to recognize Kane's authority any longer, but by bringing the crew the meat they needed, he showed that he still had the best interests of his shipmates in mind. Godfrey felt that after the abortive withdrawal, when Kane gave permission to leave the expedition, he was no longer subject to Kane's orders.[36]

Godfrey went back to Etah on foot, but eventually both he and Hendrik returned to the brig. Kane claimed that he took Godfrey back as a prisoner, while Godfrey says that he agreed to return when Kane came to Etah and asked him as a friend to go back. However much the two feared, disliked, and misunderstood each other, they must have realized, as spring approached, that if either wished to return home, they would have to work together.[37] The Inuit hunter Hans Hendrik, however, did not need Kane as much as Kane needed him, and he took the opportunity the following month to leave the expedition for good—a fact that further supports Godfrey's account. Kane reported his disappearance in *Arctic Explorations*: "Hans the faithful—yet, I fear, the faithless—was last seen upon a native sledge, driving south from Peteravik, with a maiden at his side, and professedly bound to a new principality at Uwarrow Suk-suk, high up Murchison's Sound. Alas for Hans, the married man."[38]

MEANWHILE, far to the south, Maggie Fox was impatient for Kane's return. She was not the only one worried about him. Kane's friends and family, and the friends and families of all the expedition members, looked for the return of the expedition each October as the Arctic sailing season ended. In October 1853 there was some thought that the expedition might arrive, but all knew that such an early end to the voyage was unlikely. Most expected that this expedition, like the first Grinnell Expedition, would spend one winter in the Arctic and return around October 1854. Fox even wrote an exuberant letter to Kane from Crookville, which she sent to Grinnell in New York to give to Kane in case he returned in the autumn of 1854.[39] "Oh! My dear Ly I am so happy with the idea of writing you once more," she wrote. She told him to visit Ellen Walter, then have Walter accompany him when he came for her in Crookville. Fox had it all planned. She assumed that Kane would take her to meet his family, but she was nervous at the prospect: "I would much rather go from here to Mrs. Walter's than to Judge Kane's. You know I am not at all acquainted with your father and mother. When you come after me Mrs. Walter, yourself and I will call on Mrs. Leiper, and then dear Ly I would rather go to Mrs. Walter's."[40] Fox was looking forward to announcing her engagement with Kane, indicating that no one had yet been told of it: "I often think dear Ly of your sacred promise, that is if all things met with your expectations. May I not tell that to my dear true friend Mrs. Walter? She will not mention it." She also boasted of her dedication to her lessons while he was gone. Clearly her goal was to please Kane: "I am getting along finely with all my studies. Are you not pleased? I shall commence German in a few weeks. Now dear Ly do I pray hurry hurry home. I will not let you go on another expedition very soon."[41]

In this letter, which is found in Kane's papers rather than in *The Love-Life of Dr. Kane*, Fox also took delight in teasing Kane, especially about their coming marriage and his insistence on secrecy. At one point she joked: "Ly what do you think I have done?—I have made a proposal—to—Mrs. Walter. There: you thought I meant some gentleman." Then she teased: "Some lady asked Mrs. Walter if she thought that you had any idea of marrying me. Mrs. Walter told her she thought not. If anyone should ask me that question what should I say? You say and I know it is very wrong to tell stories. I think I had better not answer the question at all."[42] Unfortunately for Maggie Fox, Kane did not return at the end of the 1854 season as she hoped, so the plans she made in the letter never transpired. The letter sat unread for over a year.

Fox was not the only one waiting for Elisha Kane's return. As the autumn of 1854 came and went, Kane's friends worried. Reports reached the United States from the whaling fleet in Baffin Bay that conditions had been unusually severe the preceding winter and summer. Some began rightly to suspect that the *Advance* had become permanently frozen in.[43] Would Kane become another Franklin—lost forever in the sublime Arctic regions? His friends and family hoped not, but they feared it was a possibility. Over the winter, plans were formed for a relief mission. This time Congress was willing to contribute more generously than it had before for Arctic exploration, appropriating $150,000 for the effort. Henry Grinnell and Judge Kane helped prepare the mission, which also had the full support of the navy.[44]

The relief expedition was organized over the winter for a planned departure in the spring of 1855. It consisted of two vessels, the brig *Release* and a new steam propeller, appropriately named *Arctic*. These vessels were put under the command of Lieutenant Henry Hartstene, an experienced naval officer from South Carolina. Hartstene was no stranger to exploration. He had been part of the famed Wilkes Exploring Expedition years before, when he had served alongside Edwin DeHaven, commander of the first Grinnell Expedition, when they were both midshipmen. Hartstene's second in command on the *Release* was William Lovell, a veteran of the first Grinnell Expedition. Kane's youngest brother, Dr. John Kane, went along as surgeon to the expedition.[45]

When the two vessels left New York on May 31, 1855, they took with them letters addressed to the lost explorers from loved ones they had not seen in two years. A letter from Thomas Kane to his brother is perhaps the most interesting. Thomas was the brother with whom Elisha most often discussed his hopes for his career and his reputation. Tom Kane knew his older brother had ambition and often acted the role of adviser in that cause. Thus Thomas's letter focused on the progress and status of his brother's reputation at home during his absence, which contrasted sharply with the actual experience of the expedition to that point.[46]

Thomas informed Elisha that he had become a hero in the eyes of the American public. Interest in the explorers had increased throughout the country during their absence. As a result, Elisha had become "the child of your whole country and not of any part of it." Thomas told him that, although in the past the Northeast had been the region most interested in the Franklin search and most willing to contribute to Arctic exploration, that was no longer the case. In the effort to secure funds for a relief expedition, the southerners in Congress had been instrumental in getting support approved.[47] In the midst of the turbulent 1850s, the decade before the Civil War, this was one of the few issues about which the different sections could agree.

Not only was Kane now the darling of every part of the country, but also his reputation was strong with every type of American. "It has been the same with the different classes of persons," wrote Thomas. "You have had the misses of the Northern Young Ladies Seminaries with you, but you have also carried the most ugly gritty of your own naval men." Not just the medical corps of the navy, which supported him before, but the officers, too, were now his supporters and admirers: "They assert that they must rescue you as a brother officer—a gallant friend—an honor to their own corp: this has become the accepted statement of the affair, and is the footing on which it, and you thereby, must hereafter stand."[48]

"It is all plain sailing with you now," Thomas happily declared, with an appropriately nautical metaphor. "When a nation makes a pet of a man, all it requires of him is to take his petting gracefully." Thomas detailed the exact nature of Elisha's new reputation, which combined expertise in Humboldtean science with heroic manly style and panache: "Your tack will be the official scientific—Science with the brevet of sword, spunk, and gentlemanly savoir faire—Hurrah Horse and Head of Bureau.—Land Turtle Maury, or American Humboldt—and so forth." He then went on to advise his brother exactly how to manage this newfound celebrity: "You have the chance of pushing this thing to its very farthest.—A worthy aim for the ambition of any man. But a little study of concise sham modesty of speech in public and a composed and courteous demeanor universally, will compass more than all the geodic schemes &

computations your head will ever master." Then, with the recognition that reputations are made as much as they are earned, Thomas advised his brother to pay heed to the growing power of American mass culture: "If as an act of grace only, remember your newspaper friends. Respect au fardeau!—It is thy who made us and not we ourselves." He counseled Elisha to oblige the reporters who would meet him on his arrival home and to be generous with his acknowledgments to his colleagues.[49]

Thomas Kane's advice was sound. Even though he knew nothing of the actual progress of the expedition when he wrote the letter, he knew how it must be portrayed to the public in order to be considered a success. Elisha Kane and his crew could not arrive home in New York and tell the whole truth of the expedition. They could not tell a story of conflict, strife, and near mutiny. They had to return as comrades. The expedition would be judged as a whole, with Kane as its personification.

UNAWARE OF THE activity on their behalf back at home, the men on board the *Advance* now directed their hopes toward the spring, when they planned to make their escape. Kane realized that they could not wait for the brig to be released from the ice as they had the previous summer. Instead he planned to abandon the *Advance* in May and haul their two whaleboats on sledges until they reached open water to the south. They would then sail to Upernavik. As spring approached, Kane organized the men in making preparations. At this Kane was at his best. His abilities as an organizer helped ensure the men's survival. He set a date for departure, May 17, and all were set to work getting ready for that day. Some sewed warm garments, while others packaged bundles of provisions or secured the whaleboats on the sledges. When at last the day of departure came, they began hauling the two boats with all their gear over the ice. Four of the men were not well enough to help in this work, so Kane shuttled them on a sledge by dog team to a hut several miles to the south.

While the men dragged the boats, Kane tended to the sick and did what he could to obtain large quantities of fresh meat from the Inuit in Etah. As usual, the assistance of the Inuit was instrumental to the men's well-being. With this important help, the journey southward went better than any of them had expected, and their spirits began to improve, as did their health, as they were now eating large quantities of nutrient-rich raw meat. The journey was not without its dangers, though. One day, as they neared the open water, one of the runners of the sledge carrying the boat *Hope* broke through the ice. Ohlsen supported the sledge while the rest pulled it up onto safer ice, but in the process he suffered internal injuries, and a few days later he died.[50]

On June 16, four days after burying Ohlsen, Kane reported: "Our boats are at the open water. We see its deep indigo horizon, and hear its roar against the icy beach. Its scent is in our nostrils and our hearts."[51] Two days later the men bade good-bye to their friends from Etah and set out on the water. In the weeks that followed, the two small boats made their way southward along the coast of Greenland. They had to contend with ice, storms, and cold temperatures, and had to stop often to wait out bad weather or restock their fresh food supply, but finally, on August 3, they arrived at Upernavik. From there they took passage to Godhaven, where they learned of the expedition that had been sent out to find them. A few days later they met up with this expedition, and at last in October 1855 they were welcomed back in New York.

When the men of the second Grinnell Expedition had left New York Harbor in the springtime of 1853, they had shared a feeling of pride in being part of an American scientific and humanitarian mission to explore new worlds and rescue a lost explorer. They had shared in the popular American curiosity about the unknown, and they had demonstrated to the world how diverse elements of American society could come together in pursuit of a cause—in this case geographic discovery. When they sailed off into the Arctic, they represented a unified American nationalism projecting itself out into the world.

The experiences of the second Grinnell Expedition, however, did not live up to these expectations. They did not remain a unified party of men driven by enthusiasm. As they left behind the cultural milieu that created their mission, social relations broke down and their differences cracked their veneer of unity. As Carl Petersen observed, the "heterogeneous elements" on board the *Advance* did not live in concord with one another.[52] Now, as they returned to the world they had left more than two years before, they faced the job of representing their experiences to the nation. In this Elisha Kane met with his greatest success.

ON THURSDAY, October 11, 1855, the members of the second Grinnell Expedition arrived in New York as passengers aboard the ships that had been sent to find them. The steamship *Union* was the first to bring the news that the survivors were on board the *Release* and the *Arctic* below

Sandy Hook, approaching Manhattan Island. As the ships came up the river, word quickly spread throughout the city that the lost explorers had returned. "An army of reporters ran to the docks," reported the *New York Daily Times* the next morning. According to the *Sun*, the news "spread with rapidity through the city, while the telegraph wafted it to near and distant parts of the country."[53] After making port, the members of the expedition talked to reporters on board the *Release* and the *Arctic*, then retired, followed by the throng of reporters and curious onlookers, to the Astor Hotel.[54]

The next morning all six columns on the front page of the *Daily Times* were devoted to the returned expedition. "Dr. Kane Home Again," read the headline. The story that followed recounted the progress of the expedition, which many had given up for lost. While it acknowledged all of the returned explorers, naturally Kane, as leader, received most of the attention. The newspapers all told of the hardships the expedition had faced, and of the strange scenes and the strange people they had met with in their travels. The reports told of the Open Polar Sea, which had, it seemed, at last been found by Morton and Hendrik, and of the skill and benevolence of the expedition's leader, who, according to the papers, was held in the highest esteem by all of his men. The *Herald* reported that the members of the expedition spoke of Kane in the most complimentary terms: "Nothing was too high for his scientific research, nor too mean for his humane action. He proved himself, indeed, a model commander."[55] The *Rochester Daily American* went even further: "Between the Doctor and his men an almost fatherly feeling seemed to exist, they looking up to him with pride and veneration, feelings which he returned by an affection for them that was truly paternal."[56]

Some stories emphasized themes of American nationalism. The *New York Evening Express* boasted that the returned expedition had shown the world that "Yankee enterprise and Yankee hardihood are equal to that of British navigators in the field of adventure."[57] The *New York Daily Times* also expressed its view that the whole country deserved a share of the honors that the expedition had won. Americans were proud, said the *Times*, of "the generosity, energy and heroism of American enterprise and American skill."[58]

Most of the reports focused on exotic details. They described the unearthly Arctic landscape of glaciers and ice and the inhospitable conditions of the far north. To express the intensity of the cold, the papers repeated what one of the expedition members must have told them at the Astor House: "Whiskey froze in November."[59] For many reporters this one fact served to sum up all that the expedition had endured.

Although some papers acknowledged that the actual accomplishments of the expedition were slight, others hailed the discoveries of the Great Glacier of Humboldt and the Open Polar Sea as important achievements. All of the papers freely admitted that the original purpose of the expedition, the search for Franklin, had been rendered moot. While Kane was gone, remains of the Franklin Expedition had been discovered by the Scots-Canadian overland explorer John Rae, who had found the remnants in the possession of the Inuit in the region of the Boothia Peninsula. This was far from Smith Sound, where Kane was searching. The Inuit had told Rae that all of Franklin's crew were dead and added the unwelcome news that, in the end, the British explorers had taken to eating the flesh of their dead colleagues to survive. This was a disturbing revelation for the pride of the British Empire, but for Americans it served only to magnify the achievement of Kane's journey. To them, Kane had set off on a brave endeavor to bring aid to a lost navigator. Although he had not succeeded, he was ennobled by the attempt. That Kane, unlike Franklin, had come back alive added to his glory. The Americans had prevailed where the British had descended into cannibalism.[60]

Surprisingly, at the same time that reports celebrated Kane's expedition, many papers called for an end to Arctic voyages. The *Troy Daily Whig* approved of the expedition on humanitarian grounds and rejoiced in Kane's return, but also called the attempt to discover a Northwest Passage "ridiculous."[61] Many felt that only the humane desire to rescue Franklin had justified American Arctic expeditions at all. Mere geographic curiosity was not worth the risk involved. The same article in the *New York Evening Express* that spoke with nationalistic pride of "Yankee enterprise and Yankee hardihood" also concluded that "with the return of Dr. Kane, we presume, ends, for this generation at least, those bootless excursions to the Arctic Seas. Human life enough has been sacrificed,—all for nothing, these few years past—to render any future enterprise of the kind, aught but the merest exhibition of human fatuity."[62] Even the *New York Daily Times*, which was giving unprecedented coverage to the returned expedition, "hoped that we shall not have many more Arctic Expeditions."[63]

WHILE ELISHA KANE was being heralded as a returned hero by the citizens of New York, Maggie Fox was staying at Ellen Walter's home at Clinton Place. She learned of Kane's arrival and heard the guns being fired on the waterfront in celebration of his return. According to Elizabeth Ellet, "All that evening, when it was known that Dr. Kane was in the city, they waited for the ring of the bell that should herald his visit."[64] But Kane did not arrive that night. Nor did he show up the next morning or all the next day. Ellen Walter, thinking that Kane must not know that Fox was in New York, sent a note to Henry Grinnell's home, where Kane was now staying. Meanwhile Fox, upset by Kane's neglect, went to her mother's home on Tenth Street.

Eventually word arrived for Fox that a carriage had pulled up in front of Walter's house on Clinton Place. Thinking that this was Kane, she went off to see him, but when she arrived, she found that the visitor had been Cornelius Grinnell, sent to inform Fox that the Kane family was up in arms about rumors circulating of an engagement between Elisha and Maggie Fox. Kane would come as soon as he could, said Grinnell. Moreover, reported Ellet, Grinnell had been sent by one of the Kanes (presumably Robert P. Kane, who had an eye for such detail) to "procure the letters addressed by Dr. Kane to Miss Fox, which he supposed to be in Mrs. Walter's keeping." As Fox was not there when Grinnell arrived, he had to leave without the letters.[65]

The following morning Kane finally arrived at Mrs. Walter's home to see Maggie Fox. Understandably, it had been difficult to slip away secretly from his family and his adoring admirers, so he had waited until the initial excitement of his return died down. Fox, her feelings nevertheless hurt by this delay, at first refused to see him, but finally she went downstairs to meet him. "The conversation was long, and Margaret listened patiently and kindly," reported Ellet, "though its purport was to inform her that all idea of their marriage must be indefinitely postponed on account of the violent opposition of Dr. Kane's family and relatives. For the present, they must be to each other only as sister and brother!" Kane then wrote out a statement alleging that the two of them had never intended to marry, but that their relationship was "merely friendly and fraternal." He asked Fox to copy it in her own handwriting and sign it to satisfy his family. This she did, according to Ellet, since "she wished to restore peace between him and his family."[66]

Ellet described this as a particularly dramatic scene, and she included a somewhat melodramatic dialogue between Fox, Kane, and Walter. Kane claimed that the written statement was only to satisfy his mother. They then called in Mrs. Walter as a witness, who read the note and then asked, "Maggie is this so?" Fox replied in tears, "No—no—it is not so! Doctor Kane knows it is not!" Kane, angered, told her, "You are not the Maggie I took you for."[67] While much of this must be taken as the construction of Elizabeth Ellet for an audience that enjoyed sentimental romance, the gist of the matter was that Kane had broken off the engagement, and Fox had agreed not to hold him to his promise. These were the days when a promise of marriage was legally binding. If Maggie Fox chose to press the issue, it would have been an intolerable scandal coming at the worst possible time for Kane's reputation. Ellet certainly had an eye toward the legal ramifications of the story, even while she presented it as a fervid romance.

All this happened in the context of Kane's attempt to ride the wave of enthusiasm generated by his return. As his brother Thomas had told him, he was now being heralded as a noble hero. His future would depend on how well he cultivated that reputation. Ellet blamed Kane's rejection of Fox on pressures from his family. She observed that Kane was still financially dependent on his father and feared a disinheritance if he married against his father's wishes. This may have been partially true, but perhaps more important to Kane was his public reception. A romantic connection or marriage with a notorious spirit rapper could damage his heroic image. He could not afford any connection that would put his judgment in doubt. Worse still would be any sort of scandal.

Fueling the growth of the antebellum penny press was a growing interest in the personal and sexual lives of public figures. Curiosity about the private lives of famous people was quickly becoming fair game in the fierce competition for newspaper sales. The sexual relationship between the murdered prostitute Helen Jewett and her alleged killer had been an integral theme of the penny press coverage of that notorious case. More common were stories of divorce, elopement, marital discord, abandonment, and seduction. These topics rated a small story if the people involved were ordinary citizens, but when they were publicly known figures, the curiosity about private matters was magnified. Recently, the highly public divorce case of the famed actor Edwin Forrest and his wife, Catherine, had been splattered across the papers. Catherine Forrest's alleged affairs with men such as the *Home Journal* editor Nathaniel P. Willis were recounted in lurid detail for all to read.[68] As the historian Thomas Baker has observed of the 1850s, "Now more than ever, celebrity scandal figured, along with celebrity gossip, as an engrossing form of entertainment for an audience raised to expect insight into the sinews and heart of private character."[69]

Kane and his family must have feared that accounts of his own dubious relationship with a spirit rapper would find their way into the penny press. The same forces of mass culture that had made the Fox sisters a nationwide sensation, and were making Kane into a national scientific hero, could drag them both down into the depths of notoriety. Nobody wanted that.

The Kanes would have been even more sensitive to public opinion because Elisha was not the only member of the family in the news. His father, the judge, had recently handed down a highly controversial ruling in the case of an abolitionist named Passimore Williamson, who was accused of harboring a runaway slave. In accordance with the divisive Fugitive Slave Laws of 1850, Judge Kane ordered Williamson to produce this missing "property." On Williamson's refusal, Judge Kane jailed him on the charge of contempt. To antislavery northerners this seemed to represent control of the nation's courts by the southern "Slave Power." Throughout October and November, newspaper stories of Dr. Kane's return from the Arctic appeared side by side with stories about Judge Kane and the Passimore Williamson case. Fortunately for Elisha, the father's unpopularity did not seem to affect the son.[70]

Rumors of Kane's connection with the Maggie Fox were another matter entirely, and his fears of scandal were realized within a week of his return. On October 19 the *Troy Daily Whig* printed a seemingly innocent announcement: "A gentleman from this city informs us that Dr. Kane, of the Arctic Expedition, is soon to be married to Miss Margaretta Fox, the second sister of the 'Fox girls' at whose residence in Hydesville, Wayne county in this State, the spirit rappings were first manifested. Dr. K. became acquainted with the Fox family in New York. During his absence Miss Fox, his said-to-be-affianced, has been attending a young ladies' school at Philadelphia."[71] While rumors had been circulating before this announcement, this was the first public link between the two. As was the practice, other papers then picked up the story. Within a week the announcement was reprinted by the *Sun* in New York.[72]

There followed a series of claims and retractions concerning the relationship, revealing various behind-the-scenes interests. On October 31 the highly respectable *New York Evening Post* brought up the rumor of an engagement but emphatically stated that "we have the best reason for saying [it] is without a shadow of foundation."[73] the *New York Daily Times* reprinted the *Post*'s denial of an engagement the next day, but two days later reversed itself.[74] On November 3 the *Times* reported that it had been "confidently assured" that the story of an engagement was true, adding that Maggie Fox had given up spirit rapping and "is said to be a beautiful, pure-minded and amiable girl."[75] Then within two days the *Times* once again changed its position, printing a retraction that stated that the *Post*'s version was indeed correct: "The parties who so 'confidently assured' us that the *Post* was in error, have announced to us that they themselves were mistaken." The rumors of an engagement, it declared, were "utterly unfounded."[76] In *The Love-Life of Dr. Kane,* Ellet explained that, after the *Times* reported the rumor to be true, "some party furious in the Kane interest . . . threatened vengeance against the person who had made the assertion."[77] Thus the retraction.

Meanwhile, Horace Greeley at the *Tribune* expressed his distaste that all these rumors were making their way into print. His reaction demonstrates how the boundaries of reporting on the private lives of public figures were still in flux. Greeley knew Maggie and her whole family, and he was also a friend of Thomas Kane's. He had reported on the careers of both Maggie Fox and Elisha Kane frequently in his paper, but he felt that reporting on their private relationship was crossing the line. Greeley made a career out of satisfying public curiosity, yet this "impertinent curiosity," was different. "We wish the several journals which have originated reports, *pro* and *con,* respecting the persons above named," wrote Greeley, "would consider whether they have or have not therein perverted their columns to the gratification of an impertinent curiosity." Greeley asked, "What right has the public to know anything about an 'engagement' or non-engagement between these young people?" Perhaps, he said, if the United States were a hereditary monarchy and Kane or Fox were royalty, the public might have a right to know of their plans, "but in the actual state of the case, such intimations as have appeared in the journals are not to be justified." Greeley concluded unequivocally, "Whether they have been, are, may be, are not, or will not be, 'engaged,'—can be nobody's business but their own and that of their near relatives."[78]

Maggie Fox apparently agreed. The one thing that prevented a true scandal from erupting was her steadfast refusal to allow her friends to talk with reporters about her private affairs. She, more than most, knew both the power and the dangers of the penny press. The last thing she wanted was a public debate in the papers about her private life. No more articles asserting an engagement appeared, although denials did, suggesting that the rumors persisted in private circles. Kane's family and friends were much more willing to talk with the papers. On November 19 the "benevolent gentleman" version of Kane's relationship with Fox came to the fore. A widely reprinted article, which appeared in the *Philadelphia Pennsylvanian* and the *New York Evening Post*, told the story Kane had so carefully fabricated before he left on his expedition:

> Sometime previous to the departure of Dr. Kane on his last expedition, a subscription was started in New York by a number of liberal, kind hearted gentlemen, for the purpose of educating one of the Fox sisters, a remarkably bright, intelligent girl, and worthy of a better employment than "spirit rapping." Dr. Kane was applied to, and feeling somewhat interested, from pure motives of humanity, subscribed with a sailor's liberality. On his return, by invitation of the gentleman superintending her education, he called to witness the improvement of his protégé; and from this simple incident has arisen the engagement story.

The article went on to discuss the benevolent generosity of all of the men in the Kane family. The four eldest Kane men were held up as models of virtuous paternalism. Apparently Judge Kane, Thomas Kane, Robert Patterson Kane, and Dr. Kane had a history of helping the unfortunate, which the writer greatly admired.[79]

Despite repudiating her to his family and the wider public, Kane continued to court Maggie Fox. Her mother and many of her friends advised her not to see him anymore, but Kane pressed the issue. He told Fox that now they were to be like brother and sister. That way he could continue to advise her on her conduct while holding on to the convenient fiction that theirs was not a romantic love. Kane wanted to continue to exert authority over Fox, but he was unwilling to make any sacrifices himself or go against the wishes of his family. Mrs. Fox and her daughter's friends saw that he was asking too much. Fearing for Maggie's reputation, they insisted that all communication between the two end. Maggie Fox seems for a time to have agreed, and she offered to return all of Kane's letters.

These love letters would become an important element in the drama that unfolded in the weeks and years that followed. Kane was clearly worried about them, since they revealed his true relationship with Fox. He feared their being made public, yet he was also ambivalent about asking Fox to return them, for that act would acknowledge a final break. So he vacillated. When Fox offered to send him the letters, he wrote: "As to your dear generous offer of returning my letters, I tremble—not at the letters—but at the fear that you have not understood me. I have never distrusted you, or even asked for those notes. With them or without them you were always the same to me." But he also made clear that he did want them. He dreaded the impertinent curiosity of strangers: "I only felt and feared that suspicious, designing friends or enemies might see and abuse these letters and give me pain and trouble. I fear for them and I fear for you. I confess that their absence makes me unhappy; but as I am an honorable gentleman, I will not deprive you of them, or give you pain by requesting them." Of course, if she wished to return them to him, he would take them: "If of your own free choice you send them to me, I will regard it as the highest proof of trust and love."[80] Ellet claimed that Fox subsequently offered Kane the letters more than once, but he refused to take them.[81]

During the winter, Kane was able once again to insinuate himself into the good graces of the Fox family and make regular visits to Maggie. Despite periodic objections by Mrs. Fox and Maggie's friends, by April the two had renewed their engagement. According to Ellet, Kane declared that he "cared no longer . . . for the world's opinion or its sneers," but he also insisted once again on secrecy, telling no one but the Fox family that they were once again engaged.[82]

The renewed engagement was on a more intimate basis than their previous relationship. The main source for this period is *The Love-Life of Dr. Kane*, in which Ellet is careful not to suggest anything scandalous, but there are indications that the two began to spend more time alone together. Maggie Fox had moved back into her mother's home in New York City, where Kate continued to hold séances. While these were going on, Kane and Fox often retreated to a third floor room which Fox had set up as a parlor. One can only speculate whether these meetings ever evolved into a sexual relationship, but the surviving evidence indicates that Kane was driven more by a desire for control than for sex. As in his dealings with his men on the expedition and with the Inuit of Smith Sound, Kane's overriding desire was to have others recognize his benevolent authority. He wanted Maggie Fox to yield control to him, and in this he was largely successful, since Fox in turn wanted the stability and respectability that Kane offered. To attain respectability, however, she had to give up much of the freedom she had known.

IT WAS NO coincidence that the story of Kane and Fox's relationship became public little more than a week after his return from the Arctic. Stories about Kane had appeared in the newspapers regularly for much of the fall and into the winter. Most dealt with the accomplishments of the expedition, but since Kane had become a celebrity, any story about him was of interest. Now that he was safely at home, the papers had fun recounting a story of his supposed death which had appeared in a Boston paper just days before his return.[83] Another paper jokingly reported a story about a medium who had claimed months before to have communicated with Kane's spirit.[84] Many stories described the numerous honors being bestowed on him. The Press Club gave a dinner in his honor.[85] He met the president. He and his officers were photographed by Matthew Brady.[86] Even Kane's dog "Toodles" became the object of public curiosity. "Poor Toodles had a narrow escape!" wrote the *Troy Daily Whig*. As the survivors of the expedition were traveling by open boat on Baffin Bay, they were running out of food. Toodles was the last remaining dog, and the men were hungry. "The pistol was already loaded, and the stew pan prepared which was to convert the shaggy body of Toodles into a savory ragout, when Providential interference! one of the party made his appearance with a seal which he had just captured." Toodles was spared.[87]

Kane had reached a new level of celebrity. In past representations of Kane, the Arctic had been the primary theme, as spirit rapping was with Fox. Upon Kane's return from his second Arctic voyage, his personal celebrity became paramount. Any story about him, his expedition, or even his dog was newsworthy. The coverage changed from stories about his expedition to stories about his private life. His earlier exploits in India, Africa, and the Philippines were now rehashed for the general public. His became the modern type of celebrity, a fame that transcended his actual achievements and focused instead, with sometimes "impertinent curiosity," on his personality and private life.

This was not an unforeseeable result of his earlier attempts to cultivate a reputation by mixing science and sensation. The antebellum culture of curiosity made an effort to combine education and progress with entertainment, but such a combination could also lead to the celebration of personality over substance.[88] Whether he liked it or not, Kane's private life was just as much a part of his public reputation as was his knowledge of geology, botany, or oceanography.

9

Becoming a Hero of Science

Science Weeps, Humanity Weeps, the World Weeps.
Pennsylvania Inquirer, March 13, 1857

WHEN ELISHA KANE returned to his native shores in the autumn of 1855, few would have guessed that he had less than a year and a half to live. Kane's health had always been poor, but he returned from the Arctic in better condition than usual. He commented to one friend, "My health is almost absurd: I have grown like a walrus."[1] At thirty-five he seemed fit and ready to embark on the next phase of his life.

His chief priority at this time, when he was not embroiled in romantic escapades with Maggie Fox, was to write an account of the second Grinnell Expedition. He wanted to capitalize on the attention given to the expedition's belated return by writing a narrative that would secure his place among the famed Arctic explorers of his day. In fact, he had begun to edit his journal of the expedition on board the rescue ship *Release* even before arriving in New York.

Soon he had a publisher as well. Judge Kane, who helped manage his son's business affairs, had not been satisfied with the handling of Kane's first book by Harper Brothers. That book had done reasonably well, and was praised by the likes of George Templeton Strong, who wrote in his diary that it was "far more attractive than any narrative of northern voyages and discovery that I've met."[2] But the judge and the doctor decided to try a different publisher this time, Childs & Peterson of Philadelphia.[3]

Meanwhile, a curious public was impatiently awaiting the narrative. Notices about the coming publication began to appear in the papers as early as November 1855, less than a month after the expedition returned. The *Philadelphia Public Ledger* reported Kane's contract with Childs & Peterson and described the contents of the anticipated account: it was to be a personal narrative rather than a scientific treatise. Kane called it "a centre-table book, fit as well for the eyes of children as of refined women."[4] The book would also include "a variety of scientific papers, and be illustrated with maps and several hundred engravings."[5] These engravings were being prepared by a well-known artist, James Hamilton, from sketches drawn by Kane.

Apparently no expense would be spared in the production of the two octavo volumes. The *Public Ledger* placed the estimated cost at $20,000.[6] Later reports, on the eve of publication the following autumn, reported that Childs & Peterson had already signed up 30,000 advance subscribers. Gambling that the book would be very popular, they planned to print 100,000 copies for the first edition.[7] Their confidence was well founded. Within the next few years the book sold close to 150,000 copies.[8]

Arctic Explorations in the Years 1853, '54, '55 became Elisha Kane's greatest legacy. Eagerly anticipated, it was even more eagerly consumed. In it Kane told the story of long dark winters in a strange and forbidding Arctic landscape. He recounted the suffering of the men from scurvy and frozen toes and fingers, and how they all were kept alive that second winter by the treaty he negotiated with the Inuit at Etah. Kane's book provided interesting and amusing ethnographic details about the lives of these strange "Esquimaux," and portrayed the dedicated process of gathering scientific data on tides, temperature, and other natural phenomena on a daily basis in harsh conditions.

More interesting for readers, however, *Arctic Explorations* told of the expedition's small, often sickly young commander, who used his medical knowledge, ingenuity, and perseverance to bring all but three of his men home alive. It was the story of a leader who faced amazing hardships and overcame a hostile nature. This was a man who had been raised with every advantage of class and position, yet who gave it all up for the sake of advancing human knowledge. Rather than an account of a failed mission that left three men dead for no tangible results, readers got a tale of a noble quest, in which a small group of survivors triumphed over adversity. The attempt to find Franklin and to sail the Open Polar Sea had failed, but for antebellum Americans, there was still value in the sacrifices made in what seemed a virtuous cause.

Arctic Explorations followed the same general pattern as Kane's first book, *The U.S. Grinnell Expedition*, covering a wide range of both practical and scientific subjects within the context of a narrative of exploration. As one reviewer noted, "The monotony of events connected with a winter in the Arctic regions is a good deal relieved in Dr. Kane's work by the little vignettes that illustrate such simple topics as storing provisions, training dogs, and drawing sledges."[9] In both books, Kane satisfied his readers' curiosity about countless aspects of the polar regions, describing in detail what he and his men did and how they survived. But *Arctic Explorations* also differed from Kane's earlier work in two important regards. First of all, it added ethnography to the list of sciences he pursued. Kane had only briefly encountered the Inuit on his first voyage, but on the second they played a central role. Detailed descriptions of Inuit life made up some of the most interesting parts of the book. Second, Kane intensified his emphasis on human suffering in the face of a terrifying yet wondrous landscape. Although danger and privation had played a part in the first expedition, it could not compare with what the second expedition endured. Popular interest revolved in large part around the explorers' suffering in the face of unprecedented adversity.

On the second expedition, Kane and his men had come to know the Polar Inuit intimately. His account of these people, however, was marked by lighthearted condescension. He combined sincere admiration for them with contempt, seemingly unaware of the contradiction between the racist ideology of his day and the obvious fact that his expedition owed its survival to the knowledge and skill of these northern hunters. Unlike earlier Arctic explorers, Kane had planned from the very start of the expedition to emulate Inuit ways as much as possible. He freely acknowledged this to his readers. While seamen of the Royal Navy continued to dress in woolens for their Arctic expeditions, Kane and his men adopted the Inuit dress of furs. Like the Inuit, Kane planned to use dogs rather than men to haul sledges. Rather than relying solely on stored provisions, he intended to supplement the crew's diet as much as possible with nutritious fresh meat. British explorers hunted mainly for sport. Kane planned to hunt for food as the Inuit did. That was why he hired Hans Hendrik. In *Arctic Explorations*, Kane explained to his readers all the advantages of Inuit ways. Furs were warmer; dogs had more endurance; fresh meat helped ward off scurvy.

In the face of harsh conditions, Kane explained, he and his men came to emulate the Inuit more closely as time passed. During their second winter they packed the cabin in the *Advance* with moss, converting it into an imitation of the stone structures in Etah. Kane and the others often joined the Inuit in hunting seal and walrus. He even took to eating his meat raw as the Inuit did. By the final spring in the Arctic, Kane had remarked, "We are now more than half Esquimaux."[10]

Kane readily acknowledged the debt his expedition owed to the Inuit, but he retained the basic assumption of a dichotomy between savage and civilized life. Because the Arctic was itself a savage region, Kane and his men needed to take advantage of the skills of the "savage" men who inhabited it in order to survive. At the same time, in Kane's view, the Polar Inuit of Smith Sound were a backward people headed for eventual extinction. He observed, "They are a declining—almost an obsolete—people."[11] He spoke condescendingly of their filthy ways and portrayed them as a childlike and thieving lot, physically, intellectually, and morally inferior to the Americans. Thus Kane managed to hold on to his basic faith in white supremacy, despite extraordinary evidence to the contrary. One British reviewer noted the contradiction when he doubted Kane's belief in "the superior endurance of the white race," pointing out that Kane's men, "with superior shelter and better resources than the Esquimaux, [were] perishing away, where the Esquimaux were thriving."[12] American readers, however, seemed not to notice.[13]

Kane also repeatedly criticized the Inuit for being improvident, which is astonishing considering how often he had to go to them for food. He claimed that they never stored food, and as a result often had to endure famine. There were times of plenty, as when they collected birds that nested by the thousands in nearby cliffs in the summertime, but these were not taken advantage of, according to Kane, to put food away for the scarce months of winter.[14] He does not explain why, despite the benefits of American planning, the Inuit usually had more food than he did.

Despite his ethnocentric notions, by the time the explorers left on their journey south, Kane was reflecting on the friendships they had formed with the northern hunters. He led his readers to feel pity rather than contempt for the Inuit. As in his relationship with Maggie Fox, Kane's admiration was mixed with a heavy dose of condescension. "My heart warms to these poor, dirty, miserable, yet happy beings," he wrote, "so long our neighbors, and of late so staunchly our friends."[15] He continued: "Whatever may have been the faults of these Esquimaux heretofore, stealing was the only grave one. Treachery they may have conceived, but the day of this has passed away." He concluded, "God knows that since they professed friendship, albeit the imaginary powers of the angekok-soak and the marvelous six-shooter which attested them may have had their influence, never have friends been more true."[16]

Readers were delighted by the tales of these quaint friends Kane had found amidst the icebergs. The *North American Review* devoted seven pages to the Inuit in its joint review of Kane's narrative and that of the Royal Navy captain Sir Edward Belcher.[17] Other reviewers did not fail to mention the unusual appearance and habits of the "Esquimaux," who, like the polar bear and the ice, were a part of the strange and wonderful Arctic landscape.

While for Kane and his men knowledge of Inuit ways had been a matter of life and death, for his readers back home the Inuit provided the thrill of a spectacle. Unlike the explorers, who merely ventured into the Arctic for a brief time, the Inuit lived, raised families, and died in the North. Theirs was a domestic world, familiar yet unfamiliar to the domestic world at home where Kane's book was consumed. Mentally venturing into the lives of these people allowed readers the voyeuristic thrill of experiencing Arctic life from the safety of their own parlors. With Kane as guide, one could venture out on a cultural excursion into the unfamiliar. One could experience the savage without ever leaving home.

Kane's narrative told the story of a small man with a small crew who ventured off in a little wooden brig to confront the worst a threatening nature had to offer. The David versus Goliath aspect of it appealed to antebellum readers. Kane triumphed over nature not by superior power but by using his wits and, more important, trusting in Providence to deliver him in the end. His focus was on the sublime grandeur of the polar regions in contrast to the insignificance and impotence of himself and his men.

As the literary scholars Chauncey Loomis and Francis Spufford have keenly observed, to British and American readers the Arctic was characterized by the sublime.[18] The sublime, as understood by the romantics, referred to awe-inspiring beauty on a grand scale. The sublime was unfamiliar, but it inspired passionate and often horrifying emotions. The strange vastness of the Arctic was certainly sublime. It had beauty and grandeur. It inspired awe, yet it also inspired terror. The landscape was magnificent, yet it also threatened imminent death to those who ventured into it. Through a compelling narrative and beautiful engravings, Kane presented his readers with a magnificent terror that thrilled them to the bone.

Elisha Kane knew how to tell a good story. One reviewer noted that "the scenes which [*Arctic Explorations*] describes are so vividly and vigorously brought before the reader, that there are few who sit down to the perusal of the narrative but will fancy, before they rise from the engrossing occupation, their own flesh paralyzed by the cold 100 degrees greater than frost, and their blood scurvy-filled by the four months' sunlessness."[19] Another called Kane's narrative "among the most stirring and the most fearful that have yet been recorded."[20] This same reviewer continued, "It is without comparison the most painfully interesting record of experience in wintering in the Far North that has ever yet been published."[21]

"Painful" is not usually a compliment, but for readers of *Arctic Explorations* the pain was a moral pleasure. The lesson they took away was that suffering in the face of adversity brought forth the noblest aspects of human character. In this sense, *Arctic Explorations* was a morality play, a modern *Pilgrim's Progress*. Like Christian in Bunyan's classic tale, Kane underwent trials and tribulations but grew morally stronger as a result. Many reviewers commented on this. "The Arctic search has been, in more respects than one, the school of character," wrote one in the *North American Review*. "It has shown what charm there is in perilous adventure to the human mind. Its dangers have been great, its hardships severe. It is remarkable to see what courage and capacity of calm endurance [the explorers] have developed."[22] Similarly, the *New York Daily Times* observed: "If we are to look for heroic and unsullied adventure anywhere at this time of day, we may search for it in the privations and purity of the atmosphere north of seventy degrees of latitude. There folly, we should think, would wither, and effeminacy expire."[23] Kane's suffering was authentic, it was noble, and it was selfless, not like the tawdry commercialism and political strife that marked the antebellum home front.

NEEDLESS TO SAY, Kane had not copied his journals for publication without some serious editing. Had he not done so, his readers would have learned that suffering had brought out the worst as well as the best in Kane and his men. He obscured the interpersonal strife that had plagued the expedition. He removed all critical references to his fellow officers, omitting his dissatisfaction with John Wilson and Henry Goodfellow and his conflicts with Carl Petersen. Of course, he could not ignore the moment in the story when half his crew abandoned him and the brig to try to escape their icy prison in the fall of 1854, but he could interpret it as he saw fit. Gone were his fantasies of administering a beating to Sonntag and Hayes. Kane was careful to hide his resentment of what he had thought of as betrayal at the time. Instead, he depicted the officers of the withdrawal party as wayward children who ran into trouble because they did not follow their commander's advice but were welcomed back into the fold upon their return. Hayes, Sonntag, and Petersen all played prodigal sons to Kane's forgiving father.

The crew did not all receive the same kind treatment in *Arctic Explorations* as the officers. Blake and Godfrey were portrayed as dangerous and unpredictable men who often taxed their benevolent commander's patience. It was Godfrey who bore the brunt of Kane's criticism, as if he alone had been the source of conflict and dissension in an otherwise happy and obedient family. This was what motivated Godfrey to respond with his own narrative, in which he portrayed himself in a better light. Kane's account was aimed at a middle-class readership, who would have been concerned about controlling the lower orders. Kane presented his attempts to control Godfrey's behavior as a microcosm of the problems of American society: How can a democratic leader rule his followers without resorting to force? In *Arctic Explorations,* Godfrey played the part of the unruly child—not fit to govern himself, yet unwilling to be governed by others. He represented the potential problem of a democratic society in which the lower classes fail to see the wisdom in deferring to their natural betters.

In short, Kane's self-presentation in *Arctic Explorations* demonstrated not the kind of leader he actually was but rather the kind of leader he wished to be. This is probably why it appealed so much to antebellum readers. He portrayed himself as a benevolent, paternal commander, admired and respected by his men. The reader witnessed him filling the men with confidence when they were in doubt, caring for them when they were ill, and instructing them when they lacked knowledge. According to his book, he led by example rather than by force. He appealed to the men's reason, and they followed him accordingly. He seemed the epitome of the democratic leader whose authority derives from his own superior abilities and skill. This paternal ideal existed in the minds of both southern slaveholders and northern employers, even if it did not exist in reality. Kane, in effect, successfully created in his writing the kind of fatherly relationship he and his society so often failed to create in real life.

Readers were drawn to the Kane they read about, seeing him as a morally upstanding example of true manhood. The *North American Review* noted, "No more gallant crew can be found than the company of Dr. Kane, and there could be no braver or better commander."[24] The *New York Daily Times* reviewer read *Arctic Explorations* "as a revelation of the genius of the man—for there was no mistaking the personal qualities which lived half masked behind the words. The sentences stood succinct, girt, the phrases of a man who lived in action. . . . There was not a particle of literary confectionery, but every page glittered with the transparent frost-work of the scenery which had inspired it."[25] Kane's words seemed to ring with the truth of authentic experience. It was art without artifice—or so his readers thought.[26]

There were a few voices of dissent, but they came mostly from the far side of the Atlantic. Some argued that Kane's claim about proving the Open Polar Sea theory was premature. They rightly observed that what Morton and Hendrik had sighted could have been merely a temporary local stretch of open water. Most critics, however, argued this point with respect. A different criticism of Kane came from the *North British Review*, in an article reprinted in America in *Eclectic Magazine*, which zeroed in on Kane's account of his troubles with Godfrey. It suggested that Kane viewed much of Godfrey's behavior "through the eyes of his imagination." Godfrey seemed to the reviewer to have been a valuable member of the expedition. Of Kane's attempt to shoot Godfrey, the writer noted that Kane was lucky he did not succeed, for then he would have been liable for prosecution for murder.[27] Such criticism, however, was the exception. Most observers on both sides of the Atlantic continued to shower Kane with admiration.

KANE FINISHED writing *Arctic Explorations* in the late summer of 1856. The uncharacteristically robust health he had enjoyed upon the expedition's return had not lasted. As the narrative was going to press in September, he wrote to his publisher, "The book, poor as it is, has been my coffin."[28] Toward the end of the summer, with work on the book done, he retired to a homeopathic spa in Brattleboro, Vermont, to try to regain his health, but he had too much to do to lie idle for long.[29] He did not yet realize how much of a success his book was going to be. At the time he only seemed beset by troubles.

One of these troubles was Wilson, the most discontented of his former officers, who was threatening to write a book of his own—one that Kane was vehemently trying to suppress.[30] There was also conflict in Congress over a bill proposing to purchase a number of copies of Kane's book to distribute to libraries, as had been done to help the sales of previous narratives of government-sponsored expeditions. The problem was that the second Grinnell Expedition had been privately funded. Afraid of the precedent this would set, Congress rejected the bill, though not without controversy. Kane's many admirers saw this as an insult to the expedition.

There was also continued discussion of further Arctic voyages, much of it inspired by the unexpected appearance of an abandoned Royal Navy ship, the *Resolute*, discovered by an American whaling ship crewless and adrift in Baffin Bay. The previous year, while locked in the pack ice in Lancaster Sound, it had been abandoned by Captain Henry Kellett of Sir Edward Belcher's search squadron. Its officers and crew had returned to England on board Belcher's other ships. It was thus a great embarrassment to the Royal Navy when the ship turned up intact the following year, having made the journey out of Lancaster Sound without the benefit of its crew. The American government bought the derelict ship from the whaling captain who found it, and then in an act of gallantry, and perhaps with a little smug satisfaction, offered to return it as a gift to the queen and the British people.[31]

Lady Jane Franklin, who had not yet given up the hope of finding more evidence of her lost husband, saw this as an opportunity. Her last appeals to the Admiralty to send out yet another expedition to search for further remains of her husband's lost expedition had been rejected on the grounds that no ship was available. The true reason, however, was that the Admiralty had realistically given up all hope of finding any survivors of the expedition and had removed Franklin and his officers from the navy lists. But now there was a ship, tested in Arctic conditions, which Lady Franklin hoped to put to her own use. She also thought that she knew the best person to send as its commander in case the Admiralty refused to provide Royal Navy officers: the bold American navy doctor who had recently returned from Smith Sound.[32] Kane was clearly flattered by Lady Franklin's faith in him, and he wanted to help her cause as best he could. Despite his failing health, he resolved to journey to England to promote another expedition. In the second week of October 1856, he left for England from New York on board the steamer *Baltic*, accompanied by his steward, William Morton, who remained his most faithful follower to the very end.[33]

MEANWHILE, Maggie Fox had spent much of August and September 1856 with her mother and Kate, visiting relatives in Canada, but by the end of September she was back in New York, as was Kane. In *The Love-Life of Dr. Kane*, Elizabeth Ellet relates that one day in early October, Kane came to Mrs. Fox's home on Twenty-second Street. He planned to take Maggie to get her photograph taken. A few times before this, according to Ellet, Kane had, in private, referred to Maggie Fox as his wife. On this day, Ellet writes, he did as well. "You know you are my own—my wife!" he told Maggie. Then, according to Ellet, he said: "Would you like me to repeat what I have said, formally, in the presence of your mother? Such a declaration, in the presence of witnesses, is sufficient to constitute a legal and binding marriage; a marriage as firm as if the ceremony took place before a magistrate. Attend to me, Maggie; listen; would you be willing *now* to enter into such a bond?"[34] Fox consented, and in front of Mrs. Fox, Kate, a servant, and "a young lady who was spending the evening there," Kane declared, "Maggie is my wife, and I am her husband." Maggie agreed. In case this was not convincing enough, Ellet provided a footnote to *The Love-Life* with numerous citations from legal authorities and court precedents that such a declaration did in fact constitute a legal marriage contract.[35] A few days later, on October 11, Kane left for England, promising that the marriage would be made public in May. But May never came for Elisha Kane, so we are left with rather tenuous evidence that the marriage ever took place at all.

KANE ARRIVED in Liverpool on October 22 and moved on to London three days later, where he visited with noted men of science such as Roderick Murchison and Edward Sabine and met frequently with Jane Franklin. His health, though, was failing fast, to the point where he could not fully participate in British scientific society as he wished, so he retired to a private residence outside London. By the middle of November he was consulting local doctors, who recommended a warmer climate. He considered making his way to southern Europe, but instead chose Cuba, since it was nearer to home. With Morton, he took passage from Southampton to St. Thomas, where he waited over two weeks before taking another ship to Cuba on December 20. As the ship neared Cuba, Kane's condition deteriorated. He experienced paralysis in his right arm and leg, from which he slowly recovered in a few days.[36]

Arriving in Havana on the Christmas Day, he was met by his brother Thomas, who had come down from Philadelphia to be with him. About two weeks later his mother and his brother John also arrived in Havana. Apparently the family had become aware that this was more than just another of Elisha's temporary bouts of ill health. Over the next month his condition fluctuated. At times he could get out of his bed at Mrs. Almy's Hotel and move around a bit. On these occasions he would make plans to return home, but then he would suffer a relapse and be confined to his bed, to be tended by Morton and his mother. On February 10 he was "seized with 'apoplexy,'" which again paralyzed him. "He was not unconscious nor insensible," wrote his biographer William Elder, "only paralyzed, with the power of emotional expression left, the power to indicate his sympathies, sufferings, and wants." Finally, on February 16, 1857, Elisha Kane died.[37]

The public reaction was immediate and overwhelming. The degree of mourning for the departed explorer shows clearly how far Kane's reputation had advanced in the last years of his life, spurred on by his return from the Arctic and the popularity of his book. At his death he was one of the most admired men in the country, a symbol of American virtue. The day after his death, between two and three hundred American citizens in Havana, "men of respectability from almost every State in the Union," met "for the purpose of agreeing on some public demonstration of respect to the memory of the intrepid Arctic navigator."[38] In doing so they set a precedent that would be repeated across the United States.

At 7:30 on the morning of February 20 a large group of Americans, and some from other countries, met the body as it was brought out of Mrs. Almy's Hotel. A procession of six to eight hundred people then accompanied it to the Plaza de Armas, where they were joined by representatives of the Cuban government, members of "various learned bodies," and a military band. This procession proceeded to the waterfront, where the remains were put on a barge solemnly decorated for the occasion. The boats of every American ship in the harbor, in addition to those of other nations, joined in a floating procession up the harbor, where "every American vessel, and indeed nearly all of those of every other country, had their colors hoisted half mast high."[39]

The body was taken to the steamer *Cahawba*, on which it would travel back to the United States, accompanied by Kane's mother and two brothers, who had tended him on his deathbed. After appropriate speeches by both Cuban and American representatives, the *Cahawba* departed.[40] It arrived in New Orleans on the morning of February 22. With the return of Kane's remains to the United States, word of his death spread throughout the country by telegraph. Meanwhile, the New Orleans city authorities began to organize. The honors they showed the departed explorer demonstrated unparalleled admiration for a man most of them had never met. Mourners carried the body to City Hall, where it lay in state overnight under a guard of honor. The next day, the *Daily Picayune* reported, the remains, taken by a military escort "and followed by a concourse of citizens, military officers, the city authorities, the Masonic fraternity, and the Keystone Association, were borne through some of our principal streets to the levee, and there placed on board the steamboat *Woodruff*, for Louisville, en route to Philadelphia."[41] As this procession passed through the streets of New Orleans, crowds gathered to pay their last respects. Between five and seven thousand observers came out to see the procession. Along the route and at the port, homes and businesses displayed flags at half-mast, and on Lafayette Square a detachment of artillery fired their guns at fifteen-minute intervals as a token of respect.[42] As the body of the explorer proceeded toward home, The *New Orleans Evening Delta* observed, "Strange that even the corpse of the Arctic wanderer is traveling still. Poor Kane was a true martyr to science, and there is a genuine sanctity in his coffin, worth the prestige of a thousand conquerors."[43] This was a theme that would emerge frequently in the course of Kane's long journey home: Kane was a hero, but his heroism was that much greater because it was based on scientific discovery and humanitarian sacrifice, not war or political conflict.

The *Woodruff* made its way up the Mississippi and Ohio rivers, passing Cairo, Illinois, on the morning of March 3. In spots, spectators lined the banks of the river to watch the funeral procession pass by. In Louisville the mayor and the Order of Free Masons prepared for Kane's arrival. The body was carried amidst great fanfare to Mozart Hall, where it lay in state overnight. The next day it was taken across the river to New Albany,

Indiana, where a committee from Cincinnati took charge, bringing it by steamboat to that city. All this was accompanied by solemn addresses by members of special committees from Louisville, New Albany, and Cincinnati.[44] These committees were made up of the first citizens of those cities, who felt that the honor of their communities depended on the respect they showed the remains of the departed explorer. Throughout the funeral journey the ceremonies were organized by America's elite male citizens, yet the newspapers consistently pointed out that the spectators who came to mourn Kane were from the working class as well as the wealthy, and included women as well as men.

As mourners carried Kane's body in a procession through the streets of Cincinnati, the city's most respected citizens gave speeches in memory of the deceased. They then accompanied the remains to the depot of the Little Miami Railroad Company, where they were placed on a railroad express car for the journey to Columbus.[45] The citizens of Columbus planned to honor Kane's memory "as a proud and dauntless warrior of science."[46] The body arrived on Saturday March 7, and was brought to the Senate chamber in the Capitol, where it lay in state over the Sabbath. On Sunday morning the chamber was opened to the public, but the crowd was so large that barely half of those wishing to gain entrance to the hall could be accommodated. A minister delivered a sermon, and mourners said prayers and sang a hymn dedicated to the memory of this "hero of science and discovery." From two to five in the afternoon the chamber remained opened to visitors, "and throughout the afternoon, the living tide, flowing and ebbing, was constant; and with saddened hearts and bowed heads all passed around the bier, in the melancholy tribute that genius and worth, unsullied by blemish, nor tainted by reproach, can alone command."[47]

As the corpse neared home, the displays of mourning intensified. Each city seemed to compete with the one before to show Kane's memory even greater honors. On Monday morning, citizens of Columbus took the remains to the station and placed them on a train heading east. At various points along the train's path through Ohio "the people assembled in great numbers, and stood uncovered while the train was passing, whilst at some points the station-houses and dwellings by the side of the road were draped in mourning, indicative of the deep and wide-spread feeling of admiration that prevailed for the character and services of the deceased, and the heartfelt sorrow for his early demise."[48]

After the train crossed the Ohio River again near Wheeling, amidst the tolling of bells from boats on the river, the body was placed on a specially prepared car of the Baltimore and Ohio Railroad to be taken to Baltimore.[49] Citizens of Wheeling, Virginia, who had planned to have Kane's body over the Sabbath, were disappointed by not being able to express their sorrow more fully.[50]

Baltimore had special reason to mourn the death of Dr. Kane, for it was the site of the Maryland Institute, of which Kane had been a member. Baltimore was the first stop along the route of this massive funeral procession where many of the participants in the ceremonies had actually known Kane personally. Many others had seen him lecture at the institute a few years before. Following observances in Baltimore, a paper observed, "On no occasion have our citizens united more generally, or with a greater earnestness of purpose, in manifesting their appreciation of distinguished worth and eminent services."[51] Another observed, "The testimonial was one of a universal character, it having been participated in by every class of our community."[52] As the body was carried from the train station to the Maryland Institute, where it was to lie in state, "the streets were walled with people, whilst windows, balconies and roof tops were occupied by spectators."[53] The funeral procession through the crowded streets included carefully arranged representatives from military, scientific, academic, fraternal, and religious organizations. When the procession reached the Maryland Institute, ceremonies were performed and a band played a dirge before a crowd so large it had to be restrained by police.[54] The body lay in state overnight before being placed on a train for Philadelphia.

The morning of March 12 in Philadelphia was clear and cold. The normal activities of this busy port did not proceed this morning; instead the whole city wore an aura of mourning. "The indications of sorrow were seen on all sides. . . . The flags of the shipping were at half-mast, . . . the public offices were closed, the bells were tolled, minute guns were discharged, and although the day was bright and clear, an anxious and solemn aspect characterized the city, and indicated the feelings of the community at large."[55] Homes and businesses draped signs of mourning from their windows. A building on Chestnut Street displayed a banner from its upper story that read, "Philadelphia mourns an illustrious son, and the world a martyr to science and humanity."[56] A banner on another building declared, "Science Weeps, Humanity Weeps, the World Weeps."[57]

Hundreds of Philadelphians congregated outside Independence Hall, the birthplace of the nation, where the body of Elisha Kane lay. Here the symbolism of the mourned explorer could mingle with the symbolism of nationhood. "At an early hour the streets were filled with people, and the city presented the aspect of an unusual occasion. Before nine o'clock the vicinity of Independence Hall presented a dense mass of citizens, and there was continual accumulation until, about ten o'clock, the crowd was almost impenetrable," one newspaper reported.[58] At eleven o'clock preparations began to form the line of procession. The city's newspapers listed the participants in great detail and appropriate order. They included Kane's shipmates from his Arctic expedition, political associations, clergy, members of scientific societies, fraternal organizations, military units, and professional groups. The pallbearers were among Philadelphia's and the nation's elite, including the governor, prominent jurists, and an Episcopal bishop.[59]

At noon the body was brought out of Independence Hall as the State House bell tolled, and the procession proceeded toward the Second Presbyterian Church. It moved slowly, taking nearly an hour to pass a single point.[60] At the church only those with invitations could fit inside to hear the eulogy delivered by the Reverend Charles Shields. Still, it was reported that 950 people were crowded into the lower floor and galleries.[61] Most had to wait until that evening or the next day to read the text of Shields's sermon in its entirety on the front pages of the city's newspapers. After the ceremony, the body of Elisha Kent Kane finally ended its journey and was laid to rest in Laurel Hill Cemetery.

In death Kane achieved his goals of nationwide fame and admiration. Coming as it did little more than a year after his return from the Arctic, and only months after the publication of his thrilling narrative, his death occurred at the apex of his career. More than any book review, the public expression of mourning shows how Kane's career as a celebrated explorer had touched not only the minds but also the hearts of the American public.

Because antebellum Americans had both a great curiosity about the unknown and a belief that uncovering the unknown led to human progress and happiness, a figure such as Kane took on even greater prominence than might otherwise have been the case. The search for scientific knowledge in remote regions could readily be presented as a noble quest. Kane did not work in a laboratory doing experiments incomprehensible to the layperson; rather he voyaged out into uncharted portions of the globe and exposed himself to physical peril in order to advance knowledge. Exploration, which combined intellectual achievement with physical courage, could be easily understood by a wide-ranging audience. Science could be read as adventure, and adventure could be read as science, the scientific motive serving to legitimate a certain degree of foolhardy risk taking. As one observer pointed out about Kane, "His earliest travel and exploits have a color of scientific enthusiasm to sanction their physical hardihood."[62]

Despite the prevalence in his obituaries of stock phrases such as "martyr to science" or "hero to science and humanity" or "science weeps," the evidence shows that Kane's actual scientific attainments were slight. In the eyes of his contemporaries, his greatest achievement was his shipmates' discovery of an "Open Polar Sea." This was, of course, an error, though at the time of his death this was not yet known.[63] His other scientific achievements consisted of ethnographic descriptions of the Inuit, data on tides, astronomical observations, and observations on the natural history of the Arctic, all interesting but hardly monumental. Kane's real fame lay instead in the values that his science seemed to promote. A broad spectrum of Americans loved Elisha Kent Kane, as one observer noted, for "the whole cluster of manly graces and virtues wedded to science."[64] The *New York Daily Tribune* declared, "Whatever the scientific results of his perilous voyages, they are of still higher significance in the example they have presented of noble, persistent, and disinterested and undismayed manhood."[65] As a polar explorer Kane exemplified admirable masculine traits such as bravery, perseverance, selflessness, intelligence, and duty. He placed the good of his men and the good of humanity above his own self-interest. Even those who did not understand Kane's scientific significance could understand and honor his virtue in a humanitarian cause.

One Philadelphia newspaper, trying to explain the honors being paid to Kane on the day of his funeral, looked not to Kane's practical discoveries but to his symbolic value for the nation, suggesting that Kane was being honored more for his motives than for his achievements. He was to be remembered for "what he has attempted and endured in the high and ennobling service of science and philanthropy."[66] The article concluded by claiming that the ceremonies in honor of Kane were really about "that abstract ideal of manly virtue and magnanimity, which his life embodied." His life was to serve as a moral inspiration and example to the young.[67] It was this side of Kane that brought his reputation out of the specialized confines of the scientific community, made him an accessible hero for a wider public, and turned mourning his loss into a national public ritual.

Kane's funeral procession had developed into a nationwide celebration of the values he was held to represent. Thousands of Americans in New Orleans, Columbus, Louisville, Baltimore, Philadelphia, and other cities, who knew neither one another nor Kane, all could imagine themselves as part of the same nation, despite the growing sectional conflict of the era.[68] The mayor of Cincinnati put it this way: "[Kane] was our countryman, and his life has made a bright page for our country's history, and added to the consideration which the world abroad is daily disposed to concede to us as a nation."[69] Eight members of the Louisville bar expressed the same theme in a public letter of condolence to Judge Kane: "You must know that the reputation of your son belongs to the American public, and will be cherished as a part of the nation's wealth. His heroic devotion to humanity and science has conferred imperishable glory upon his country."[70] Kane was often compared with the national icon Columbus, the explorer who over 350 years earlier had sailed to the New World, and had later become a symbol of the United States. *Harper's Weekly* printed a poem on its first page after Kane was buried, one stanza of which treats Kane, the scientific traveler, as a unifier of the nation, as all the regions of the country, from "Maine's deep woods" to "Hot Southern lips" to "the large-lunged West" proclaim "Honor to Kane!" Interestingly, this poem appeared right next to, and in stark contrast with, a story on continuing violence in "Bleeding Kansas," the site of intense sectional conflict over the slavery issue.[71]

Newspapers, too, depicted Kane as a national hero, not just the hero of a particular class, region, or faction.[72] Some noted the journey of the corpse through both southern and northern states.[73] The *Baltimore Sun* observed that the mourning for Kane in Baltimore "was of universal character, it having been participated in by every class of our community."[74] Others pointed to the symbolic value of Kane's lying in state in Philadelphia's Independence Hall, where the nation had been born. The Reverend

Charles Shields observed, "Fittingly we have suffered his honored remains to repose a few pensive hours at the shrine where patriotism gathers its fairest memories and choicest honors."[75] Shields used the image of geographic lines of longitude converging at the North Pole as a symbol of Kane's role as a unifier of disparate people. To Shields, Kane's journey in search of Franklin was "a beautiful tribute to the sentiment of national amity."[76] Similarly, the mayor of Cincinnati observed that the citizens of his city had come together "to pay respect to the remains, not of a party leader, nor of him who lost his life in party strife or in the broils of faction, but of one whose fame is world-wide, gained by distinguished services rendered to the intelligence and the humanity of the age."[77] The intellectual and moral progress of the nation through science, as symbolized by Kane's image, transcended the corrupting influences of faction and section at a time when little else did.

10

Private Lives, Public Legacy

Dr. Kane often seemed to think of the possibility of his love-letters being published. He would say—intimating that something might happen at a future time to render a publication necessary—"Maggie, never fear, you hold a fortune in my letters."

The Love-Life of Dr. Kane

More than eight years after the heartfelt public mourning for Elisha Kane, a little volume appeared in American bookshops called *The Love-Life of Dr. Kane.* Containing what was alleged to be the private correspondence between the heroic Arctic navigator and the love of his life, Margaretta Fox, it told of a romance and a secret marriage between them, and claimed a place for Maggie Fox in the nation's memory of Elisha Kane. The story of how this book came into being indicates that the public's curiosity about well-known figures had moved into a realm of sensation and celebrity more characteristic of a later phase of American popular culture. Control over Kane's private letters to her gave an otherwise powerless Maggie Fox some limited control over her situation. From Kane's death in 1857 to her own in 1893, Fox made numerous attempts to turn public curiosity to her own advantage while retaining a modicum of self-respect. In this she met with only limited success.[1]

With the death of Elisha Kane, Maggie Fox was left in an ambiguous position. She had taken no part in the great outpouring of grief over Kane's death. She could not play the role of the widow, since her secret marriage to Kane, if it had indeed taken place, was known to only a few. Rather, upon hearing of Kane's death, Fox fell seriously ill and remained ill for months. According to Elizabeth Ellet, "during the greater part of the time she was shut up in a dark room, utterly inconsolable, and unable to bear the light of day."[2]

Had the romance between Elisha Kane and Maggie Fox truly followed the course of the sentimental novel it so much resembled, Fox would have withered away and died there and then, but instead she was destined to live on for another thirty-five years. For most of this time she would be torn between conflicting influences, which continually mingled private with public concerns. Her every significant action was noted by strangers and reported in the newspapers. Rumors still circulated about the alleged affair between her and Elisha Kane. Even though Kane's official biographer, William Elder, made no mention of her, two other biographical treatments of Kane from around the same time suggest that the rumors had not ceased. When William Godfrey wrote his account of the second Grinnell Expedition in order to clear his name after the criticism he had received in *Arctic Explorations*, his publisher included a short biographical sketch of Kane at the end. This account, published in late 1857, described the relationship between the doctor and the spirit rapper as a passionate love affair, and lamented that Kane had succumbed to the aristocratic prejudices of his family and broken off the engagement. "The name of 'spirit-rapper,' with the pointings and gazings of the mob, the sneers of the ribald newspaper press, and the imputations of charlatanry," wrote the author of this sketch, "seemed dreadful to the man who had fearlessly confronted the weapons of both savage and civilized foes." This version of the story ends with Kane's cowardly renunciation of Fox on his return from the second expedition.[3] Samuel Schmucker's biography of Kane, which appeared sometime in 1858, also recalled the romance, but Schmucker too wrote that Kane had broken off the engagement shortly before his death.[4] These accounts undoubtedly reflected prevailing rumors that Kane and Fox had indeed been engaged but had never been married.

Conflicting forces vied for control over Maggie Fox in the years after Kane's death. On one side were the demands of her family and the public life of a spirit rapper. On the other side was the memory of Elisha Kane and the ideals of middle-class propriety he had tried to instill in her. When he was alive, he had done everything in his power to separate Fox from the influences of her family and spiritualist circles. To live up to his expectations, she had promised Kane never to go back to spiritualism, and now that he was dead, she would keep that promise, for a time.

Her promise, however, left Maggie Fox in a predicament. Kane had pressured her to separate herself from everything and everyone she knew, but he had offered nothing to fill their place except his own empty promises. Now Kane was dead, and his family did not recognize her as his widow. To be fair, the Kanes knew nothing of the supposed secret marriage, since Elisha had continually lied to them about his relationship with Maggie Fox. But despite this, Fox at first looked to the Kane family for her future. She hoped to gain from them the opportunity for a respectable private life, away from the gaze of strangers.

Before leaving for England, Kane had made a will in which he set aside five thousand dollars to be held in a private trust by his brother Robert Patterson Kane for the benefit of Margaret Fox.[5] Not long after Kane's death, Fox became aware of this bequest through Henry Grinnell's wife, who had witnessed the will. Sometime in March or April 1857, Mrs. Fox wrote to Robert Kane: "My dear sir, a few days after the Dr.'s death, Mrs. Grinnell called to tell Margaret that she had been 'remembered to the last,' and that he had made a request which was left with you to deliver to Margaret. Her trials have been (as you must already know) greater than she could bear, and we fear that unless changes soon take place she cannot survive them much longer. I wish you would come at once. . . . I send this note unknown to my daughter, still your presence cannot be unexpected."[6]

On June 1, having recovered somewhat from her illness, Maggie Fox also wrote to Robert Kane. Clearly she was looking for emotional as well as financial support from someone whom she saw as her link to her lost love as well as the only means to continue on the path toward respectability that Elisha Kane had urged her to take. "I know the Doctor must have left some message for me," she wrote, "and I know that you will not refuse to deliver it, even though it gives you much pain in recalling the name of him whose memory is and ever will be sacred." She continued, in the sentimental language of the day, "I have always held a religious faith in the deep sincerity of the Doctor's love, and his memory will always remain a beautiful green in my unchanged affections."[7] Robert Kane was the only member of the family whom she knew at all. She saw him as someone she could go to in her grief, and she repeatedly appealed to him to visit her.[8]

Robert Kane, however, wanted nothing to do with Maggie Fox. He knew that his brother had been involved with the notorious spirit rapper, but it is doubtful that he knew anything of the supposed marriage or even believed the rumors of a serious engagement between the two. All he knew was that his elder brother had recklessly formed a secret relationship with Fox against his family's wishes and despite the threat of public scandal. To him she was a dark shadow that threatened to obscure the bright reputation his brother had achieved in death. Above all else, he wanted her to go away. Moreover, Robert Kane was not the best person in whom to rest one's fate. The Philadelphia diarist Sidney George Fisher, a relative by marriage, observed that Robert Kane was "clever & designing" as well as "ambitious of political success, with the talents of an attorney & unable to understand an abstract principle or to feel enthusiasm for a just cause."[9] Apparently he was hardly the type of man from whom to expect fair play or noble sentiment.

Unfortunately for Robert Kane, his brother's celebrity along with Maggie's own had given Maggie Fox some control over her situation. She still had a large bundle of letters, which gave evidence that a romantic relationship had existed between her and the doctor. In at least one of these letters Elisha Kane referred to Maggie Fox as his wife, and in almost all of them Kane presented himself as her ardent lover. Moreover, the letters revealed Kane's fear of public exposure. Even if Maggie Fox could not, others reading the letters would be able to see that Kane's behavior had at times been cowardly, snobbish, and less than gentlemanly, and that the great man had been more concerned with his public reputation than with the feelings of the woman he claimed to love.

Fox, however, was not out to ruin Elisha Kane's reputation. All she wanted was recognition from the Kane family and help in avoiding further public sensationalism. Her first job, then, was to prove to Robert Kane that his brother had loved her and planned to marry her. She had to demonstrate that theirs had been no tawdry sexual affair that needed to be hushed up, so she showed Robert Kane some of the letters his brother had written to her, which made clear to him that Elisha had repeatedly promised to marry her. At first Fox shied away from making any claims about the secret marriage that would later be described in *The Love-Life*. She may have mentioned it, but at this point she did not yet assert that it was a legal marriage that gave her the rights of a widow. She continued to call herself Margaret Fox rather than Mrs. Kane, as she would later be known.[10]

Although Fox's motive seems primarily to have been to gain recognition and respectability, she also needed money. She did not want to be a burden on her mother and Kate, with whom she was then living. Kate Fox was still an active medium, and it was her money that supported the household. Maggie Fox could not live as a dependent on her sister for long without being drawn back into spiritualism herself. To retire from public life and lead the virtuous existence that Dr. Kane had urged her toward, she needed the help that Robert Kane was in a position to give. This was not an unreasonable expectation, especially since Elisha Kane's estate had grown significantly since his death. At the time he wrote his will, five thousand dollars may have been all he could afford to leave Fox, but *Arctic Explorations* was bringing in many thousands of dollars to his estate. In August, just six months after Kane died, one newspaper reported that his share of the profits from his book had reached sixty thousand dollars.[11]

Out of necessity, Robert Kane began to cultivate a relationship with Fox. He sincerely tried to protect her from what he thought were evil spiritualist influences, and he provided her with small sums of money to help pay her bills. Yet as months passed, it gradually became clear that his motives were not solely altruistic, and he did not appear willing to pay the entire sum left with him for Fox's support. Maggie Fox was, ultimately, an annoyance and a threat, someone who had the power to expose his brother's private life to a curious public. He wanted to gain control over the letters, even though she assured him that they would never leave her hands. "The letters are mine to guard and cherish so long as I live," she told him, "and when I am no longer able to guard them, I will place them with you, but do not think me so lost as to ever allow them to be published."[12] To make sure that Maggie would keep her promise, Robert Kane had to cultivate good relations with her. He did not trust her with the letters, and wished to get them out of her hands as soon as possible.

KANE RIGHTLY feared the influence of others on Maggie Fox, especially Elizabeth Fries Ellet, who had become friendly with the Fox family. Ellet was a well-known figure in antebellum America, and is remembered today as the first major historian of American women. In 1848, the same year the Fox sisters began their knockings, Ellet wrote the pathbreaking *Women of the American Revolution*, which recounted the role played by women in the early years of the nation. She was the author of a number of other books, and her shorter writings often appeared in popular magazines such as *Godey's Lady's Book* and *Graham's Magazine*. By all indications, Ellet was a formidable personality. She was making a way for herself not only as a sentimental "scribbler" but also as a serious historian, an area dominated by men. She skillfully used the means available to her to advance as far as she could both professionally and personally.[13]

It is not clear when Ellet and Fox came to know each other. Perhaps Ellet had been acquainted with the Foxes for many years, as she too was originally from western New York, but she first appears in Fox's limited surviving correspondence in July 1858. Ellet soon learned of Maggie Fox's situation, and she came to the conclusion that young spirit rapper was not getting what she deserved from the Kanes. When she heard of the alleged secret marriage between Fox and Dr. Kane, she decided that it was a legally binding union under common law and the laws of New York State, which should have given Fox the rights of a widow. Ellet began to pressure Fox to stop deferring to Robert Kane, who treated her with a lack of proper recognition, and instead to fight for what she deserved. Fox was clearly torn. Robert Kane was helping her a little, though not as much as she wished. If she made waves, even that little bit of support might disappear. Besides, the last thing she wanted at this point was publicity or scandal.

Meanwhile, Robert Kane thought he had the matter in hand. He claimed to take a genuine interest in Fox's welfare, and Fox seems to have deferred to his wishes when it came to the letters.[14] On August 11, when Kane was about to depart on a trip to the South, he sent her his good wishes and fifty dollars. While he was away, however, Ellet's pressure appears to have influenced Maggie Fox's thinking. Two and a half weeks later Kane returned home to Philadelphia to find a letter waiting for him on his table. It must have come as a dreadful shock when he opened it and began to read this message from a New York lawyer named Rush C. Hawkins:

> Dear Sir:
>
> I have been requested by a gentleman of this city to communicate with you in regard to the wife of your deceased brother, Elisha K. Kane.
>
> I am of the opinion that Margaretta Fox was on the [blank] day of Oct. 1856 lawfully married to your brother, and that she is now justly entitled to bear his name: It seems that there has been some doubt existing in the minds of the friends and relatives of your brother, in relation to this marriage: of the marriage above referred to there exists abundant proof.

Hawkins went on to express an interest in seeing Kane's will on behalf of "Mrs. Kane," because, he said, he had reason to believe "her husband" had provided for her in it. He closed by claiming that he was acting "not as a lawyer, but as a friend, on behalf of a woman ignorant of her rights and the laws of her country." The implication was that there was still time to settle the matter in an informal and private manner, but that if necessary, legal steps would be taken, which would naturally attract publicity.[15]

Robert Kane must have been mortified to hear Maggie Fox referred to as "Mrs. Kane" and Elisha referred to as "her husband." Here was a notorious woman claiming membership in his own family. He could stomach giving Fox small sums of money as a charity case, but he certainly had no wish to acknowledge her as a relative. Kane reacted to Hawkins's letter by immediately trying to regain control over Maggie Fox. He met and "explained to her at some length how ill-judged had been the action of her so called friends."[16] Propriety dictated that Fox behave humbly and place herself in the hands of those who knew what was best for her. To a surprising degree, Fox was convinced by this argument. She craved what she saw as a normal life, and she wanted to be well thought of by genteel people. Most of all, she did not want to be the object of further public scrutiny.

Robert Kane solicited the help of other respectable personages in his cause and the cause, he claimed, of Maggie Fox. Horace Greeley had remained on friendly terms with the Fox family ever since they had first traveled to New York City in 1850. Though not a believer in spiritualism, he still thought that the Fox sisters might have unique unexplained mesmeric or clairvoyant powers. Greeley continued to take an interest in their welfare, paying for Kate's education, for instance, and inviting the Fox family to stay at his house in New York. He advised Maggie that she was better off appealing to Robert Kane's goodwill as a gentleman than demanding what was hers through the law and attracting publicity to herself. Despite being a newspaper man, Greeley thought that private matters should remain out of the public eye. At the same time, Greeley may have believed that Robert Kane ought to be providing for Fox better than he was doing.[17]

Fox was also getting advice from Father William Quinn, a Roman Catholic priest. Elisha Kane had once told Fox of his admiration for the Roman Catholic faith, and he had urged her to consider converting.[18] On

August 15, 1858, in a ceremony attended by her mother, father, sister Kate, and Horace Greeley, Maggie was baptized a Roman Catholic at St. Peter's Church in New York.[19] Her Methodist family disapproved, but they went along with her wishes. Given the extreme antiauthoritarian posture of most spiritualists, the hierarchic structure of the Catholic Church was about as far as one could get from spirit rapping. Becoming a Roman Catholic was thus Maggie Fox's way of turning her back on spiritualism in favor of tradition and paternalistic authority. She did not, however, publicly repudiate the rapping. That would have been too much of a blow to her family members who were still involved in it. She preferred simply to separate herself from spiritualism and conform to the teachings of the Catholic faith. Of course, this did not prevent the papers, which remained interested in the former spirit rapper, from debating the significance of her conversion. The *Herald* saw it as a recantation of spiritualism, while Greeley's *Tribune* disagreed, saying that Fox had "never dreamed of saying or implying that any of her family were guilty of fraud or deception in the matter of the 'Rappings.' "[20]

Fox's conversion was a blessing for Robert Kane, since Father Quinn, Fox's new spiritual mentor, would be a great help to him in his efforts to keep Fox away from the influences of spiritualists and her family. Kane worried less about a legal suit claiming a portion of Elisha's estate than he did about publicity. His greatest fear was that Elisha's letters to Maggie Fox might be published, which he believed would bring shame on the Kane family. Once again, the effort to publish was being driven chiefly by Elizabeth Ellet. At some point in the summer or fall of 1858, Kane received a letter from a friend of the family touching on this delicate matter. Through it, Kane was made aware of what was going on behind enemy lines. "I've something to tell you that is none of my business," wrote the friend, who seems to have been witness to a conversation between Ellet and members of the Fox family, who were unaware of the listener's connection with the Kanes. "It relates to Dr. Kane's correspondence with Miss Fox, which is about to be published. That is, it is in the hands of Mrs. Ellet (of magazine celebrity) to whom publishers have made large offers for the publication." The letter went on to say that Fox had not yet given her consent, chiefly because of the influence of Ellen Walter, who disapproved of the idea, but that Maggie's sister and mother favored publication. "Her family are urging her strongly, and Mrs. Ellet tells her it is due to her own reputation which the [Kane] family have injured etc., and altogether they are endeavoring to make her feel that she is deeply aggrieved by the family in various ways, and that it is only justice to herself and family that these letters should be published." The correspondent then went on to suggest that publication could probably be prevented with some action on the part of the Kanes.[21]

Word was reaching Robert Kane from a variety of fronts concerning Ellet's interest in and influence over Maggie Fox. Cornelius Grinnell returned to his home in New York in early October, after a cruise aboard his yacht, to discover that Ellet had been talking with his mother, who had witnessed Elisha Kane's will. Grinnell had the chance to speak with Ellet and promptly reported to Robert Kane that "the drift of her plans . . . are to make out that Miss Fox was married to the Doctor from the fact (as she states) that he had several times before witnesses addressed her as his wife." Grinnell clearly thought that Ellet's case had no merit: "The idea was so absurd that I may have received it rather too jocosely for Mrs. Ellet's ire was aroused. I regret extremely the turn this affair has taken, and I await your arrival with some impatience."[22]

For her part, Maggie Fox was growing angry at the attempts on both sides to control her and the letters. She did not want to go public, but she did need support. In early September she wrote to Robert Kane, telling him that the letters were safe from publication, yet she also refused to hand them over to him. "The letters are sacred to me, little as you have appreciated it," she said. Only when she died, she told him, would they pass to the Kane family. She also reassured him that, despite Ellet's urgings, she did not claim the status of Elisha Kane's widow: "The private marriage you can think of as you please. My ideas of a private marriage are very different from Mrs. Ellet's. To me a private marriage is quite as disgraceful, as to stand in another light, but our honorable engagement you can never deny, at least to me."[23] Fox was trying to do what she thought was right, but without any tangible support from Robert Kane or the Kane family, the costs were high. As it so often was for Fox, the respectable course was the least profitable.

For a time, Robert Kane seemed to have won her over. The book was put on hold, and Kane heard no more word of legal recourse. He supplied Fox with enough money for a modest existence, and she in turn behaved with a meekness that pleased him. Soon she was even contemplating entering a convent to live out her life in piety and seclusion.[24] But Maggie

Fox was far from happy. Elisha Kane's death seems to have triggered a decline into depression and alcoholism. By early 1859 she was renting her own rooms in New York so that she did not have to live with her sister and mother, in constant association with spiritualists. But this isolation hurt her more than it helped. Soon, Maggie's family and friends became aware that she was drinking heavily.[25]

All of her money now came from Robert Kane, in whose hands she had placed her fate. Early in 1859 she began to negotiate with Kane and Father Quinn about depositing all of the letters with Quinn at the church. In return, she would get a steady allowance from Kane, sufficient to allow her to live modestly, while Father Quinn would act as her chief adviser and as a mediator between her and Kane.[26] Yet Fox was reluctant to release her hold on the letters, and they had not yet settled on an arrangement.

By the end of 1859 Maggie was still behaving properly, in the opinion of Father Quinn. She held on to the letters, but received an allowance from Kane, which ensured that they would be kept private. Quinn wrote to Kane in December: "I must say that she conducts herself very well. She attends church very regularly, confession also; and the other obligations of our church are not neglected. I am sure these observances will keep her from all improper influences." But Quinn still worried about those influences: "Still you know mother, Kate and many others of the same sort, who have little judgment, are constantly with her and urging her to contract obligations beyond her means." Quinn assured Kane that he would work to keep Fox under his benevolent control: "I will advise her and obtain a promise that she will consult with me on all matters of even moderate importance."[27]

One of Quinn's worries, which he passed on to Kane, was the continued influence of Elizabeth Ellet. "That woman Ellet," Quinn wrote, "fills her mind with nonsense in the hope that she may be able to make a book and get the lion's share." He suggested that if Fox's allowance were increased, he might finally be able to get her to place the letters in his safekeeping.[28] These same concerns continued to plague Kane and Quinn throughout the following year. Fox was unhappy, and she was drinking. Many of her letters from this time deteriorate into an incoherent scrawl. By the autumn of 1860, Quinn was still telling Kane that he feared "the influence of a certain class of book makers who are less or more acquainted with her."[29]

Over the course of the next year, Robert Kane's control slowly began to unravel. Ellet was still at work trying to find out what others such as the Grinnells knew about the affair, and she was urging Fox to see a lawyer. At the same time, Fox was telling Robert Kane that she feared she was going insane. She was unhappy and constantly in need of money.[30] She was also isolated, owing largely to the efforts of Quinn and Kane. Their paternalistic control guaranteed her an income, though a meager and insecure one, while their efforts to remove her from "improper influences" served to alienate her from most sources of emotional support. She had set up her private rooms as a morbid shrine to Elisha Kane. On Sundays, Kate, who was also developing a drinking problem, would visit her there. According to Mariam Pond, who married a descendant of the Fox family and wrote a semifictionalized history based in part on family tradition,

> Kate could not find the words to tell their mother of the strangeness that was changing Maggie. She did not tell her of the black-curtained shrine Maggie had arranged in a large closet, where she mourned before the candle-lighted, flower-bedecked portrait of Elisha, sobbing hysterically in tearless grief, for tears had ceased to flow from Maggie's eyes. Nor could Kate speak of the more shameful fact, that after each exhausting outburst of emotion, Maggie would stumble blindly to the outer room and drink until sleep came with dreams which bore her far away. Her grief found other forms of violent expression; she played and sang in frenzied outbursts which brought protest and interference from her long-suffering neighbors.[31]

Robert Kane and Father Quinn apparently considered such isolation better than the "improper influences" of her family.

Robert Kane's own influence over Maggie Fox had always been tenuous, and in 1862, most likely because of financial pressures, she finally consented to publish Elisha's letters. Ellet made arrangements with a New York publisher, George W. Carleton, to print the volume. Carleton apparently thought that Elisha Kane's celebrity was still great enough, five years after his death, to draw interest even now in the midst of the Civil War.[32] Fox also hired a lawyer and brought suit against Robert Kane in Orphan's Court in Philadelphia. Kane, no longer able to constrain Fox with a few dollars and an appeal to her sense of propriety, hired his own lawyers, and negotiations commenced to halt both the lawsuit and the book.[33]

Kane succeeded, but only by entering into an out-of-court settlement in which he agreed to pay Fox a specified allowance, presumably higher than the one he had been paying her. In return, publication of the letters was stopped, and they were placed in the hands of a third party, Dr. Edward Bayard, who had tended to Fox's medical needs for many years. As long as Fox received the agreed-upon payments from Kane, the letters would remain with Bayard. If the payments stopped for any reason, Fox could retrieve her letters.[34]

This arrangement lasted another three years, until 1865, when, for some unknown reason, Kane discontinued the payments. In accordance with the terms of the agreement, Bayard returned the letters to Fox, and they were promptly published by Carleton. *The Love-Life of Dr. Kane* appeared anonymously. Ellet's name appears nowhere on the book, but it is clear that it was she who edited the volume and wrote the introduction and the narrative that connects the letters.[35]

Ellet began *The Love-Life* by apologizing "for presenting to the world that which was never intended to meet the public eye."[36] She was well aware that the public exposure of private matters, while becoming more common, was still looked upon as unseemly. She addressed this issue in a preface, saying, "Perhaps many will think that no circumstances could justify the publication of the letters contained in this volume." But, she continued, Maggie Fox "has borne the sneers of the world, and the neglect of those whose regard for the deceased should have induced them to protect, comfort, and befriend her."[37] She had been slandered in the press and humiliated by the Kane family, said Ellet, and was denied the money left to her by Kane. To make matters worse, the papers were repeating the Kanes' claim that Maggie Fox had never married Elisha Kane. "Could any woman who respected herself, submit to such an indignity?" asked Ellet. "What was there about her whom Dr. Kane had wooed and wedded, that she should be thus insulted, and denied common justice under an outrageous imputation? Her sole means of defense," continued Ellet, "her only vindication—was the publication of this correspondence."[38]

Thus depicting Maggie Fox as a meek girl being mistreated by the rich and powerful Kane family, Ellet asserted that the personal letters of Dr. Kane were being published as a last resort in defense of the defenseless: "The world usually sides with the rich, the proud, and the powerful; and it is not expected that the poor, the humble and the weak, will receive either justice or sympathy."[39] Before the American public, however, the humble could attain justice. The private dispute between Maggie Fox and the Kanes was being presented to the public much as spirit rapping had been: Let the public decide who was right and who was wrong.

Ellet's task was not only to justify publication of the letters but also to construct a compelling narrative. Readers would not purchase *The Love-Life of Dr. Kane* just to vindicate Maggie Fox; Ellet also had to claim that they would gain insight into the character of Dr. Kane by reading his love letters. Here, as in her better-known women's histories, Ellet combined scholarship with sentiment.[40] She asserted that great men could not be properly understood without knowledge of the women they loved. As the title suggests, *The Love-Life of Dr. Kane* is more about Elisha Kane than it is about Maggie Fox, yet it claims a place for her at his side, for, as Ellet explains, "the loves of eminent men, through the world's literary history, have not only shared their renown, but have aided them to deserve it."[41]

The Love-Life was typical of the sentimental literature of the day. It set out to expose the heart of the man through his emotional life. By witnessing the character of his love for Maggie Fox, claimed Ellet, "we are all the more touched by his tenderness, and wonder at the depth and ardor of the love that impelled him." Ellet continued, linking the sentiment behind Kane's heroic Arctic travels with his feelings for Maggie Fox: "So the little incident of his carrying the portrait of his beloved one strapped to his back, through the dreary Arctic wastes, gives us a better insight into a true and noble heart than all the anecdotes collected by his biographer."[42] This was hardly a feminist argument, but it did claim some value for the roles of women as shapers of history. Above all, Ellet was using sentimental notions of a woman's sphere to gain Fox some power over her situation.

The Love-Life of Dr. Kane is the classic story of a love that transcends social boundaries. Like Pamela and Mr. B. of Samuel Richardson's novel *Pamela,* or Jane Eyre and Rochester of Charlotte Brontë's *Jane Eyre*, Kane and Fox were not evenly matched. Ellet played on democratic sensibilities to present Fox and Kane as lovers tormented by social prejudice, which derived not only from class difference but also from cultural difference. "That one so distinguished and highly esteemed as Dr. Kane should love and wed an untutored girl, with only beauty and virtue for her dower, was scarcely pardonable by a proud family," she wrote; "but the added odium of the spirit-rapping association his family could not possibly bear; his friends shrank from it; he, himself, with all his bravery, trembled to encounter it."[43] The antagonists here are the Kane family, who, according to Ellet, impeded the course of Elisha's true expression of love. She trusted that the democratic sensibilities of American public opinion would help right the wrongs of aristocratic prejudice.

Had *The Love-Life of Dr. Kane* appeared shortly after Kane's death, it would no doubt have caused a sensation. As it was, the little book received some notice but was hardly a best-seller. When the *New York Times* reviewed the work, it commented that, despite the excuses made in the preface, the volume should not have been published. The reviewer regarded it as "an intrusion of private matters before that many-headed monster, the Public—the last body in the world that should be selected to exercise the functions of a court of appeal for the redress of individual grievances."[44] Nor did the Kane family back down. They denounced *The Love-Life* as a "canard."[45] Although we have no records to tell us how many readers bought the volume, we do know that, in at least one sense, publication was a success. For the remainder of her life, Maggie Fox was known as Mrs. Kane. She had gained some of the recognition she desired, but she needed to find a stable source of income now that she could no longer look to Robert Kane.

THE IDEALS of genteel behavior that Elisha Kane had tried to instill in Maggie Fox did not work very well when she tried to put them into practice. She had become a public celebrity early in life, and sensational public activity seemed to be the only kind that now brought her any rewards. For the remainder of the 1860s, after *The Love-Life* appeared, Fox remained faithful to her decision to abandon spirit rapping, but by 1871 the financial pressures had become too strong. Now approaching forty, Maggie Fox took up her old career again.[46]

Even though she resumed the rappings, she never embraced theological spiritualism as her sister Leah had. She maintained the old investigative model the sisters had used years before. On the back of her cards she printed a notice: "Mrs. Kane does not claim any Spirit power; but people must judge for themselves."[47] She continued to perform simple rappings for her clients, though by this time there were many other mediums, including her sister Kate, who could produce far more sensational phenomena, such as materializations, spirit writing, and even spirit photography. Fox seems to have got by with simple knocks and name recognition. Since she attracted little notice, there are few sources for her life at this time. Mariam Pond describes this phase in Maggie Fox's career, which lasted through the 1870s and much of the 1880s: "Maggie made a few tours to other cities and to other sections of the country, but there was little in her work which merited recording. She was remembered as a sad, almost morbid little woman, who had occasional periods of intemperance which interrupted her professional career. Neither her work nor her intemperance attracted much attention. Maggie had become unimportant to the general public."[48]

Fox remained isolated, and her drinking may soon have been supplemented by drug use.[49] The Fox family was no longer intact. Mrs. Fox had died in 1865, shortly before *The Love-Life* was published. Mr. Fox, too, was dead. Kate spent much of the 1870s and early 1880s in England, where she married an Englishman named Henry Jencken and had two children. Leah was still in New York City, but she and Maggie were becoming increasingly estranged from each other. Leah had given up professional rapping after marrying a wealthy man named Daniel Underhill, but she remained an advocate for theological spiritualism. Although Daniel Underhill sometimes contributed to Maggie's support, the sisters' relationship was not very good, and Maggie's drinking and distaste for her spirit rapping career did little to help.[50]

While Fox's activities went largely unnoticed, she did play a role in the University of Pennsylvania's Seybert Commission. A wealthy spiritualist named Henry Seybert, for whom Fox had sometimes rapped, left a legacy in his will funding scientific investigations of spiritualist phenomena. In 1887 Fox gave the Seybert Commission some demonstrations of spirit rapping. Although the commissioners had exposed some other frauds, they were not able to expose Maggie Fox, but this was mainly because she simply refrained from rapping when the scrutiny was too close. They were nevertheless unconvinced by her performance.[51]

Fox's dissatisfaction and the problems within her family came to a climax in the late 1880s, with nationwide repercussions for the spiritualist movement. Kate returned from England after the death of her husband, but she, like Maggie, had become strange and unpredictable. The two of them were by this time confirmed alcoholics and mentally unhinged. Kate quickly began to alienate other family members, a situation Mariam Pond attributes to Kate's overprotected and spoiled children. Leah and Kate soon had a falling-out, caused in part by Kate's alcohol abuse. To make matters worse, Leah considered Kate an unfit mother, and she may have taken part in a highly publicized attempt by the Society for the Prevention of Cruelty to Children to remove Kate's children from her.[52]

Maggie Fox, meanwhile, had left New York for England in late March 1888, so she was in London when she learned, through a story in the *New York Herald,* of Leah's conflict with Kate and Kate's efforts to keep her children. Her response was to go public in a scathing letter to the *Herald* in which she blamed all of her family's and her own problems on spiritualism. "Spiritualism is a curse," Fox declared. "No matter in what form Spiritualism may be presented, it is, has been and always will be a curse and a snare to all who meddle with it." She complained of fanatics who gravitated toward the most sensational manifestations and who ignored simple rappings, which Fox still claimed were the "only part of the phenomena that is worthy of notice."[53]

These were harsh words coming from one of the best-known names in spiritualism. Even if her career was in decline, she was still one of the famed Fox sisters, who had begun the whole thing. Although Fox had not denounced spiritualism as a total fraud, she had come close. Her words contrasted sharply with those of her sister Leah Underhill, who, just three years before, had written *The Missing-Link in Modern Spiritualism,* which told the history of the rappings from their beginnings in Hydesville (or at least her version of the history) and celebrated the movement as the dawning of a new age.[54] Reporters were thus ready for Maggie Fox when she returned to New York in September 1888. They were not disappointed. Fox told them that she planned to expose spiritualism for the fraud it was.

A reporter from the *Herald* described the scene when he called on Maggie Fox in her home on West Forty-fourth Street in New York. He depicted her as a "small, magnetic woman of middle age, whose face bears the traces of much sorrow and of a world-wide experience." Her behavior was erratic. She paced the floor and periodically burst into tears in front of the reporter, as she told him of her plans to expose the deception. At times she would sit down suddenly at the piano and "pour forth fitful floods of wild, incoherent melody."[55]

Fox's plans came to fruition the following month in New York's Academy of Music. Responding to posters and advertisements that promised the death of spiritualism, on October 21 an audience made up of "a mixed assemblage of many grades of society" came together to witness Fox's renunciation.[56] It was an immense audience, according to the *Tribune*: "One could easily pick out in the crowded seats professional men of all sorts—ministers, physicians and lawyers, scholarly men and women, men of repute in legitimate scientific research, others notorious in the walks of humbug, women well-known by the frequenters of materialization séances, and distinguished 'cranks' who adorn every such occasion, and Sunday night idlers who came from the same motive from which Artimus Ward's 'Uncle Simon, he clum up a tree,' namely, to see what they could see."[57]

In other words, Maggie Fox's renunciation attracted the same sort of audience her performances always had. For her it must have been very much like the early days of spirit rapping almost forty years before, except this time she was in the role of an antispiritualist like Chauncey Burr. Once again, Fox allied her skills with those of an experienced male lecturer. Dr. Cassius M. Richmond, a dentist who was known for exposing frauds, mounted the podium and delivered a lecture in which he asserted that the age of miracles was over. Telling his audience, "You are judge and jury," he gave some demonstrations of slate writing and other tricks by which, he claimed, professional mediums made their living.[58]

Soon it was Maggie Fox's turn to take the stage. Kate was there too, sitting in the audience in silent affirmation of her sister's actions. Finally Fox came onstage, "a little, compact woman, dark eyed and dark haired and dressed in black, and using eyeglasses with black cord and heavy black rims." She was obviously frightened, and appeared so pathetic that some in the audience began to heckle her. She read her statement that spiritualism was a fraud, then sat down and put her feet up on a board. Richmond, like Chauncey Burr and the Buffalo Doctors many years earlier, explained that the raps were made with the bones of the big toe. While the audience members in the gallery made "irreverent remarks," a committee of doctors examined her feet. Then, moving to various parts of the stage, Maggie produced rapping sounds that could be heard clearly throughout the hall.[59]

Maggie Fox's exposure of spirit rapping was a shock to the spiritualist movement, but one it could get over. Fox was known to be mentally unbalanced and addicted to alcohol and perhaps other drugs. Believers claimed that she had simply come under the control of evil men who wanted to exploit her name in order to embarrass them. Spirit rapping was not the fraud, they claimed, the renunciation was. Kate, too, was by now a pathetic remnant of her former self, so when both women signed their names to authenticate *Death-Blow to Spiritualism,* a little book exposing the history of spirit rapping which was published that same year, the truly dedicated spiritualists ignored it. Kate and Maggie found only limited success as antispiritualists, even though they toured the country for a time, now exposing spirit rapping. As audiences for Chauncey Burr had discovered years before, it was more fun to wonder how the trick was done than to be shown how it was done. Eventually, the two sisters even took up rapping again.[60]

Elisha Kane would have been horrified to see Margaret Fox's final days, little more than four years after her renunciation of spiritualism. She was destitute and lonely—prematurely old. Kate was gone, having died the previous year. Only days before her death, the *New York Times* reported that Maggie was shortly to be evicted from her tenement house in New York.[61] She was taken in by a sympathetic spiritualist, only to die on March 8, 1893, at fifty-nine years of age.[62] The *Daily Evening Telegraph* of Philadelphia reported: "Her face, once beautiful, was at the last marked by age and dissipation, and her one appetite was for intoxicating liquors. This wreck of womankind had been a guest in palaces and courts. The powers of mind, later almost imbecile, were the wonder and study of scientific men in America, Europe, and Australia."[63]

The one group who still had some use for Margaret Fox were the spiritualists. They organized her funeral. The ceremony was presided over by the departed Benjamin Franklin, who spoke through an entranced Reverend Charles Hicks. In addition to the hundreds of living mourners, the funeral was allegedly attended by the spirits of Leah Fish Underhill and Horace Greeley, both of whom had been dead for many years.[64] It was perhaps the paradox of Margaret Fox's life that all the while she strove for gentility and respectability, her only real support came from the spiritualists she so often despised.

Conclusion

Science, Showmanship, Celebrity, and Sensation

Fame is a fickle food
Upon a shifting plate.
Emily Dickinson, *Poems*

IN OCTOBER 1861, while reporting on the early days of the Civil War, the British journalist and diarist William Howard Russell reflected on the nature of American celebrity. "A public man in the United States is very much like a great firework," wrote Russell. "He commences with some small scintillations which attract the eye of the public, and then he blazes up and flares out in blue, purple, and orange fires, to the intense admiration of the multitude, and dying out suddenly is thought of no more, his place taken by a fresh Roman candle or Catherine wheel which is though to be far finer than those which have just dazzled the eyes of the fickle spectators."[1] Russell might well have been referring to Margaret Fox and Elisha Kane. Few today have ever heard of the explorer and the medium, regardless of how brightly their fleeting flames once burned.

The flames of public figures flare out for particular historical reasons that tell us something of the times in which they lived. Fox and Kane became famous because they lived at a time when mass commercial culture was taking on some of its modern characteristics, yet still retained vestiges of older ideals. Antebellum commercial culture embraced curiosity about life's mysteries and had a growing taste for sensation. Kane and Fox both appealed to these desires. Each mixed aspects of "high" and "low" culture in a way that addressed both the minds and moral sense of a wide audience. Yet, as their lives illustrate, this could be a problematic enterprise. Scientists and showmen, scholars and sensation mongers all competed for the attention and dollars of the American public in similar public forums, which fledgling institutional structures could not always sort out. Elisha Kane, with his tales of polar exploration, and Margaret

Fox, with her communications with the dead, are located somewhere in the borderlands between enlightenment and commercial entertainment.

From the perspective of a later age more used to the ways of commercial mass media, it is easy to see only the folly of Kane's and Fox's activities. The futile quest for an open sea at the North Pole, the quixotic attempt to rescue the lost explorer Franklin after he was surely dead, and the colorful stories presented in lectures and books make Kane seem nothing but a thrill-seeking adventurer, a hopeless romantic who led himself and others into needless danger. In turn, solemn séances and strange knockings make Margaret Fox appear either a fanatic or a fraud who coarsely manipulated the sorrows of her clients. But understanding Kane and Fox in the context of antebellum curiosity allows us to see that their activities were often understood by their contemporaries in terms of science, democratic learning, and American progress. Science, to antebellum Americans, was not an exclusively professional activity that went on only behind the closed doors of university laboratories or in the specialized pages of academic journals, though many at the time wanted to make this so. Rather, science was often a democratic endeavor that took place in the minds of citizens. While not "scientists" in any modern sense of the word (which was only coined during their lifetimes), Kane and Fox were understood by their contemporaries as guides in a wide-ranging search for knowledge. They encouraged their fellow Americans to explore other worlds using their senses and their reason rather than relying on the pronouncements of authorities. They presented strange phenomena for public consumption, and in doing so they promoted a type of popular scientific interest that was in decline even during their own lifetimes. Their personal experiences, particularly the sensationalism that came to surround their private lives, point to the reasons why the popular democratic manner of understanding science was already being overtaken by science as a profession engaged in by specialists with academic credentials.[2]

Science and mass culture turned out not to be as compatible as some Americans had hoped. Curiosity about new scientific discoveries was a great source of sensationalism in the media of mass culture, and those who sought to educate the nation about the mysteries of the world could not always be distinguished from those who sought to profit in the nation's growing economy. The mass media spread knowledge to an ever-expanding public. To some this represented democratic progress, since even the most humble mechanic could better himself and his family through intelligent amusements. To others, however, these endeavors represented crass commercialism at odds with republican virtue, for the knowledge transmitted in these forums was often superficial and not always reliable. How could scientists and intellectuals remain disinterested when the profit motive was taking over public life?

When Elisha Kane looked at the similarities between his own science and what he saw as the sensationalism of Margaret Fox's spirit rapping, he recognized that showmanship and commercialism, for better or worse, played a part in both their careers. He observed this with a certain degree of disgust, for comparison with a woman whom he saw as beneath him made him doubt his own worth. At the same time that he appealed to popular curiosity, he feared that publicity could obscure the difference between worthwhile knowledge, such as he thought he produced, and the deception and popular pandering of spiritualism. Kane's fear and mistrust of the public that he appealed to came to the fore in his personal relationship with Fox (and with William Godfrey), a relationship that was always hindered by the paradox of Kane's thinking. He was an elitist who achieved success as a popularizer. Perhaps the recognition of something of himself in Margaret Fox evoked in him an aversion to the sensational side of his own career, but it did not prevent him from promoting his explorations before a mass audience.

As their own lives became part of the sensational blend of the American culture of curiosity, their moral attributes, or perceived attributes, and their personal lives became the object of attention as well. The focus shifted from genteel learning to voyeuristic curiosity about issues of personality. Arctic exploration ceased being about icebergs and polar bears and became a measure of personal virtue. Kane's moral attributes were finally of greatest concern, as demonstrated by the rhetoric and ritual that surrounded his funeral. For those not converted to belief, spirit rapping ceased being an entertaining puzzle and became instead a sign of delusion. While Kane stood as a shining example of moral purity for American youth, Fox struggled to remain a respectable woman in the eyes of middle-class America. *The Love-Life of Doctor Kane* was the ultimate demonstration that voyeuristic curiosity about individual personalities was gaining ascendancy over anything that could even remotely be called learning. The Enlightenment was over, but inquiring minds still wanted to know.

If the culture of the age brought Kane and Fox together, the social structure of the age kept them apart. Elisha Kane may have admitted to his love that the two of them were similar, but in saying this he was only partially correct, as he well knew. Outside of the culture of curiosity, they remained worlds apart. Popular culture does much to unite a democratic society. It can provide a set of shared experiences to a diverse nation.[3] But, as we see in Margaret Fox's decline, there are social boundaries that popular culture may obscure but cannot overcome. Spirit rapping could draw the interest of both the Tammany thug Isaiah Rynders and the middle-class reformers Amy and Isaac Post; Elisha Kane's funeral could touch the feelings of rich and poor, North and South; the culture of curiosity could attract men and women from various social and economic backgrounds. But none of this could prompt Elisha Kane to admit publicly a connection with Margaret Fox or, later, prompt Robert Kane to embrace her as his sister-in-law. Social prejudice remained powerful, despite the fact that on one level Elisha Kane and Margaret Fox were "not so far removed after all."

Notes

Introduction: A Culture of Curiosity

1. Anonymous, *The Love-Life of Dr. Kane* (New York: George Carleton, 1865), 62 (hereafter *Love-Life*).

2. Ibid., 62.

3. William Shakespeare's characterization (in *Hamlet*) of death as an "undiscovered country" was a geographic metaphor well suited to the spiritual investigation of death in the nineteenth century. William Dean Howells used the phrase as the title of his novel about spiritualism. See William Dean Howells, *The Undiscovered Country* (Cambridge: Riverside Press, 1880). Fittingly, a romantic historical novel based on the relationship between Kane and Fox also uses the metaphor as a title. See Jay Walz and Audrey Walz, *The Undiscovered Country* (New York: Duell, Sloan & Pearce, 1958).

4. Howard P. Chudacoff and Judith E. Smith, *The Evolution of American Urban Society*, 5th ed. (Upper Saddle River, N.J.: Prentice Hall, 2000), 55.

5. On the changing nature of work in the early nineteenth century and its influence on social relationships see Paul E. Johnson, *A Shopkeeper's Millennium: Society and Revivals in Rochester, New York, 1815–1837* (New York: Hill and Wang, 1978). On the growth of the middle class, see Mary P. Ryan, *The Cradle of the Middle Class: The Family in Oneida County, New York, 1790–1865* (New York: Cambridge University Press, 1981). The uses of leisure time by working-class men and women in New York City is described in Christine Stansell, *City of Women: Sex and Class in New York, 1789–1860* (Chicago: University of Illinois Press, 1987).

6. Lawrence Levine, *Highbrow/Lowbrow: The Emergence of Cultural Hierarchy in America* (Cambridge: Harvard University Press, 1988). A good synthesis of the emergent popular culture of the era is Jim Cullen, *The Art of Democracy: A Concise History of Popular Culture in the United States* (New York: Monthly Review Press, 1996), 41–90.

7. Eric Lott, *Love and Theft: Blackface Minstrelsy and the American Working Class* (New York: Oxford University Press, 1993); David Roediger, *The Wages of Whiteness: Race and the Making of the American Working Class* (London: Verso, 1991).

8. Neil Harris, *Humbug: The Art of P. T. Barnum* (Chicago: University of Chicago Press, 1973); Andrea Stulman Dennett, *Weird and Wonderful: The Dime Museum in America* (New York: New York University Press, 1997); James L. Crouthamel, *Bennett's New York Herald and the Rise of the Popular Press* (Syracuse: Syracuse University Press, 1989).

9. Harris, *Humbug*, 61–89; also James W. Cook, *The Arts of Deception: Playing with Fraud in the Age of Barnum* (Cambridge: Harvard University Press, 2001).

10. Carl Bode, *The American Lyceum: Town Meeting of the Mind* (Carbondale: Southern Illinois University Press, 1956); Thomas Bender, *Intellect and Public Life: Essays on the Social History of Academic Intellectuals in the United States* (Baltimore: Johns Hopkins University Press, 1993), 3–46.

11. Bender, *Intellect*, 3–46.

12. The intellectual's response to the new urban audience is explored in Bender, *Intellect,* 30–46.

13. For a defense of the narrative approach to history and an overview of innovative new work in narrative history, see James Goodman, "For the Love of Stories," *Reviews in American History* 26, no. 1, (1998): 255–74. Also Jill Lepore, "Historians Who Love Too Much: Reflections on Microhistory and Biography," *Journal of American History* 88, no. 1 (June 2001): 129–44.

14. Ann Braude, *Radical Spirits: Spiritualism and Women's Rights in Nineteenth-Century America* (Boston: Beacon Press, 1989). Braude emphasizes the ways mediumship served to empower women. My view does not contradict Braude's thesis but gives greater emphasis to the drawbacks of public mediumship for one particular woman. Karen Halttunen's discussion of the tension between commercial success and the achievement of gentility is helpful to an understanding of Fox's position. See Karen Halttunen, *Confidence Men and Painted Women: A Study of Middle-Class Culture in America, 1830–1870* (New Haven: Yale University Press, 1982), 194–95, passim.

15. Goodman, "For the Love of Stories"; Lepore, "Historians Who Love Too Much"; Clifford Geertz, "Thick Description: Toward an Interpretive Theory of Culture," in *The Interpretation of Cultures* (New York: Basic Books, 1973), 3–30.

16. The idea of popular culture as a unifying force in American history is treated in Cullen, *Art of Democracy*.

1. Geographic Curiosity

1. Fletcher Webster, quoted in William Elder, *Biography of Elisha Kent Kane* (Philadelphia: Childs and Peterson, 1858), 75–76.

2. Nicholas B. Wainwright, ed., *A Philadelphia Perspective: The Diary of Sidney George Fisher Covering the Years 1834–1871*, (Philadelphia:Historical Society of Pennsylvania, 1967), 390.

3. *Dictionary of American Biography,* S.V. "John Kintzing Kane"; Elder, *Biography,* 13–17.

4. Quoted in Charles Coleman Sellers, *Mr. Peale's Museum: Charles Willson Peale and the First Popular Museum of Natural Science and Art* (New York: W. W. Norton, 1980), 167.

5. Ibid., 271, passim.

6. Elder, *Biography,* 18–31.

7. Ibid., 32–33; George Washington Corner, *Doctor Kane of the Arctic Seas* (Philadelphia: Temple University Press, 1972), 23–24.

8. Elder, *Biography*, 36–38; Corner, *Doctor Kane*, 24–25.

9. Elder, *Biography*, 40.

10. Ibid., 37.

11. Ibid., 53.

12. Corner, *Doctor Kane*, 26–28.

13. Peter Raby, *Bright Paradise: Victorian Scientific Travelers* (Princeton: Princeton University Press, 1996), 28–41.

14. Corner, *Doctor Kane*, 32–33.

15. Claude M. Fuess, *The Life of Caleb Cushing* (New York: Harcourt Brace, 1923), 397–454.

16. Ibid.

17. Elisha Kent Kane (hereafter EKK), "Rio de Janeiro," Elisha Kent Kane Papers, American Philosophical Society Library (hereafter EKK Papers).

18. Ibid.

19. Ibid.

20. "Description of a visit to Ceylon and India," William H. Weaver Papers, Margaret Elder Dow Collection, Dartmouth College, Rauner Special Collections Library (hereafter Dow Collection).

21. Corner, *Doctor Kane*, 36; Elder, *Biography*, 55–56; Fuess, *Cushing*, 422–25. There is some disagreement as to dates here: Corner says that Cushing arrived on November 28, while Elder incorrectly states that the *Brandywine* waited for "some months" in Bombay.

22. Quoted in Elder, *Biography*, 77.

23. Elder, *Biography*, 56.

24. Fuess, *Cushing*, 425–38.

25. Elder, *Biography*, 58; EKK, "Notebooks on Travels . . . [1844]," no. 1, EKK Papers.

26. Thomas Kane to EKK, February 12, 1847; January 26, 1851; April 12, 1851, EKK Papers.

27. EKK, "Notebooks on Travels . . . [1844]," nos. 1, 3, 4, 5, 6, 8, and one unnumbered; EKK, "Travel Notes"; "EKK Items," no. 4, EKK Papers.

28. EKK, "Notebooks on Travels . . . [1844]," no. 1, EKK Papers.

29. Ibid.

30. Ibid.

31. "EKK Items," no. 4, EKK Papers.

32. Ibid.

33. EKK, "Notebooks on Travels . . . [1844]," nos. 3, 4, and 5, EKK Papers.

34. EKK, "Notebooks of Travels . . . [1844]," no. 8, EKK Papers.

35. Ibid.

36. Ibid.

37. EKK, "Notebooks of Travels . . . [1844]," unnumbered, EKK Papers.

38. Ibid.

39. Ibid.

40. EKK to Kane family, April 14, 1844, EKK Papers.

41. EKK, "Travel Notes—The Crater," EKK Papers.

42. Elder, *Biography,* 63–65; EKK, "Travel Notes—The Crater," EKK Papers. Describing non-Western people as "Indians" far from either North America or India was common in the nineteenth century.

43. Elder, *Biography,* 64–65.

44. "Elisha Kent Kane," in Henry Simpson, *Lives of Eminent Philadelphians Now Deceased, Collected from Original and Authentic Sources* (Philadelphia: Brotherhead, 1859), 618–20.

45. Elder, *Biography,* 65–74; Corner, *Doctor Kane,* 40–42. Corner, a medical doctor, presumes rice fever to have been cholera.

46. Corner, *Doctor Kane,* 43–44; "EKK Items," no. 7, "Journal of a trip in Egypt," EKK Papers.

47. EKK, "Journal of a trip in Egypt."

48. Brian Fagan, *The Rape of the Nile: Tomb Robbers, Tourists, and Archeologists in Egypt* (New York: Charles Scribner's Sons, 1975), 11, passim.

49. EKK, "Journal of a trip in Egypt."

50. Ibid. On Samuel Morton, see William Stanton, *The Leopard's Spots: Scientific Attitudes toward Race in America, 1815–59* (Chicago: University of Chicago Press, 1960), 28–40, passim.

51. Elder, *Biography,* 96.

52. Elder, *Biography,* 97; Corner, *Doctor Kane,* 46–48.

53. Ahmed M. Metwalli, "Americans Abroad: The Popular Art of Travel Writing in the Nineteenth Century," in Steven E. Kagle, ed., *America: Exploration and Travel* (Bowling Green, Ohio: Bowling Green State University Popular Press, 1979), 68.

54. Charles Darwin, *The Voyage of the Beagle* (1839; reprint, New York: Penguin Books, 1989); Alexander von Humboldt, *Personal Narrative of a Journey to the Equinoctial Regions of the New Continent,* trans. Jason Wilson (1834; reprint, New York: Penguin Books, 1995); Charles Wilkes, *Narrative of the United States Exploring Expedition during the Years 1838, 1839, 1840, 1841, 1842,* 5 vols. (Philadelphia: Lea and Blanchard, 1845); John L. Stephens, *Incidents of Travel in Egypt, Arabia Petraea, and the Holy Land* (New York: Harper & Brothers, 1837); John L. Stephens, *Incidents of Travel in Central America, Chiapas, and Yucatan* (New York: Harper & Brothers, 1841); John Charles Frémont, *Report of the Exploring Expedition to the Rocky Mountains in the Year 1842, and to Oregon and North California in the Years 1843–44* (Washington, D.C.: Gales and Senton, Printers, 1845); V. Ponko Jr., "Science in the Exploration Narratives Authored by U.S. Naval Officers," in Kagle, *America: Exploration and Travel,* 92–100.

55. Bode, *American Lyceum,* 217–219.

56. Harris, *Humbug,* 33–57; Dennett, *Weird and Wonderful,* 32, passim.

57. Robert V. Bruce, *The Launching of Modern American Science, 1846–1876* (New York: Alfred A. Knopf, 1987), 187–200, 251–68.

58. *Knickerbocker,* 37 (April 1851): 371.

59. Robert Bogdan, *Freak Show: Presenting Human Oddities for Amusement and Profit* (Chicago: University of Chicago Press, 1988), 176–99.

2. "Come and Investigate"

1. Fox and her mother both were named Margaret. The daughter, who is our primary concern here, was generally called Maggie or Margaretta. Some accounts place the sisters' ages at as young as six and eight when the rappings began, but these accounts stem from Maggie Fox's later wish to disassociate herself from spiritualism by presenting herself as an innocent child drawn in against her will. Samples of Maggie's and Kate's writing from 1850 appear to be those of girls in at least their middle teens. The ages fifteen and twelve were given by Mrs. Fox in her signed statement published in E. E. Lewis, *A Report of the Mysterious Noises Heard in the House of Mr. John D. Fox, In Hydesville, Arcadia, Wayne County, N.Y. Authenticated by the Certificates, and Confirmed by the Statements of the Citizens of that Place and Vicinity* (Canandaigua, N.Y.: E. E. Lewis, 1848), 6. These approximate ages are also supported by the testimony of most people who met them at around this time.

2. Reuben Briggs Davenport, *The Death-Blow to Spiritualism, being the True Story of the Fox Sisters, as Revealed by Authority of Margaret Fox Kane and Catherine Fox Jencken* (New York: G. W. Dillingham, 1888), 84.

3. "Certificate of Mrs. Margaret Fox," in Lewis, *Mysterious Noises*, 5. A slightly different, but less reliable, version of Mrs. Fox's statement is also recounted in A. Leah Underhill, *The Missing Link in Modern Spiritualism* (New York: Thomas R. Knox & Co., 1885). Underhill was a later married name of Leah Fox Fish. More or less similar accounts, which derive largely from Lewis, include Eliab W. Capron and Henry D. Barron, *Singular Revelations: Explanation and History of the Mysterious Communion with Spirits* (Auburn, N.Y.: Finn & Rockwell, 1850); D. M. Dewey, *History of the Mysterious Noises, Heard at Rochester and Other Places, Supposed to be Spirit Communications together with many Psychological Facts and New Developments* (Rochester, N.Y.: D. M. Dewey, 1850).

4. "Certificate of Mrs. Margaret Fox," 6.

5. Davenport, *Death-Blow*, 90.

6. Ibid., 92.

7. "Certificate of Mrs. Margaret Fox," 6–7.

8. "Statement of Mrs. Mary Redfield," 30–31.

9. Ibid., 31.

10. "Certificate of Mrs. Margaret Fox," 8.

11. Ibid., "Statement of Wm. Duesler, of Arcadia," and "Certificate of Mrs. Elizabeth Jewell," in Lewis, *Mysterious Noises*. Although the name is left blank in the statements of these witnesses, a statement attesting to the character of John C. Bell tacked on to the end of Lewis's pamphlet makes obvious the identity of the accused.

12. Capron and Barron, *Singular Revelations*, 15.

13. "Certificate of Mrs. Margaret Fox" and "Statement of Wm. Duesler," 8–9, 14–16.

14. *Rochester Republican*, April 19, 1848.

15. Adelbert Cronise, "The Beginings of Modern Spiritualism in and near Rochester," *Publication Fund Series* (Rochester Historical Society), 5, (1926): 1–2.

16. "Statement of Lucretia Pulver," in Lewis, *Mysterious Noises*, 37–39.

17. Wayne County is not far west of Oneida County, the subject of Mary Ryan's study of the middle-class family during this era. Ryan, *Cradle of the Middle Class*.

18. Whitney R. Cross, *The Burned-Over District: The Social and Intellectual History of Enthusiastic Religion in Western New York, 1800–1850* (New York: Octagon Books, 1981), 3.

19. Herbert Jackson, *The Spirit Rappers* (Garden City, N.Y.: Doubleday, 1972), 2; "Statement of Walter Scotten," "Certificate of Mrs. Elizabeth Jewell," and "Statement of Wm. D. Storer," in Lewis, *Mysterious Noises*, 16–17, 19–20, 26–27; Capron and Barron, *Singular Revelations*, 12.

20. Cronise, "The Beginnings of Modern Spiritualism," 2.

21. One prevalent problem in secondary historical accounts of the rappings at Hydesville is that they often refer to later accounts by Leah Underhill or Eliab Capron for information. Both Capron and Underhill are very partisan sources who tend to exaggerate and embellish the original story. There is as yet no good biography of any of the sisters, although there have been attempts. Jackson, *Spirit Rappers*, is useful, but it consists mainly of lengthy quotations from newspaper reports without any citation. An unreliable and very poor biography of Margaret Fox is Earl Wesley Fornell, *The Unhappy Medium* (Austin: University of Texas Press, 1964).

22. Lewis, *Mysterious Noises*, 3–4, 42.

23. Davenport, *Death-Blow*, 90–91.

24. *Rochester Daily American*, April 4, 1848. On the theme of antebellum responses to deception, see Cook, *Arts of Deception*.

25. *Rochester Republican*, April 19, 27, 1848.

26. *Rochester Daily American*, April 22, 1848.

27. *Rochester Republican*, May 4, 18, 1848; *Auburn Daily Advertiser*, May 12, 27, 1848.

28. Underhill, *Missing Link*, 31–32. This book, written much later by Leah Fish (now Leah Underhill), needs to be read with a great deal of skepticism, as much of it is embellished and exaggerated in order to support the reality of spiritualist phenomena. It was described by Maggie Fox as a "lying book." Davenport, *Death-Blow*, 89.

29. Davenport, *Death-Blow*, 102–4.

30. Jackson, *Spirit Rappers*, 2, 20–23; Underhill, *Missing Link*, 30–31.

31. Underhill, *Missing Link*, 30–31.

32. Ibid., 32–33; Davenport, *Death-Blow*, passim.

33. Underhill, *Missing Link*, 33–40; Wheaton Phillips Webb, "Peddler's Protest," in *New York History*, 24 (April 1943): 228–50.

34. Davenport, *Death-Blow*, 36.

35. Ibid., 112.

36. Ibid., 92.

37. Johnson, *Shopkeeper's Millennium*; Nancy A. Hewitt, *Women's Activism and Social Change, Rochester, New York, 1822–1872* (Ithaca: Cornell University Press, 1984); Ronald G. Walters, *American Reformers, 1815–1860* (New York: Hill and Wang, 1978); Alice Felt Tyler, *Freedom's Ferment: Phases of American Social History to 1860* (Minneapolis: University of Minnesota Press, 1944); Jon Butler, *Awash in a Sea of Faith: Christianizing the American People* (Cambridge: Harvard University Press, 1990).

38. *Dictionary of American Biography*, S.V. "Isaac Post"; Jackson, *Spirit Rappers*, 25.

39. I use "spiritualists" and "spiritualism" to refer to those who believed in the spiritual nature of the raps and their beliefs, while I use "spirit rapping" to refer to the production of the noises by those who may or may not have believed in spiritualism.

40. On the relationship between spiritualism and reform, see Braude, *Radical Spirits*; Walters, *American Reformers;* Robert Delp, "American Spiritualism and Social Reform," *Northwest Ohio Quarterly*, 44, no. 4 (1972), 85–99.

41. Frederick Douglass, *The Life and Times of Frederick Douglass, Written by Himself* (Hartford, Conn.: Park Publishing Company, 1881), 232.

42. William Cooper Nell to Amy Post, August 11, December 12, 1849, Amy and Isaac Post Family Papers, Department of Rare Books and Special Collections, University of Rochester Library (hereafter Post Papers).

43. John Willis to Amy Post, June 21, 1849, Post Papers.

44. Walters, *American Reformers*, 163–172.

45. Braude, *Radical Spirits*, 18–19.

46. Spiritualist philosophy is another matter, but one not directly tied to the activity of the sisters. Spiritualist beliefs were very much connected to the reformist ideals of believers, but there is no evidence that the Fox sisters ever held any such beliefs.

47. Underhill, *Missing Link*.

48. A typical example of this upward mobility was Abby Warner, a disfigured teenage orphan who rapped for middle-class spiritualists in Ohio. Dr. Abel Underhill, *The Arrest, Trial, and Acquittal of Abby Warner for Spirit Rapping in St. Timothy's Church in Massillon O.* (Cleveland: Gray & Wood/Plain Dealer Steam Press, 1852). Victoria Woodhull, a famous spiritualist and advocate for women's rights in later years, also came from a background of poverty; see Barbara Goldsmith, *Other Powers: The Age of Suffrage, Spiritualism, and the Scandalous Victoria Woodhull* (New York: Knopf, 1998), 8–27. Interestingly, this tendency can also be seen in the creation of Mormonism by the poverty-stricken Joseph Smith and the less successful "Kingdom of Matthias" by Robert Mathiews; Tyler, *Freedom's Ferment*, 86–88; Paul Johnson and Sean Wilentz, *The Kingdom of Matthias: A Story of Sex and Salvation in Nineteenth-Century America* (New York: Oxford University Press, 1994).

49. Margaret Fox Kane to Amy Post, August 21, 1849, Post Papers.
50. Underhill, *Missing Link*, 47–56.
51. Webb, "Peddler's Protest."
52. Ibid., 236.
53. Ibid., 237.
54. Ibid., 239.
55. Ibid., 245–46.
56. *Auburn Daily Advertiser*, November, 3, 1848.
57. E. W. Capron, *Modern Spiritualism, its Facts and Fanaticisms, its Consistencies and Contradictions* (New York: Partridge and Brittan, 1855), 66–67.
58. Capron and Barron, *Singular Revelations*, 40.
59. Underhill, *Missing Link*, 62–65.
60. *Rochester Daily Democrat*, November 15, 16, 1849.
61. *Auburn Daily Advertiser*, December 30, 1848.
62. Ibid., July 8, 1848.
63. Ibid., September 4, 1849.
64. Ibid., September 5, 1849.
65. Ibid., September 11, 1849.
66. Ibid., October 20, 23, 26, 1849.
67. *Rochester Republican*, November 29, 1849.
68. *Rochester Daily Democrat*, November 16, 1849.
69. R. Laurence Moore, *In Search of White Crows: Spiritualism, Parapsychology, and American Culture* (New York: Oxford University Press, 1977).
70. Edgar Allan Poe, "Mesmeric Revelation," in *The Short Fiction of Edgar Allan Poe* (Chicago: University of Illinois Press, 1990), 139–145.
71. Capron, *Modern Spiritualism*; Alison Winter, *Mesmerized: Powers of Mind in Victorian Britain* (Chicago: University of Chicago Press, 1998); Robert Darnton, *Mesmerism and the End of Enlightenment in France* (Cambridge: Harvard University Press, 1968); Robert C. Fuller, *Mesmerism and the American Cure of Souls* (Philadelphia: University of Philadelphia Press, 1982).
72. *Rochester Republican*, November 29, 1849.
73. *Auburn Daily Advertiser*, November 17, 1849.
74. *Rochester Republican*, November 29, 1849.
75. *New York Tribune*, November 29, 1849.
76. Moore, *White Crows;* Walters, *American Reformers;* Braude, *Radical Spirits;* Bret E. Carroll, *Spiritualism in Antebellum America* (Bloomington: Indiana University Press, 1997).
77. Braude, *Radical Spirits*, 18.

3. Humboldtean Science and the Search for Franklin

1. Elder, *Biography,* 101–141; Corner, *Doctor Kane*, 49–70.
2. Hugh Richard Slotten, *Patronage, Practice, and Culture of American Science: Alexander Dallas Bache and the U.S. Coast Survey* (New York: Cambridge University Press, 1994), 1.

3. Susan Cannon, *Science in Culture: The Early Victorian Period* (New York: Science History Publications, 1978), 73–110; Michael Dettlebach, Intro. to Alexander von Humboldt, *Cosmos: A Sketch of the Physical Description of the Universe* (Baltimore: Johns Hopkins University Press, 1997), vii–xlii; William H. Goetzmann, *Army Exploration in the American West* (New Haven: Yale University Press, 1959), 16–19, 423; Slotten, *Patronage*, 112–46.

4. Cannon, *Science*, 73–110. For an interesting treatment of Humboldt's influence in South America, see Mary Louise Pratt, *Imperial Eyes: Travel Writing and Transculturation* (New York: Routledge, 1992), 111–43.

5. Benjamin A. Gould, "An Address in Commemoration of Alexander Dallas Bache," quoted in Slotten, *Patronage*, 116.

6. EKK to Alexander Dallas Bache, December 24, 1849, EKK Papers.

7. EKK to J. D. L Kane, April 8, 1850, EKK Papers.

8. Slotten, *Patronage*, 172.

9. Cannon, *Science*, 86; Andrew Rolle, *John Charles Frémont: Character as Destiny* (Norman: University of Oklahoma Press, 1991), 142; John Muir, *The Story of My Boyhood and Youth* (Boston: Houghton Mifflin, 1938), 259.

10. Humboldt, *Personal Narrative* and *Cosmos*.

11. Edgar Allan Poe, *Eureka: A Prose Poem* (Amherst, N.Y.: Prometheus Books, 1997), 3, 6–7.

12. *New York Daily Times*, May 5, 1853.

13. *New York Herald*, November 3, 1849.

14. *Eclectic Magazine*, 40 (1857): 388; *Littell's Living Age*, 52 (1857): 400.

15. *Eclectic Magazine*, 15 (1848): 133.

16. Jeannette Mirsky, *To the Arctic! The Story of Northern Exploration from Earliest Times* (Chicago: University of Chicago Press, 1970), 95–129; Pierre Burton, *The Arctic Grail: The Quest for the North West Passage and the North Pole, 1818–1909* (Toronto: McClelland and Stewart, 1988); Ann Savours, *The Search for the North West Passage* (New York: St. Martin's Press, 1999); Trevor Levere, *Science and the Canadian Arctic* (New York: Cambridge University Press, 1993).

17. "What does Africa, what does the West, stand for? Is not our own interior white on the chart? black though it may prove, like the coast, when discovered. Is it the source of the Nile, or the Niger, or the Mississippi, or a Northwest Passage around this continent, that we would find? Are these the problems which most concern mankind? Is Franklin the only man who is lost, that his wife should be so earnest to find him? Does Mr. Grinnell know where he himself is?" Henry David Thoreau, *Walden*, in *Henry David Thoreau: Three Complete Books* (New York: Gramercy Books, 1993), 389.

18. Leslie H. Neatby, *The Search for Franklin* (New York: Walker and Company, 1970), 119; Mirsky, *To the Arctic!* 130–40; "The Arctic Expeditions," in *Littell's Living Age*, 20 (1849): 289–97; *New York Herald*, December 3, 1849.

19. Jane Franklin to Zachary Taylor, April 4, 1849, in *New York Herald*, May 6, 1849.

20. John M. Clayton to Jane Franklin, April 25, 1849, in *New York Herald*, May 4, 1849.

21. *New York Herald*, May 10, July 17, 1849.

22. For an excellent discussion of the sublime appeal of the Arctic, see Francis Spufford, *"I May Be Some Time": Ice and the English Imagination* (Boston: Faber and Faber, 1996), 16–40.

23. *New York Herald*, July 17, 1849.

24. *Dictionary of American Biography,* S.V. "Henry Grinnell."

25. EKK to Thomas L. Kane, March 8, 1850, EKK Papers.

26. *New York Herald*, February 23, 1850.

27. *New York Herald*, May 15, 1850.

28. Elisha Kent Kane, *The U.S. Grinnell Expedition in Search of Sir John Franklin: A Personal Narrative* (New York: Harper & Brothers, 1853), 17.

29. Ibid., 18.

30. Robert Randolph Carter, "Private Journal of a Cruise in the Brig Rescue in Search of Sir John Franklin," in Harold B. Gill Jr. and Joanne Young, eds., *Searching for the Franklin Expedition: The Arctic Journal of Robert Randolph Carter* (Annapolis: Naval Institute Press, 1998), 18.

31. Kane, *U.S. Grinnell Expedition,* 24.

32. Carter, "Journal," 21.

33. Elder, *Biography,* 151.

34. Kane, *U.S. Grinnell Expedition*, 50–51.

35. Ibid., 71–72, 100–105; EKK to J. D. L. Kane, August 21, 1850, EKK Papers; EKK to Thomas L. Kane, August 23, 1850, EKK Papers.

36. EKK to Thomas Kane, August 23, 1850.

37. Kane, *U.S. Grinnell Expedition,* 151–55; Carter, "Journal," 54–57; Gill and Young, *Searching*, 7.

38. Kane, *U.S. Grinnell Expedition,* 155–68; Carter, "Journal," 59–63.

39. Kane, *U.S. Grinnell Expedition,* 164–69.

40. Ernest S. Dodge, *The Polar Rosses: John and James Clark Ross and Their Explorations* (New York: Barnes & Noble, 1973), 43–93, 222–40.

41. Kane, *U.S. Grinnell Expedition,* 171.

42. Ibid., 170–76; Carter, *Journal*, 59–72.

43. Kane, *U.S. Grinnell Expedition*, 32, 39, 145–46, passim; EKK to "Bessie" Kane, n.d. (ca. August 1850), EKK Papers.

44. Carter, "Journal," 23, 24, 28, 52, 53, passim.

45. Kane, *U.S. Grinnell Expedition*, 30, 32–34, 48, 137, passim.

46. Ibid., 37–40, 132–33.

47. Carter, "Journal," 89–90.

48. William Ballard Preston to Edwin DeHaven, May 15, 1850, printed in *Littell's Living Age*, 26 (1850), 45; also reported in many other contemporary newspapers and periodicals.

49. This theory is laid out in Matthew Fontaine Maury, *The Physical Geography of the Sea* (New York: Harper & Brothers, 1857); Elisha Kent Kane, "Access to Open Polar Sea," in *U.S. Grinnell Expedition*, 543–52; John Kirkland

Wright, *Human Nature in Geography* (Cambridge: Harvard University Press, 1966), 89–118.

50. Wright, *Human Nature*, 89–118.

51. The orders mention Maury by name. *Littell's Living Age*, 26 (1850): 45.

52. Wright, *Human Nature*, 102, 104.

53. Mary Shelley, *Frankenstein: Or the Modern Prometheus* (1818; reprint, New York: Penguin Books, 1992), 13; Edgar Allan Poe, "Narrative of Arthur Gordon Pym," in *The Fall of the House of Usher and Other Tales* (New York: Signet Classic, 1980), 200–373; Edgar Allan Poe, "Manuscript Found in a Bottle" and "Hans Pfaal," in *The Short Fiction of Edgar Allan Poe* (Chicago: University of Illinois Press, 1990), 558–88, 623–29; Jules Verne, *The Adventures of Captain Hatteras* (Westport, Conn.: Associated Booksellers, 1961); Sarah Orne Jewett, *The Land of the Pointed Firs and Other Stories*, ed. Sarah Way Sherman (1896; reprint, Hanover, N.H.: University Press of New England, 1997), 20–30.

54. John Cleves Symmes Jr., quoted in William Stanton, *The Great United States Exploring Expedition of 1838–1842* (Berkeley: University of California Press, 1975), 8.

55. See Poe's stories "Hans Pfaal," "Manuscript Found in a Bottle," and "The Narrative of Arthur Gordon Pym," and Verne, *Captain Hatteras*, and Jules Verne, *Journey to the Centre of the Earth*, trans. William Butcher (1864; reprint, Oxford: Oxford University Press, 1992).

56. Stanton, *Great United States Exploring Expedition*, 8–40.

57. *New York Evening Post*, June 4, 1850; *New York Tribune*, November 21, 1851; *New York Daily Times*, October 11, 1851; *Cincinnati Daily Times*, October 18, 1851; *Cleveland Daily Plain Dealer*, October 21, 1851.

58. John C. Symmes to EKK, October 20, 1851, EKK Papers.

59. *New York Herald*, May 22, 1850.

60. Winter, *Mesmerized*, 122–25; *Daily Albany Argus*, April 17, 1850.

61. *Troy Daily Whig*, May 16, 1850; *Albany Daily State Register*, May 16, 1850.

62. These tables were prepared by Charles Schott of the Coast Survey. Schott proved Carter's criticism of armchair Humboldteans by complaining with Kane of the quality of the meteorological data collected by the first Grinnell Expedition; Charles A. Schott to EKK, November 29, 1852; EKK to Charles A. Schott, May 8, 1852, EKK Papers.

63. Kane, *U.S. Grinnell Expedition*, 67.

64. Ibid., 66.

65. Ibid., 67.

66. Ibid., 552.

4. The Spirit of Inquiry in New York City

1. Despite frequent misstatements to the contrary, Barnum's Hotel and the Fox sisters were connected with neither P. T. Barnum nor his American Museum. The misconception that P. T. Barnum was the Fox sisters' publicist arose because,

when they visited New York City in the summer of 1850, they stayed in a hotel called Barnum's Hotel. This hotel was run by an entirely different Barnum. The mistake was made at the time by non–New Yorkers who were not aware of a distinction between Barnum's Hotel and Barnum's Museum, but was corrected in the *New York Tribune*, July 6, 1850. More recently the misconception has been reinforced in Fornell, *The Unhappy Medium*, 24–27, which later historians have sometimes taken as an accurate biography.

2. The evening was reported on by George Ripley in the *New York Tribune*, June 8, 1850, and by Nathaniel P. Willis in the *Home Journal*, June 15, 1850.

3. *New York Tribune*, June 8, 1850.

4. Ibid.

5. Ibid.

6. *Home Journal*, June 15, 1850.

7. *New York Tribune*, June 8, 1850.

8. Underhill, *Missing Link*, 141.

9. James Fenimore Cooper to Mrs. Cooper, June 9, 1850, in *The Letters and Journals of James Fenimore Cooper*, ed., James Franklin Beard (Cambridge: Harvard University Press, 1968), 4: 193.

10. *New York Tribune*, June 8, 1850; *Home Journal*, June 15, 1850.

11. *New York Evening Post*, June 15, 1850.

12. *New York Tribune*, November 29, 1849.

13. *New York Tribune*, December 5, 1849.

14. Valentine Nicholson to Amy and Isaac Post, December 16, 1949, Post Papers.

15. Edmund P. Willis to Isaac Post, April 26, 1850, Post Papers.

16. Why Mr. Fox was not involved in this decision is unclear, and for this time period seems very odd. After the initial rappings in Hydesville, John D. Fox receded into the background and remained in Acadia Township, while his wife and daughters constantly moved about the country.

17. Eliab W. Capron to Margaret Rutan Fox, February 10, 1850, Post Papers.

18. Barbara Goldsmith, in her biography of Victoria Woodhull, has claimed that Greeley made a trip to Rochester in August 1849 to see the sisters and "fetch Kate Fox." It is unclear where she got this information, as none of the sources listed in her endnotes say anything of the sort. Kate did, however, stay with the Greeleys for a time in the late summer and fall of 1850. Goldsmith, *Other Powers*, 55.

19. Eliab W. Capron to Margaret Rutan Fox, February 10, 1850, Post Papers.

20. Capron, *Modern Spiritualism*, 183; Davenport, *Death-Blow*, 121–30.

21. Davenport, *Death-Blow*, passim.

22. *New York Tribune*, June 29, 1850.

23. *New York Evening Post*, April 30, 1850; *Daily Albany Argus*, May 10, 1850; *New York Tribune*, June 27, 1850.

24. The best source for theologically oriented spiritualism is Carroll, *Spiritualism in Antebellum America*; see also Ernest Isaacs, "A History of Nineteenth-

Century American Spiritualism as a Religious and Social Movement" (Ph.D. diss., University of Wisconsin, 1975).

25. *Troy Daily Whig*, May 1, 1850; Underhill, *Missing-Link*, 117–22.

26. Underhill, *Missing Link*, 117–22. There was little notice of the sisters' presence in Albany and Troy in those cities' newspapers. I found no mention of the visit in the *Daily Albany Argus, the Albany State Register*, or the *Albany Evening Journal*, but the *Troy Daily Whig* did report on the visit on May 1, 3, 11, 20, and 25, 1850.

27. Leah Fish states that they arrived in New York City on June 4, 1850; Underhill *Missing Link*, 128. But newspaper reports indicate that they were in the city as early as May 29. *New York Evening Post*, June 1, 1850; *New York Tribune*, June 5, 1850.

28. *New York Herald*, June 17, 1850.

29. Underhill, *Missing Link*, 128.

30. Ibid., 128–130.

31. Newspaper accounts primarily mention men attending these public séances. Whether this is because men predominated as guests or because newspapers simply omitted any mention of women who were present is unclear. Most likely there was some distinction between the public and private séances with regard to gender. Women may have gravitated more toward private séances in homes.

32. *New York Tribune*, June 5, 1850.

33. Greeley's position on the raps has often been misinterpreted. Many have taken his statement that there was no deception out of context as an endorsement of spirits and spiritualist philosophy. Greeley was interested, but that interest should not be read as any sort of acceptance of spiritualist beliefs. He was one of the many (perhaps even the majority) who attended séances with an open, curious mind, yet never came to a definitive conclusions.

34. *New York Evening Post*, June 6, 1850.

35. *New York Herald*, June 17, 1850.

36. *New York Tribune*, June 5, 1850.

37. *New York Tribune*, June 8, 1850.

38. *Home Journal*, June 15, 1850.

39. *New York Herald*, June 17, 1850.

40. Halttunen, *Confidence Men*, 40, passim.

41. Ibid., 57.

42. Davenport, *Death-Blow*, 127

43. *New York Tribune*, June 5, 1850.

44. *New York Tribune*, July 17, 1850.

45. Gustavus Myers, *The History of Tammany Hall* (New York: Gustavus Myers, 1901), 161.

46. Anthony Gronowicz, *Race and Class Politics in New York City before the Civil War* (Boston: Northeastern University Press, 1998), 141–42.

47. M. R. Werner, *Tammany Hall*, (Garden City: Doubleday, Doran & Company, 1928), 65.

48. *New York Herald*, July 12, 1850.

49. Ibid.

50. John D. Stevens, *Sensationalism and the New York Press* (New York: Columbia University Press), 1–28.

51. Crouthamel, *Bennett's New York Herald*, 19–42, passim; Don C. Seitz, *The James Gordon Bennetts, Father and Son, Proprietors of the New York Herald* (Indianapolis: Bobbs-Merrill, 1928), 46–47; Patricia Cline Cohen, *The Murder of Helen Jewett: The Life and Death of a Prostitute in Nineteenth-Century New York* (New York: Knopf, 1998).

52. On the emergence of the murder mystery genre at this time in American culture as well as literature, see Halttunen, *Murder Most Foul: The Killer and the American Gothic Imagination* (Cambridge: Harvard University Press, 1998), 91–134.

53. *New York Herald*, January 23, 1850.

54. *New York Herald*, February 6, May 9, 1850.

55. *New York Herald*, June 16, 1850.

56. *New York Tribune*, December 10, 1849.

57. *New York Tribune*, January 11, 1850.

58. *New York Tribune*, January 18, 1850; Capron and Barron, *Singular Revelations*.

59. Capron and Barron, *Singular Revelations*, 8.

60. *New York Tribune*, January 23, 1850.

61. Halttunen, *Confidence Men*.

62. *New York Tribune*, January 31, 1850.

63. *New York Tribune*, February 4, 1850.

64. Ibid.

65. Ibid.

66. Ibid.

67. *New York Tribune*, February 11, 1850.

68. *New York Tribune*, August 10, 1850. Greeley's wife was another matter entirely. She had been mentally ill for a long time, and she and her husband had recently lost their youngest child, Pickie. As a result, she came to believe strongly in the spirits. Goldsmith, *Other Powers*, 55–62.

69. *New York Tribune*, July 3, 1850.

70. Isaacs, "A History," 141–147.

71. *New York Tribune*, July 9, 1850.

72. *New York Tribune*, July 17, 1850.

73. Ibid.

74. *New York Tribune*, July 31, August 1, 1850.

75. *New York Tribune*, July 31, 1850.

76. *New York Evening Post*, August 3, 1850.

77. *New York Tribune*, January 11, 1851.

78. *New York Tribune*, January 11, 13, 17, 1851.

79. *New York Tribune*, January 13, 1851.

80. *New York Tribune,* January 17, 1851.

81. *New York Tribune*, February 5, 1851.

82. Buffalo Doctors, *Rochester Knockings! Discovery and Explanation of the Source of the Phenomena Generally Known as the Rochester Knockings* (Buffalo: George H. Derby and Co., 1851), 6.

83. Ibid., 7.

84. Ibid.

85. Underhill, *Missing Link*, 173.

86. The letter is reprinted ibid., 171–72, and in Buffalo Doctors, *Rochester Knockings*, 9.

87. Underhill, *Missing Link,* 196.

88. *New York Tribune*, June 3, 1851.

89. *New York Tribune*, October 18, 1851.

90. Ernest Isaacs, "The Fox Sisters," in Howard Kerr and Charles L. Crow, eds., *The Occult in America: New Historical Perspectives* (Urbana: University of Illinois Press, 1983), 82.

91. Braude, *Radical Spirits,* 19.

92. Isaacs, "The Fox Sisters."

93. Carroll, *Spiritualism*, passim; Isaacs, "A History."

94. Harris, *Humbug*, 4.

5. Curiosity and Values in the Antebellum Lecture Hall

1. EKK to Lady Jane Franklin, November 15, 1851, EKK Papers.

2. *The New York Daily Times,* January 10, 1852. It was normal for newspapers to print detailed reviews of popular lectures the day after they were given, but usually these were not more than a single column in length and appeared only in the papers of the city where the lecture was given.

3. *Philadelphia Public Ledger*, January 6, 1852.

4. *New York Daily Times*, January 10, 1852.

5. Ibid.

6. Ibid.

7. Ibid.

8. "Notice of Elisha's Lecture" (clipping from *Philadelphia Evening Bulletin,* February 21, 1852), in Thomas L. Kane Papers, American Philosophical Society Library.

9. This can be determined from the many invitations from lecture halls and lyceums around the country which can be found in his papers. He accepted only a fraction of the offers he received.

10. Bode, *American Lyceum;* Bender, *Intellect and Public Life*, 3–46.

11. David Mead, *Yankee Eloquence in the Middle West: The Ohio Lyceum, 1850–1870* (East Lansing: Michigan State College Press, 1951).

12. *New York Daily Tribune*, October 21, 1852.

13. Donald B. Smith, "The Life of George Copway or Kah-ge-ga-gah-bowh

(1818–1869)—and a Review of his Writings," *Journal of Canadian Studies*, 23, no. 3 (1988): 5–38. Reviews of Copway's lectures also frequently appeared in periodicals of the day. See, for instance, *New York Herald*, February 20, 1849.

14. George Gilfillian, "Popular Lecturers.—Professor Nichol," *Eclectic Magazine*, 14 (1848): 98.

15. *New York Daily Tribune*, October 28, 1852.

16. *New York Daily Tribune*, November 24, 1852.

17. *Troy Daily Whig*, December 4, 1855; *Eclectic Magazine*, 14 (1848): 98–99; *Philadelphia Public Ledger*, February 5, 1853.

18. Underhill, *Missing Link*, 221.

19. *Cleveland Daily Plain Dealer*, April 14, 1851.

20. Moore, *White Crows*, passim; Carroll, *Spiritualism*, 53, 152, 161, passim. Carroll deals primarily with Tiffany as an advocate of individual freedom and "Spiritualist Republicanism."

21. *Cleveland Daily Plain Dealer*, April 14, 1851.

22. Moore, *White Crows*, passim. Moore traces the continuing attempt to reconcile spiritualism with the scientific method and acquire objective and experimental proof of its authenticity.

23. *Cleveland Daily Plain Dealer*, April 29, May 1, 1851.

24. *Cleveland Daily Plain Dealer*, May 5, 1851.

25. Ibid.

26. *Cleveland Daily Plain Dealer*, May 6, 1851.

27. Ibid.

28. *Cleveland Daily Plain Dealer*, May 9, 1851.

29. Ibid.

30. Ibid.

31. *Cleveland Daily Plain Dealer*, May 12, 1851.

32. There is some question whether Leah Fish sued Burr herself or if Joel Tiffany, who was also a lawyer, sued him on her behalf.

33. *Cleveland Daily Plain Dealer*, May 15, 1851.

34. *Cleveland Daily Plain Dealer*, May 26, 1851.

35. Underhill, *Missing Link*, 228; *Cleveland Daily Plain Dealer*, August 4, 30, 1851.

36. George Templeton Strong, *Diary of George Templeton Strong: The Turbulent Fifties, 1850–1859*, ed. Allan Nevins and Milton Halsey Thomas (New York: Macmillan, 1952), 15–16, 93, 119, 125.

37. Holmes quoted by Moore, *White Crows*, 41.

38. Horace Greeley, *Recollections of a Busy Life* (New York: J. B. Ford & Co., 1868), 234–41.

39. *Daily National Intelligencer* (Washington, D.C.), March 19, 1853.

40. *Daily National Intelligencer* (Washington, D.C.), March 14, 1853.

6. Private Lives, Public Curiosity

1. *Love-Life*, 60.

2. Henry Grinnell to EKK, February 11, 1852, EKK Papers; *Philadelphia Public Ledger*, February 18, 1852.

3. EKK to Henry Grinnell, May 7, 1852, EKK Papers.

4. Pierre Berton, *The Arctic Grail: The Quest for the North West Passage and the North Pole, 1818–1909*, (Toronto: McClelland and Stewart, 1988).

5. EKK to Henry Grinnell, May 7, 1852.

6. Corner, *Doctor Kane*, 102–24; Elder, *Biography*, 166–86.

7. A. Leah Fish to Amy Post, July 22, 1851, Post Papers.

8. Ibid.

9. Ibid.

10. Moore, *White Crows*, 27.

11. Margaretta Fox to Amy Post, "Wednesday afternoon" (n.d.), Post Papers.

12. Catherine Fox to Amy Post, November [1851], Post Papers.

13. Ibid.

14. Margaretta Fox to Amy Post, "Wednesday afternoon" (n.d.), Post Papers.

15. *Love-Life*, 237–39; Winter, *Mesmerized*, 122–24; *Daily Albany Argus*, April 17, 1850; *Troy Daily Whig*, May 16, 1850; *Albany Daily State Register*, May 16, 1850.

16. *Love-Life*, 23.

17. Ibid., 24.

18. Ibid., 28–30.

19. Cornelius Grinnell to EKK, January 31, February 2, 1853, EKK Papers.

20. This controversy is discussed in greater detail in chapter 10.

21. See especially Mrs. E. F. Ellet to J. P. Green, "in re R. P. Kane, M. Fox dispute," n.d. (ca. 1862–66), Robert Patterson Kane Papers, American Philosophical Society Library; Margaret Fox to Mrs. Ellet, n.d., EKK Papers. Although she was well known in her time, there is very little historical work on Elizabeth Ellet. The best source is Scott Casper, *Constructing American Lives: Biography and Culture in Nineteenth-Century America* (Chapel Hill: University of North Carolina Press, 1999), 158–78. See also "Elizabeth Fries Ellet," in *Notable American Women 1607–1950*, ed. Edwaral T. James (Cambridge: Belkazo Press of Harvard University Press, 1971), 569–570.

22. *Love-Life*, 27.

23. Ibid., 50.

24. Ibid., 30.

25. Ibid., 33.

26. The importance of "respectability" in antebellum culture is explored by Richard L. Bushman, *The Refinement of America: Persons, Houses, Cities* (New York: Vintage Books, 1993).

27. *Love-Life*, 34.

28. Ibid., 66.

29. Stansell, *City of Women*, 76–101.

30. Corner, *Doctor Kane*, 51–52; "J.T.L." to EKK, February 4, 1846, EKK Papers; C. C. Van Wyck to EKK, May 27, 1846, EKK Papers; EKK to Helen Patterson, May 7, [1846], EKK Papers.

31. Robert Patterson Kane to EKK, November 12, 1846, EKK Papers; indenture contract, "Miscellany #5," EKK Papers.

32. *Love-Life*, 48.

33. Underhill, *Missing Link*, 251–52; *Love-Life*, 51.

34. Of the three Fox sister, Leah best fits Ann Braude's description of a woman empowered by involvement with spiritualism, but even she eventually solidified her advancement with an advantageous marriage and gave up rapping. Braude, *Radical Spirits*.

35. *Love-Life*, 52.

36. Ibid., 54.

37. Cornelius Grinnell to EKK, January 31, 1853, EKK Papers.

38. Cornelius Grinnell to EKK, "Thursday," EKK Papers.

39. Cornelius Grinnell to EKK, January 31, 1853, EKK Papers.

40. Cornelius Grinnell to EKK, February 2, 1853, EKK Papers.

41. EKK to Cornelius Grinnell, n.d., EKK Papers (misfiled as EKK to Henry Grinnell).

42. *Love-Life*, 64.

43. Ibid., 67.

44. Ibid., 68–69.

45. Ibid., 72.

46. Ibid., 74.

47. Ibid., 78.

48. "Fox-Kane correspondence in re. schooling," EKK Papers.

49. *Dictionary of American Biography*, S.V. "Francis Hawks."

50. Francis Hawks to Dr. Croswell, March 26, 1853, "Fox-Kane correspondence in re. schooling."

51. EKK to Eliza Leiper, May 1, 1853; EKK to Robert Patterson Kane, June 1853, EKK Papers.

52. Eliza Leiper to EKK, April 7, 1853; EKK to Eliza Leiper, April 11, 1853; EKK to Eliza Leiper, n.d.; EKK to Eliza Leiper, May 1, 1853; "Fox-Kane correspondence in re. schooling."

53. Maggie Fox to EKK, "Fox-Kane Correspondence in re. schooling." This letter is one of a group, tied together with a ribbon, concerning Fox's placement during Kane's absence, all of which support the story that Fox's schooling was being driven by paternalistic sentiments. In another letter, EKK to Robert Patterson Kane, n.d., EKK Papers, Kane tells his brother, "I want to place it in your power documentarily to set me right in case of misrepresentation or false construction reaching dear Mother's ears." The "Fox-Kane correspondence in re. schooling" are most likely the documents to which he was referring. They seem to form a carefully selected collection that would provide cover in case the story of his interest in Fox went public.

7. Departure

1. William C. Godfrey, *Godfrey's Narrative of the Last Grinnell Arctic Exploring Expedition, in Search of Sir John Franklin, 1853–4–5* (Philadelphia: J. T. Lloyd & Co., 1857), 18–19 (hereafter *Godfrey's Narrative*).

2. Ibid., 19–20.

3. Oscar M. Villarejo, *Dr. Kane's Voyage to the Polar Lands* (Philadelphia: University of Pennsylvania Press, 1965), 11–12; Corner, *Doctor Kane*, 125–26.

4. Villarejo, *Dr. Kane's Voyage*, 11–12; Corner, *Doctor Kane*, 125–26.

5. EKK to family, June 8, 1853; EKK to Cornelius Grinnell [misfiled as EKK to Henry Grinnell], July 20, 1853, EKK Papers.

6. *Godfrey's Narrative*, 31–32.

7. *New York Daily Times*, June 1, 1853.

8. EKK to family, June 8, 1853.

9. Elder, *Biography*, 18–28; Corner, *Doctor Kane*, 67–68.

10. EKK to family, June 8, 1853.

11. John Wall Wilson, Diary, May 18, 1854, American Philosophical Society Library.

12. EKK to family, June 8, 1853.

13. *Godfrey's Narrative*, 62.

14. Ibid., 62.

15. Ibid., 63.

16. Thomas Hickey, *Thomas Hickey's Narrative of the Last Arctic Expedition of Dr. Kane* (Newark: Newark Daily Mercury Office, 1858), 3 (hereafter *Hickey's Narrative*). Copy found in the New-York Historical Society collection.

17. The native people of Greenland are popularly known as Eskimo, and they are culturally connected with the Inuit of northern Canada. Either Inuit or Native Greenlander is their preferred name, rather than Eskimo.

18. Elisha Kent Kane, *Arctic Explorations: The Second Grinnell Expedition in Search of Sir John Franklin, 1853, '54, '55* (Philadelphia: Childs and Peterson, 1856), 1:23–24; Hans Christian Hendrik was sometimes called Hans Christian.

19. Ibid., 1:24; Hans Hendrik, *Memoirs of Hans Hendrik, the Arctic Traveler, Serving under Kane, Hayes, Hall, and Nares, 1853–1876*, trans. Dr. Henry Rink (London: Trubner & Co., 1878), 22.

20. EKK to Cornelius Grinnell, July 20, 1853.

21. *Hickey's Narrative*, 4.

22. EKK to Cornelius Grinnell, July 20, 1853.

23. Ibid.

24. Carl Petersen, *Dr. Kane's Voyage to the Polar Lands*, in Villarejo, *Dr. Kane's Voyage*, 57–60.

25. Kane, *Arctic Explorations*, 1:34.

26. *Hickey's Narrative*, 5.

27. EKK to Cornelius Grinnell, July 20, 1853.

28. EKK, "Journal," January 29, 1855.

29. Berton, *Arctic Grail*, 236.

30. Kane, *Arctic Explorations*, 1:47.

31. Ibid., 1:60–62; *Godfrey's Narrative*, 61–63.

32. Petersen, *Dr. Kane's Voyage*, 63–65.

33. *Godfrey's Narrative*, 77; Kane, *Arctic Explorations*, 1:83–84.

34. Kane, *Arctic Explorations*, 1:79.

35. Ibid., 82.

36. Ibid., 102.

37. *Love-Life*, 163; *Dictionary of American Biography*, S.V. "John Cochrane."

38. Margaret Fox to Cornelius Grinnell, n.d. [early autumn 1853], EKK Papers.

39. *Love-Life*, 101.

40. Margaret Fox to Cornelius Grinnell, "Wednesday Evening," August 9, [1854], EKK Papers.

41. Margaret Fox to Cornelius Grinnell, August 15, 1854, EKK Papers.

42. Margaret Fox to Cornelius Grinnell, n.d., EKK Papers.

43. Margaret Fox to Cornelius Grinnell, n.d., EKK Papers.

44. Margaret Fox to Cornelius Grinnell, "Wednesday Evening," August 9, [1854]; "Thursday Evening," August 24, [1854]; September 1, 1855, EKK Papers.

45. Susannah Turner to Cornelius Grinnell, December 29, 1853, EKK Papers;

46. A large correspondence between Cornelius Grinnell and Margaret Fox survives among Kane's papers at the American Philosophical Society Library, most of which consists of Fox's requests for money. Apparently Grinnell kept all these letters as receipts to present to Kane on his return from the Arctic.

47. Kane's salary during the first Grinnell Expedition was seventy-five dollars a month. Edwin J. DeHaven, "Papers Relating to the Grinnell Arctic Expedition of 1850," New-York Historical Society.

48. Cornelius Grinnell to Robert Patterson Kane, February 4, 1854, EKK Papers.

49. Robert Patterson Kane to Cornelius Grinnell, February 13, 1854, EKK Papers.

50. In a letter to Robert Patterson Kane a few years later, Grinnell claimed that the idea that Kane and Fox were ever married was absurd. Cornelius Grinnell to Robert Patterson Kane, October 5, 1858, Robert Patterson Kane Papers, American Philosophical Society Library.

51. Cornelius Grinnell to EKK, June 2, 1855, EKK Papers.

52. Margaret Fox to Cornelius Grinnell, April 21, 1854, EKK Papers.

53. Susannah Turner to Cornelius Grinnell, July 2, 24, September 27, October 15, 1855, EKK Papers.

54. Kane, *Arctic Explorations*, 1:109.

55. *Godfrey's Narrative*, 83–100.

56. Kane, *Arctic Explorations*, 1:145.

57. *Hickey's Narrative*, 9; Kane, *Arctic Explorations*, 1:145–46.

58. *Godfrey's Narrative*, 108.

59. Kane, *Arctic Explorations*, 1:165–167.

60. Ibid., 167.

61. *Godfrey's Narrative*, 107.

62. Kane, *Arctic Explorations*, 2:417.

63. Petersen, *Dr. Kane's Voyage*, 77–78; Kane, *Arctic Explorations*, 1:175.

64. Kane, *Arctic Explorations*, 2:417.

65. Kane, *Arctic Explorations*, 1:180; Petersen, *Dr. Kane's Voyage*, 78–79; *Godfrey's Narrative*, 113–15.

66. August Sonntag, "Report of the Advance Party, and attempt to reach the Northern Shore, in charge of Henry Brooks," in Kane, *Arctic Explorations*, 2: 348–52, app. 5.

67. *Godfrey's Narrative*, 118.

68. Ibid., 126.

69. Kane, *Arctic Explorations*, 1:195–96.

70. *Godfrey's Narrative*, 134.

71. Ibid., 134.

72. Kane, *Arctic Explorations*, 1:196.

73. *Godfrey's Narrative*, 144.

74. On the prehistory of Smith Sound, see Karen M. McCullough, *The Ruin Islanders: Early Thule Culture Pioneers in the Eastern High Arctic* (Hull, Quebec: Canadian Museum of Civilization, 1989).

75. The native people of Smith Sound in northern Greenland were called Arctic Highlanders by John Ross, who was the first European to encounter them. More recently they have been referred to as the Polar Eskimo, Thule Eskimo, or Smith Sound Eskimo to distinguish their distinct culture from that of other Inuit people. For anthropological perspectives of the encounter between these far northern Native Greenlanders and the expedition led by Kane, see Wendell H. Oswalt, *Eskimos and Explorers* (Novato, Calif: Chandler & Sharp Publishers, 1979), 109–36; Barry Alan Joyce, "'As the Wolf from the Dog': American Overseas Exploration and the Compartmentalization of Mankind, 1838–1959" (Ph.D. diss., University of California at Riverside, 1995), 328–59. For interesting, more recent accounts of the Inuit from Etah, see Jean Malaurie, *The Last Kings of Thule: A Year among the Polar Eskimo of Greenland*, trans. Gwendolen Freeman (New York: Thomas Y. Crowell, 1956); Dagmar Freuchen, ed., *Peter Freuchen's Book of Eskimos* (New York: World Publishing Company, 1961).

76. Kane, *Arctic Explorations*, 1:201.

77. *Godfrey's Narrative*, 144.

78. Kane, *Arctic Explorations*, 1:209.

79. *Godfrey's Narrative*, 230; Petersen, *Dr. Kane's Voyage*, 84; EKK, "Journal of the brig *Advance*," July 3, 1854, copy in Dow Collection. The original of the first part of Kane's personal journal of the expedition is in the possession of the Historical Society of Pennsylvania. The original of the second part is in the Stanford University Library. William Morton, *Dr. Kane's Arctic Voyage: Explanatory of a Pictorial Illustration of the Second Grinnell Expedition* (New York: Barton and Sons, 1857), 18–19.

8. Homeward Bound

1. EKK, "Journal" June 9, 1854, Dow Collection.
2. Ibid., July 10, 1854.
3. Kane, *Arctic Explorations*, 1:310–14.
4. Ibid., 312.
5. Wilson, Diary.
6. Henry Goodfellow, "Facts Relating to the Separation of the Ship's Company of the Brig ADVANCE In the Fall of 1854," EKK Papers, B:K 132g.
7. EKK, "Journal," August 23, 1854.
8. Ibid., August 25, 26, 1854.
9. Ibid., December 9, 1854.
10. Ibid.
11. Ibid., August 26, 1854.
12. Ibid., August 28, 1854.
13. Ibid., September 5, 1854.
14. Petersen, *Dr. Kane's Voyage*, 86.
15. Ibid., 86–87.
16. EKK, "Journal," September 2, 1854.
17. Kane, *Arctic Explorations*, 1:353.
18. Ibid., 365.
19. Ibid., 367.
20. Ibid., 368.
21. Farley Mowat, *The Polar Passion, The Quest for the North Pole* (Toronto: McClelland and Stewart, 1967), 113.
22. Kane, *Arctic Explorations*, 1:369.
23. EKK, "Journal," December 7, 1854.
24. The experience of the withdrawal party is recounted in Isaac Hayes, *An Arctic Boat Journey in the Autumn of 1854* (Boston: Ticknor and Fields, 1860).
25. EKK, "Journal," December 13, 1854.
26. Ibid., December 13, 25, 1854.
27. Ibid., November 20, 1854; Wilson, Diary.
28. Petersen, *Dr. Kane's Voyage*, 148.
29. EKK, "Journal," January 10, 1855; Wilson, Diary, December 13, 1854.
30. Petersen, *Dr. Kane's Voyage*, 150, 153.
31. Kane, *Arctic Explorations*, 2:75.
32. *Godfrey's Narrative*, 145.
33. Ibid., 179–84.
34. Ibid., 185.
35. Kane, *Arctic Explorations*, 2:89.
36. *Godfrey's Narrative*, 182.
37. Kane, *Arctic Explorations*, 2:111; *Godfrey's Narrative*, 199.
38. Ibid., 2:235. Despite his desertion, Hans Hendrik went on to have an illustrious career as a polar explorer, working with Charles Hall and George Nares on later American expeditions.

39. Maggie Fox to EKK, n.d., EKK Papers. Although this letter is not dated, the contents indicate that it was written in late summer or early fall 1854. Moreover, in letters to Cornelius Grinnell dated August 1854, Fox refers to a note she had sent him to give to Kane on his return. Most likely this is that note. Maggie Fox to Cornelius Grinnell, August 20, 1854, August 24, [1854], EKK Papers.

40. Maggie Fox to EKK, n.d., EKK Papers.

41. Ibid.

42. Ibid.

43. *Littell's Living Age*, 46 (1855): 108.

44. Ibid.

45. *New York Daily Times*, June 1, 1855.

46. Thomas Leiper Kane had an interesting history in his own right. During the conflict between the U.S. government and the Mormons in 1850, he had traveled to Utah to help keep the peace. He became known as "the friend to the Mormons." Always the most radical of the Kane brothers, he would soon abandon his Democratic roots to become a supporter of the newly formed Republican Party. When the Civil War came, he raised a company in Pennsylvania known as the "Bucktails."

47. Thomas L. Kane to EKK, May 31, 1855, EKK Papers.

48. Ibid.

49. Ibid.

50. Kane, *Arctic Explorations*, 2:240–41.

51. Ibid., 244–45.

52. Petersen, *Dr. Kane's Voyage*, 148.

53. *New York Daily Times*, October 12, 1855; *New York Sun*, October 12, 1855.

54. *New York Daily Times*, October 12, 1855. Bonsall, Hayes, Sonntag, and Kane, as well as three of Kane's brothers, Thomas, Robert Patterson, and John, are all listed as "arrivals" at the Astor House in the *New York Evening Express*, October 12, 1855. Interestingly, Henry Goodfellow was listed as an arrival at the Irving House Hotel. Whether this indicates continued bad feeling between Goodfellow and his companions is a matter of speculation.

55. *New York Herald*, October 13, 1855.

56. *Rochester Daily American*, October 15, 1855.

57. *New York Evening Express*, October 12, 1855.

58. *New York Daily Times*, October 13, 1855.

59. *New York Sun*, October 12, 1855; *New York Evening Express*, October 12, 1855; *Troy Daily Whig*, October 13, 1855; *Philadelphia Public Ledger*, October 13, 1855.

60. Berton, *Arctic Grail*, 266–69.

61. *Troy Daily Whig*, October 15, 1855.

62. *New York Evening Express*, October 12, 1855.

63. *New York Daily Times*, October 13, 1855.

64. *Love-Life*, 191.

65. Ibid., 193.

66. Ibid., 195.

67. Ibid., 196.

68. Thomas N. Baker, *Sentiment and Celebrity: Nathaniel Parker Willis and the Trials of Literary Fame* (New York: Oxford University Press, 1999), 115–57; Norma Basch, *Framing American Divorce: From the Revolutionary Generation to the Victorians* (Berkeley: University of California Press, 1999), 172–76.

69. Baker, *Sentiment and Celebrity*, 115.

70. Corner, *Doctor Kane*, 225.

71. *Troy Daily Whig*, October 19, 1855.

72. *New York Sun*, October 26, 1855.

73. *New York Evening Post*, October 31, 1855.

74. *New York Daily Times*, November 1, 1855.

75. *New York Daily Times*, November 3, 1855.

76. *New York Daily Times*, November 5, 1855.

77. *Love-Life*, 218.

78. *New York Tribune*, November 6, 1855.

79. *New York Evening Post*, November 19, 1855.

80. *Love-Life*, 212–13.

81. Ibid., 213.

82. Ibid., 228.

83. *New York Sun*, October 13, 1855.

84. *Rochester Daily American*, October 25, 1855.

85. *Philadelphia Public Ledger*, October 26, 1855.

86. *New York Herald*, October 20, 1855.

87. *Troy Daily Whig*, October 24, 1855.

88. This theme is discussed in Bender, *Intellect and Public Life*, 3–46.

9. Becoming a Hero of Science

1. Elder, *Biography*, 215.

2. Strong, *Diary*, 165.

3. Corner, *Doctor Kane*, 230–31.

4. Elder, *Biography*, 216.

5. Philadelphia *The Public Ledger*, November 9, 1855.

6. Philadelphia *The Public Ledger*, December 15, 1855.

7. *Knickerbocker*, 48 (October 1856): 417.

8. For sales figures, see Carl Bode, *The Anatomy of American Popular Culture, 1840–1861* (Westport, Conn.: Greenwood Press, 1983), 223; Mirsky, *Kane and the Seafaring Frontier*, 180.

9. *Littell's Living Age*, 52 (February 1857): 330.

10. Kane, *Arctic Explorations*, 2:98.

11. Ibid., 119.

12. *Littell's Living Age*, 52 (February 1857): 331.

13. On Kane's racial attitudes toward the Inuit, see Joyce, "'As the Wolf from the Dog,'" 328–59; Barry Alan Joyce, "Elisha Kent Kane and the Eskimo of

Etah," in Edward C. Carter II, ed., *Surveying the Record: North American Scientific Exploration to 1930* (Philadelphia: American Philosophical Society, 1999), 103–17.

14. Kane, *Arctic Explorations*, 2: 202–204.

15. Ibid., 248.

16. Ibid., 250.

17. *North American Review*, 84 (January 1857): 110–16.

18. Spufford, *I May Be Some Time*, 16–40; Chauncey Loomis, "The Arctic Sublime," in *Nature and the Victorian Imagination*, (Berkeley: University of California Press, 1977), 95–112.

19. *Littell's Living Age*, 52 (March 1857): 485.

20. *Littell's Living Age*, 52 (February 1857): 329.

21. Ibid., 334.

22. *North American Review*, 84 (January 1857): 116–117.

23. *New York Daily Times*, February 25, 1857.

24. *North American Review*, 84 (January 1857): 117.

25. *New York Daily Times*, February 25, 1857.

26. Halttunen, *Confidence Men and Painted Women*.

27. *Eclectic Magazine of Foreign Literature, Science, and Art*, 40 (April 1857): 448–49.

28. Elder, *Biography*, 218.

29. Corner, *Doctor Kane*, 242.

30. EKK to John K. Kane, September 2, 1856; September 30, 1856; "Tuesday," EKK Papers.

31. Berton, *Arctic Grail*, 259–63. Interestingly, when the *Resolute* was retired, the British government had a desk made from its timbers that was then sent back to the United States as a gift in 1880 from Queen Victoria to President Rutherford B. Hayes. The desk now sits in the Oval Office.

32. Corner, *Doctor Kane*, 239–241; Berton, *Arctic Grail*, 313–314.

33. Elder, *Biography*, 231.

34. *Love-Life*, 269.

35. Ibid., 269–271. My own sense is that there might be some embellishment of the basic story here. Kane undoubtedly made many promises of eventual marriage, and may even have called Fox his wife in front of witnesses in her family. Whether the scene was actually as formal as Ellet described is debatable. The words about New York's marriage laws that Ellet puts in Kane's mouth seem a bit of a stretch.

36. Elder, *Biography*, 232–39; Corner, *Doctor Kane*, 245–49.

37. Elder, *Biography*, 240–41; Corner, *Doctor Kane*, 249–50.

38. *New York Herald*, February 27, 1857.

39. Ibid.

40. Ibid.

41. *New Orleans Daily Picayune*, February 25, 1857.

42. Ibid.

43. *New Orleans Evening Delta*, February 23, 1857.

44. Elder, *Biography,* 309.
45. Ibid., 315–20.
46. *Ohio Statesman* (Columbus), March 6, 1857.
47. Ibid.
48. Elder, *Biography,* 340.
49. *Baltimore American*, March 11, 1857; Elder, *Biography,* 340.
50. Elder, *Biography,* 341.
51. *Baltimore American*, March 11, 1857.
52. *Baltimore Sun,* March 11, 1857.
53. *Baltimore American*, March 11, 1857.
54. *Baltimore Sun*, March 11, 1857.
55. *Pennsylvania Inquirer*, March 13, 1857.
56. Ibid.
57. Ibid.
58. *Philadelphia Evening Journal*, March 12, 1857.
59. *Philadelphia Public Ledger*, March 13, 1857.
60. *Pennsylvania Inquirer*, March 13, 1857; *New York Herald*, March 13, 1857.
61. *Philadelphia Evening Journal*, March 12, 1857.
62. Review of *Elisha Kent Kane; A Biography* by William Elder, in *Philadelphia Press*, January 14, 1858.
63. Corner, *Doctor Kane,* 167; Mirsky, *Kane and the Seafaring Frontier,* 145–46.
64. *Philadelphia Sun*, March 13, 1857.
65. *New York Daily Tribune*, February 18, 1857.
66. *Philadelphia Evening Journal*, March 12, 1857.
67. Ibid.
68. See Benedict Anderson, *Imagined Communities: Reflections on the Origin and Spread of Nationalism* (New York: Verso, 1983).
69. *Cincinnati Daily Enquirer*, February 23, 1857.
70. *Louisville Courier*, March 4, 1857.
71. *Harper's Weekly*, March 14, 1857.
72. *Boston Pilot*, July 18, 1857; *Louisville Courier*, March 4, 1857.
73. *Philadelphia Inquirer*, March 13, 1857.
74. *Baltimore Sun*, March 11, 1857.
75. Charles Shields, "Funeral Discourse," in Elder, *Biography,* 371.
76. Ibid., 373.
77. *Cincinnati Daily Enquirer*, February 27, 1857.

10. Private Lives, Public Legacy

1. *Love-Life.*
2. Ibid., 280.
3. *Godfrey's Narrative*, 250–54.
4. Samuel M. Schmucker, *The Life of Dr. Elisha Kent Kane, and of Other*

Distinguished American Explorers (Philadelphia: John E. Potter & Co., 1858), 73–75.

5. Elisha Kent Kane Will (copy), EKK Papers. Fox is not named in the will; rather the money was left in the keeping of Robert Kane for an unspecified private purpose, but Robert Kane never denied that it was meant for Fox.

6. Mrs. Margaret Fox to Robert Patterson Kane, EKK Papers.

7. Margaret Fox to Robert Patterson Kane, June 1, 1857, EKK Papers. The letter also appears in *Love-Life*, 283.

8. For example, Margaret Fox to Robert Patterson Kane, n.d.; Margaret Fox to Robert Patterson Kane, June 1858, EKK Papers.

9. Wainwright, *Philadelphia Perspective*, 390, 431.

10. Margaret Fox to Robert Patterson Kane, June 1, 1857, EKK Papers; *Love-Life*, 283.

11. *National Era* (Washington, D.C.), August 6, 1857.

12. Margaret Fox to Robert Patterson Kane, May 27, 1858, EKK Papers.

13. Casper, *Constructing American Lives*, 135–78.

14. Robert Patterson Kane to Margaret Fox, July 4, 1858, EKK Papers.

15. Rush C. Hawkins to Robert Patterson Kane, August 20, 1858, EKK Papers.

16. Robert Patterson Kane to William Quinn, August 30, 1858, EKK Papers.

17. Robert Patterson Kane to William Quinn, August 30, 1858; Horace Greeley to Robert Patterson Kane, September 21, 1858, EKK Papers.

18. *Love-Life*, 284–85.

19. *New York Evening Post*, August 16, 1858; *New York Daily Tribune*, August 17, 1858; *Philadelphia Public Ledger*, August 16, 1858. Fox's baptism was reported as far away as South Carolina, indicating the degree to which she was still of public interest. *Charleston Mercury*, August 20, 1858.

20. *New York Herald*, August 16, 1858; *New York Daily Tribune*, August 17, 1858.

21. "Letter *in re* publication of Kane-Fox correspondence," EKK Papers.

22. Cornelius Grinnell to Robert Patterson Kane, October 5, 1858, EKK Papers.

23. Margaret Fox to Robert Patterson Kane, September 2, 1858, EKK Papers.

24. Margaret Fox to Robert Patterson Kane, November, 1858, EKK Papers.

25. Mariam Pond, *Time Is Kind: The Story of the Unfortunate Fox Family* (New York: Centennial Press, 1947), 217–29.

26. William Quinn to Robert Patterson Kane, January 20, 1859; William Quinn to Robert Patterson Kane, March 16, 1859; William Quinn to Robert Patterson Kane, March 12, 1860, EKK Papers.

27. William Quinn to Robert Patterson Kane, December 12, 1859, EKK Papers.

28. William Quinn to Robert Patterson Kane, March 12, 1860, EKK Papers.

29. William Quinn to Robert Patterson Kane, October 14, 1860, EKK Papers.

30. Margaret Fox to Robert Patterson Kane, September 15, 1860, EKK Papers.

31. Pond, *Time Is Kind*, 217.

32. On Carleton, see Madeleine B. Stern, "G. W. Carleton: His Mark," *Publisher's Weekly*, August 17, 1946.

33. *Love-Life*, vii–x.

34. Ibid.

35. Ibid. Mariam Buckner Pond identifies a man named Joseph LaFumee as the author of the preface and attributes the rest of the work to Maggie Fox alone, with some help from LaFumee. She makes no mention of Elizabeth Ellet. Pond, *Time Is Kind*, 219. Primary sources in the Elisha Kent Kane Papers, however, discussed earlier, clearly indicate Elizabeth Ellet's central role in the preparation of the volume.

36. *Love-Life*, vii.

37. Ibid., vii.

38. Ibid., x.

39. Ibid.

40. This aspect of Ellet's writing is discussed in Casper, *Constructing American Lives*, 159–178. Casper, however, was not aware of Ellet's connection with *The Love-Life of Dr. Kane*.

41. *Love-Life*, 14.

42. Ibid., 16–17.

43. Ibid., 17–18.

44. *New York Times*, December 15, 1865.

45. *New York Daily Tribune*, September 11, 1865.

46. Pond, *Time Is Kind*, 242.

47. Davenport, *Death-Blow*, 236.

48. Pond, *Time Is Kind*, 285.

49. Ibid., 289.

50. Ibid., 232–79; Jackson, *Spirit Rappers*, 183–211. The best evidence of Maggie Fox's dislike for her sister Leah is Davenport, *Death-Blow*, which reports repeated verbal jabs at her older sister.

51. *Preliminary Report of the Commission Appointed by the University of Pennsylvania to Investigate Modern Spiritualism in Accordance with the Request of the Late Henry Seybert* (Philadelphia: J. B. Lippincott Company, 1887).

52. Pond, *Time Is Kind*, 287–90; Jackson, *Spirit Rappers*, 197–99.

53. *New York Herald*, May 27, 1888.

54. Underhill, *Missing Link*.

55. *New York Herald*, quoted in Davenport, *Death-Blow*, 32–33.

56. *New York Times*, October 22, 1888.

57. *New York Daily Tribune*, October 22, 1888.

58. *New York Times*, October 22, 1888; *New York Daily Tribune*, October 22, 1888.

59. *New York Daily Tribune*, October 22, 1888.

60. Jackson, *Spirit Rappers*, 212–13.

61. *New York Times*, March 5, 1893.

62. *New York Times*, March 10, 1893.

63. *Philadelphia Daily Evening Telegraph*, March 9, 1893.

64. *New York Times*, March 11, 1893; unidentified newspaper clipping, Dow Collection.

Conclusion: Science, Showmanship, Celebrity, and Sensation

1. William Howard Russell, My *Diary North and South,* ed. Eugene H. Berwanger (New York: Knopf, 1988), 319.

2. Bender, *Intellect and Public Life*, 3–46.

3. Cullen, *Art of Democracy*.

Index

DAVID CHAPIN earned his B.A. in anthropology/sociology at Kenyon College, his M.A. in history at Colorado State University, and his Ph.D. in American social and cultural history at the University of New Hampshire. He has taught at Colorado State University, the University of New Hampshire, and Prescott College. He was awarded a Mellon Resident Research Fellowship at the American Philosophical Society Library to work on *Exploring Other Worlds*, which is his first book. He lives in Nottingham, New Hampshire.